The Beginner's Guide to PSoC Express
Microcontroller Development without Writing Code

Oliver H. Bailey

Timelines Industries Inc.

The Beginner's Guide to PSoC Express:
Microcontroller Development without Writing Code
By Oliver H. Bailey

Published by Timelines Industries Inc.
5107 Greenwood Pl
McHenry, IL 60050-2376
Phone: 815-759-1404
www.time-lines.com

Editors: Keith Kehl, John Wilczynski
Cover Photography: Oliver H. Bailey
Cover and Book Design: Wordware Publishing

ISBN 10: 0-9790344-0-X
ISBN 13: 978-0-9790344-0-4

CD ORDER FORM

5107 Greenwood Pl
McHenry, IL 60050-2376
USA

Sold To: Ship To:
Company: Company:
Name: Name:
Address: Address:

City   City:
State   State:
Zip   Zip:
Phone   Phone:

Email: Email:

Qty	Description	Unit Price	Total
1	The Beginner's Guide to PSoC Express CD	$19.95	$19.95
		Shipping	US $6.00 Intl $10.00
		Subtotal	
	(ILLINOIS RESIDENTS ONLY add 6.5%) Sales Tax		$1.30
		Total	

Credit Card Information:

Name on Card_____   Expiration Date:

Card Number:_____   Month ____ Year ____

Signature_____   Visa   MasterCard

Credit Card Billing Address: _____

By signing I agree to the terms and agreement of my credit card contract.

Intended Audience

The Beginner's Guide to PSoC Express is for beginners and experts alike. Anyone who wants to understand the PSoC mixed-signal microcontroller, and learn how to develop using PSoC Express will benefit from this book. I write in a conversational style, and while I do not explain what resistors, capacitors, and LEDs are, even a beginner who has no electronics experience should be able to follow along if they get a good electronics reference book. There are many electronics reference books available so pick one that is easy for you to understand. If you have had experience with the BASIC Stamp, or PIC microcontrollers, then you should have no problem following the text and doing the projects.

The projects in this book are simple by intent, to explain the concepts of PSoC Express and get the reader comfortable with visual microcontroller development. The point of the projects are to give the reader experience using different types of I/O, and decision logic, to reach a level of comfort in using PSoC Express. Because PSoC Express virtually eliminates manual coding, sometimes the transition from traditional tools can be intimidating. By keeping the projects simple, the reader can gain confidence both in the quality of PSoC Express generated projects, and in their ability to develop projects that work the first time.

For Beginners

If you've never worked with the PSoC, BASIC Stamp, or other microcontroller, then I suggest you start with chapter 1 and read the entire book. Chapters 1 through 5 explain how PSoC Express works and how to develop and test applications using simulation mode.

I should note that simulation mode replaces source line debugging and allows the developer to test logic before doing a build. Since PSoC Express is the author of all source code, this approach eliminates single-stepping through unfamiliar code, while allowing program logic to be quickly and easily tested.

For Experienced Developers

If you have experience with the PSoC or PSoC Designer, then you may wish to glance over chapters 1-5, and start developing the projects in chapter 6. I would still recommend reading chapters 4 and 5 to gain experience with developing PSoC Express projects and running them in simulation mode.

If your interest is in the advanced topics area, then jump right in at chapter 8, WirelessUSB and follow with USB, CapSense, finishing with how to modify custom.c in chapter 11. Chapter 12 is short but contains many resources for additional information and support.

Dedication

During the course of writing this book, my wife, Susan, was diag-
nosed with Multiple-Myeloma, or bone marrow cancer. While this
form of cancer is considered "very-treatable," its effect and the effect
of the drugs used in combating this disease are devastating. The worst
part of this disease is how it steals a person's energy, making simple
tasks painful and uncomfortable.

For me personally, it has been difficult to stand by, unable to take
the pain away or do anything other than watch. And so it to my loving
wife, friend, partner, and love of the past 20 years that I dedicate this
book. And so, this is for you, love. God really blessed me the day we
met.

Oliver H. Bailey

Contents

About the Author

Oliver H. Bailey has been involved with mechanical, electrical, and software systems for over 30 years. Originally a mechanical engineer designing machine tools, he became involved with machine tool electronics in the early 1970s and software control systems shortly thereafter. In 1982, he was one of the original developers at Sam's Software; the software development division of Howard W. Sam's publishing that later became Advance Operating Systems. There he wrote some of the first developer tools for the Radio Shack, Commodore, and IBM PCs. In 1984, he moved to Chicago and eventually became development director for one of the first online Videotext services, KeyFax, a joint venture between a major phone company, a computer company, and a newspaper. That venture was shut down in 1986 and he then went back to developing machine tool control systems. Since that time, he has developed machine control systems for printing presses, machine vision systems for the manufacturing of telephone equipment, motion control systems for printer manufacturers, robotic guidance systems for material handling, and telephone tracking and follow-up systems for the automotive industry.

In 2003, he decided to share his knowledge and move into training and education. In 2005 his first book, *Embedded Systems Desktop Integration* was introduced. *Embedded Systems Desktop Integration* is about how to design and implement embedded communication systems that interface to a host computer. In addition to this book, he is working on three other books that deal with other microcontroller architectures and wireless communications techniques.

Acknowledgments

If you want to know how little you know about a particular subject, just write a book about it. Writing a book on any topic is a humbling but rewarding experience. That is of course under ideal conditions, which we rarely work under, but the support that Cypress Semiconductor has given me during the writing of this book has made my chore easy and pleasurable.

Without exception, Cypress employees are always helpful and courteous when it comes to answering questions and providing support. In an age where most companies are cutting support and further removing their employees from the telephones, Cypress has live people that answer the technical support lines and actually enjoy helping customers. So many people helped me out at Cypress that I hope I do not miss any of them. Steve Gerber, Jon Pearson, David Cooper, and Dave Funston are the marketing and technical gurus that make the PSoC Express work. Hardik' Dave and Dee Bender fulfilled all my parts and developer kits needs. Dave Van Ess, Blair Wilson, and Corey Wilner were always available to listen to ideas and provide input.

John Wilczynski and Keith Kehl are my reviewers and provide great criticism on content, layout, and the words used to explain the concepts and ideas. I would also like to thank Tim McEvoy and the folks at Wordware Publishing for the excellent layout and cover on this project. I could not have done it without you. Finally to my wife, Susan, who puts up with the strange hours and the laptop implant I had. It seems that my laptop goes everywhere these days. Moreover, heartfelt thanks go to everyone who made this book possible.

God bless each one of you
Oliver H. Bailey

Introduction

When I first started this book, PSoC Express 2.0 had just been released. When I got my first copy, I installed it, played with it for 20 minutes, and then put it aside. When Cypress approached me to write a book on PSoC Express, I started using PSoC Express on a daily basis. As I used it more, I found it more useful but something else happened along the way. The amount of time it took me to develop using PSoC Express became shorter and shorter. I can now develop just about anything in 8 hours or less. It reminded me of when I took speed-reading years ago. As my comprehension increased, so did my speed and that kept going until my reading abilities improved by a factor of five. So you may be asking yourself, why should I try PSoC Express or why do I care about PSoC Express? There are several answers to that question.

In many years of developing electronic systems, there is one common denominator that all projects have. Somewhere during the prototype stage the design always take a major course change. At that point there is too much invested in the project to cancel it and too little time left to overhaul it. So what happens? The first generation product is obsolete before it ships. PSoC Express reduces the time to develop a prototype from weeks and months, to hours and days. That means you can make major design changes during the prototype phase without impacting the final development phase and, because the prototype phase has been reduced to weeks instead of months, you can make major design changes early enough to benefit first generation production. So using PSoC Express extends a product's lifecycle.

The next reason for using PSoC Express involves training. PSoC Express is an excellent education tool. It allows students to learn how to develop with mixed-signal microcontrollers without the distraction or prerequisite of learning a programming language. That's a big feature and here's why. We've all known many people who abandoned microcontroller courses because learning the architecture and programming languages were simply too much to comprehend in a short time period. With PSoC Express, the focus can remain on the device architecture without the distraction of learning a programming language or the frustration of determining if a problem lies in the software, the hardware, or the logic. If you employ engineers, break-ing in the junior people with PSoC Express allows them to develop useful products or prototypes almost immediately, building their con-fidence to take on larger projects and graduate to PSoC Designer with greatly reduced training.

The third reason for using PSoC Express is to jump-start your PSoC Designer projects. By starting out in PSoC Express, the devel-oper can visually create a desktop of needed components, add foundation logic, simulate, test, and then bring the project into PSoC Designer to be "fine tuned." With a library of over 130 components that include WirelessUSB, USB, and CapSense, there is little that can't be done in PSoC Express.

Therefore, the purpose of this book is to help you, the developer, get up to speed in using and understanding PSoC Express in minimal time. We start by developing several projects and running them in the simulator to get comfortable with a new thought process. Then we learn how to develop, build, and program projects using the traditional thought process used with old-fashioned microcontrollers. Afterwards, we learn how to develop projects that run across multiple PSoC devices using the I2C protocol. We then learn how to use WirelessUSB, CapSense, and USB Bridge devices connected to a desktop PC. We then finish up by learning how to write custom code.

There's something in PSoC Express for everyone. If you're a hob-byist, you can now develop applications visually, without the need to understand any programming language. If you're a student, you can learn how to use the PSoC at a faster pace, and if you're an engineer, you can try your design out in minutes, instead of hours, days, or weeks, and never write a line of code in the process.

I believe that in time PSoC Express will become the development tool by which others are measured.

Conventions Used in This Book

Several special shaped information boxes are used to draw attention to important information. These are used for the following purposes:

Critical Information Box

Critical or important information is displayed in a box like this. This box can be identified by the simulated curl at the lower right corner.

General Information Box

General information is displayed in this box. Items of importance but not considered critical are considered general information. This box differs from the critical information box by having rounded edges and no curl in the lower right corner.

Code and Expression Box

```
Code and expressions appear in a box like this. Information that is
provided by PSoC Express is italicized. Information added by the
user appears in either normal or bold text.
```

Remember these conventions. They are the keys to finding critical and important information.

What is PSoC Express

There are several factors that have an effect on how PSoC Express is used and the value placed on it within an organization. To account for these differences I will explain PSoC Express as viewed from different roles. In general PSoC Express is a tool that can be used to:

▶ Kick Start PSoC Based Projects

▶ Shorten Proof-of-Concept Stages

▶ Shorten the Development of Early Prototypes

▶ Shorten Time-to-Market for PSoC Based Device

▶ Train Junior Engineers

▶ Use Senior Engineers More Productively

▶ Teach Microcontrollers without Learning How-to-Program

▶ Introduce Hobbyists to the PSoC

I know, you may be saying that PSoC Express is being oversold and I'm trying to make it the solution to all the engineering problems in the world. Don't worry, I'm not and it isn't! But from personal experience with this product and 30 years of hardware and software development experience, I can say with certainty that the future of microcontroller **development will be defined by this product, and in the future other microcontroller development tools will be measured by it**.

The above statement is very clear and the long term effect this product will have on an entire industry will be enormous and here's why; PSoC Express is the first development tool for microcontroller development that separates logic and programming. The PSoC Express developer is not required to ever write a line of code in any language in order to build fully functional PSoC based products. In simple projects a developer can use PSoC Express from start to finish. In projects of medium complexity PSoC Express can handle a large portion of the development, leaving the most complicated parts that require programming to PSoC Designer. But even in the most complicated project, PSoC Express can be employed to increase senior engineers' productively, and shave large amounts of time off early and mid-stage product development. This saves money through reduced time-to-market and reduced labor costs. This translates directly to lower cost products that can be priced below products using conventional microcontroller development techniques.

More and more over the years electronic logic and software have converged. It is far too easy to make a well designed circuit ill-perform due to a single line of code that was written or interpreted incorrectly. With PSoC Express the programming equation is left out so the engineer can concentrate fully on how the logic works and not how a programming language syntax works. By dragging and dropping visual components on a desktop an electronics engineer can define all inputs, outputs, valuators (Logic Control), and interfaces needed to make a complete PSoC project.

Finally, while not obvious, PSoC Express makes internal interrupt usage totally transparent to the Embedded Developer. No writing and debugging tedious interrupt service routines. When an object is added to the design desktop that is interrupt driven, PSoC Express creates the interrupt service routine (ISR) automatically, allowing you, the developer to simply set the conditions which measure input state and set output conditions.

PSoC Express has Benefits for Everyone

There is really something for everyone in using PSoC Express. In the remainder of this section I will present the importance of this product as I see it, from the views of different types of developers, managers, educators, students, and hobbyists.

Existing PSoC Developers

For new projects, PSoC Express should become your starting point for proof-of-concept, early, and mid-cycle prototype development. Remember, the more code that would normally be written in early stages of development, the more PSoC Express will reduce your labor and time-to-market for many types of projects.

While PSoC Express can benefit your development efforts in most areas, there are still a few exceptions. Interrupts, precision timers, and manipulating the internal bus will have to be implemented by either manually coding them in PSoC Express or through the use of PSoC Designer (preferred).

> **Note:** It's important to note that if you intend to move PSoC Express projects to PSoC Designer you will need to purchase a C compiler license. In addition, the move from PSoC Express to PSoC Designer is one-way. Once a PSoC Express project has been imported to PSoC Designer, it cannot be edited further in PSoC Express. So, if you intend to move PSoC Express projects to PSoC Designer, backup your original PSoC Express project, and use a copy of the project for PSoC Designer so you can return to the original PSoC Express project.

Using PSoC Express in your new designs will save time and allow you or other developers to focus on product functionality instead of code checking. If you normally use C, you'll find that the time from concept to completion will be much shorter once you master the PSoC Express tool. If you write assembly, you will be even more pleased as your time savings should be even greater.

For CYPros Consultants

If you are a registered CYPros consultant, and you are not looking seriously at this tool, you are in trouble! PSoC Express opens up opportunities in new areas that will increase your revenue. For early stage development, proof-of-concept, and prototyping, this tool will make you look like a hero. No one is going to be able to compete with your estimates unless they are recycling an old job. Bringing in projects ahead of schedule and under budget is not only possible but a real savings in most cases.

Once you've done the early stage development, you can make additional revenue by offering your services to either train your client's employees on the use of PSoC Express, or by providing custom components that are specific to your customers needs. At this point you are probably concerned about losing a clients business to PSoC Express but remember that no employee stays on the same job forever. Your training services will be needed from time-to-time and no one will understand components you write better than you will. Even if you give (or sell) the components to the client, there will be plenty of opportunity to get additional work.

If you happen to be one of those people that resists change and think that PSoC Express is a passing fad, then you had better find a new line of work. This tool has implications that reach beyond just the PSoC. It is a new type of tool that other microcontroller manufacturers will be forced to implement over time. It will be the "Visual Studio" of microcontrollers. If you don't jump on this wagon now, you will regret it very quickly because someone else who does accept the product and becomes proficient at it will be taking your customers and you will be stuck with shrinking revenue from assembler and C jobs that you will be competing to get.

For PIC Developers

Before going any further, let me say that I use almost all of the microcontrollers that are available. Each manufacturer's product line(s) have strengths they excel at, plain and simple. I favor the PSoC when I can because it allows the protection of intellectual property through the flexibility of its internal bus, which is more flexible than those of other manufacturers. I also like the mixed-signal capability and wide variety of products. I also find that combination of the PSoC, PSoC Express, and PSoC Designer offer a level of productivity unmatched by others. For many non-interrupt driven projects, combining PSoC Express combined with a PSoC reduces time-to-market and less microcontroller specific skills to implement a PSoC based product. This is especially true for small companies and microcontroller based products that don't require interrupts or precision timers. Those types of projects can be written completely in PSoC Express today.

Keep in mind that some other microcontroller manufacturers offer parts as low as $.50 with 6 or 8 pins and only 500-700 bytes of program space. Even though the PSoC may not get down to this price point, the PSoC has a minimum of 4K Flash that should be considered when factoring in component and development costs. These facts, combined with low ongoing maintenance costs, make the PSoC highly competitive.

For BASIC Stamp Developers

I both like and use the BASIC Stamp in most of my writings. It is a great tool for fast proof-of-concept designs without spending a large amount of time coding. Some consider the BASIC Stamp expensive but the Stamp is popular among educators and hobbyists alike. While it doesn't eliminate programming, it makes programming easier to understand. But the BASIC Stamp uses an on-board interpreter and there is no way to address the core processor directly. That's where PSoC Express comes in. PSoC Express can be used by BASIC Stamp users to move their ideas into a full speed microcontroller without writing code, while still affording them the flexibility to choose a part with a pin count most effective for their designs. In addition, PSoC Express is a natural progression for BASIC Stamp users who want to move up to a full microcontroller, but don't want to get bogged down in a more complicated language.

For Project Managers

PSoC Express translates into money saved. This can happen in a variety of ways. First, because PSoC Express doesn't require pro-gramming knowledge, a junior engineer or lab technician can be used as a development resource in simple projects and for a considerable amount of work in more complicated projects. This equates to lower labor costs.

PSoC Express also reduces the time-to-market by shortening change cycles to a few minutes. As the product evolves from proto-type to completion, these cost savings add up quickly. But by shortening the development cycle, PSoC Express can greatly reduce overall development costs, providing for a lower cost product or higher profit margins on the end result. Because PSoC Express is a visual design environment, requirements are developed in parallel with prototype development and prototype testing can be used for immediate feedback into the project requirements allowing for contin-uous loop development during project development.

For Senior Engineers

PSoC Express allows more work to be performed by junior people, freeing up the senior architects to work more in an implementation capacity during the early phases of a project, and be more directly involved when later phases of a project require either more skill, or the ability to add and enhance features in PSoC Designer. Since PSoC Express doesn't require programming skills, any electronics engineer can quickly become productive in developing PSoC applications. This makes the pool of resources that can be used much larger and reduces the programming requirements reducing costs, improving time-to-market, and assuring that the developed intellectual property is documented and properly credited.

For Junior Engineers

One of the biggest challenges facing junior engineers is adapting to a new work environment quickly and gaining the confidence to do their jobs without hesitation. PSoC Express can help junior engineers get familiar with their work environment while focusing on learning the methods and standards in use at their place of employment without being distracted by a programming language. They can load existing PSoC Express projects and graphically see how the project is laid out and the underlying logic that make the heart and soul of the PSoC come to life. And all this can be accomplished without programming and without knowing a programming language.

For Educators

Educators have completely different requirements than industry. The role of higher education is to provide a workforce adept and skilled enough to be productive upon being hired. Microcontrollers combine electronics, logic, software, and firmware programming together to build intelligent devices. Since programming has always been a requirement, many an engineering student has changed course to avoid the software development aspect. Electronic engineering teachers must combine programming languages with electronics logic and teach combined classes, with programming always distracting from the rules of electronics and microcontroller logic.

With PSoC Express, engineering teachers can now focus on pure microcontroller logic without the distraction of a programming language. This means that basic microcontroller logic can be taught without any required programming skills, and a higher level class can be added for advanced topics such as interrupts, communications protocols, external memory addressing, and other topics.

And finally, PSoC Express allows educators to custom develop components or adapt existing components to their curriculum, tailoring PSoC Express to their own needs and the needs of their class.

For Students

Move over BASIC Stamp. PSoC Express combined with the PSoC, lower grade level students (junior high school) can now do development on a full-fledged microcontroller. This means that younger students who master the PSoC Express tool are free to advance to learning more advanced topics such as assembler or C, and more in-depth understanding of how logic, components, and software come together to provide a more well rounded learning experience. But most important of all, because PSoC Express and PSoC Designer are free, even the most financially limited budgets will be able to work with these remarkable software tools.

Chapter Summary

In this chapter we learned what PSoC Express is and the benefits it brings to different groups of engineers and students. As we work through the exercises and projects in later chapters, you will begin to see how PSoC Express can benefit your job the best.

Looking Ahead

In Chapter 2 we will see how our thought process needs to change in order to make the best use of PSoC Express and utilize it to its full potential.

Thinking in PSoC Express

This chapter covers two topics. The first is an overview of how PSoC Express fits into the development cycle. This will also give you some background into where PSoC Express fits in the Cypress development tools list, and insight that will help you be more productive faster in understanding and using PSoC Express. Afterwards, we'll take a quick look at the PSoC Express development cycle, and the steps necessary to make the most of PSoC Express.

The Missing Link to Microcontroller Development

PSoC Express fills a void that has existed in microcontroller development since the inception of the device. Traditionally, the developer would design an electronic circuit, of which the microcontroller would be the heart of the circuit. Afterwards, the firmware would be designed, then written in assembler or C, tested, refined, and the cycle would start over again. The point is that firmware has been mostly "seat-of-the-pants" development and firmware designs have been by "trial and error" development. Then came PSoC Designer. PSoC Designer is a visual designer that has drag and drop capability at a much lower level. PSoC Designer allows the developer to drag-and-drop internal peripheral components and visually manage the internal bus, inputs, outputs, then join the internal peripherals together and map them to external I/O pins. PSoC Designer gives the developer complete control over: interrupts, communications, internal bus connections, and external pin mapping. This magnitude of control requires a high degree of knowledge to use properly and much of the design must be implemented by hand in C or assembler.

But PSoC Designer has some very nice drag-and-drop features that could make PSoC development even easier. Therefore, the developers at Cypress came up with PSoC Express, a complete visual designer for simple to intermediate level PSoC projects and for "kick-starting" more advanced PSoC Designer projects. With PSoC Express the developer never sees a native code screen. Instead there are Inputs, Outputs, Valuators, and Communications Interface components. The code is still there, but, like the engine in an automobile, it is under-the-hood, being driven by PSoC Express. So, how do you remove the traditional code editor and replace it with a visual design environment that both new and experienced developers are comfortable with? Cypress software engineers created a very intuitive desktop that contains a menu system with the logical development order from left to right. By starting at the left side of the menu, the developer is provided with each logical step of the development process in progression moving to the right. Figure 2-1 shows the main PSoC Express desktop after the program starts.

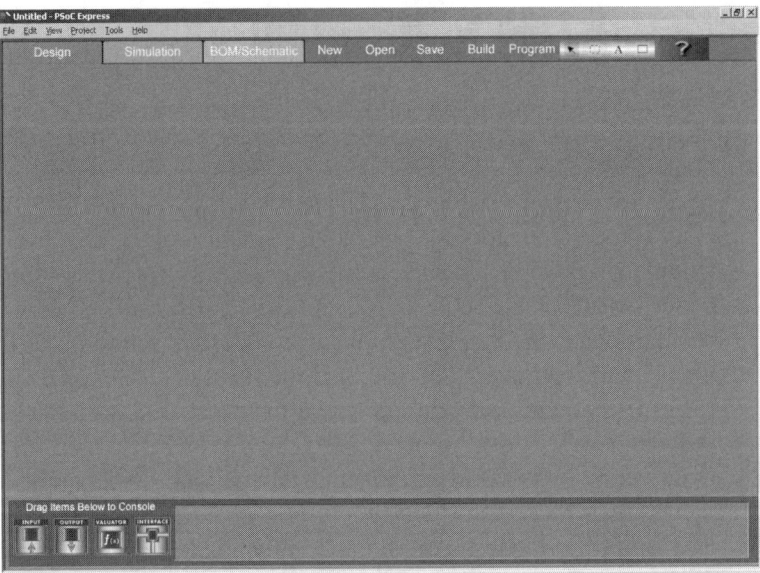

Figure 2-1 – Main development desktop

PSoC Express Menus and Tabs

Across the top, the development choices are listed in logical order. The development process begins with a blank desktop that has a main menu and tabs and buttons across the top of the screen. These allow development, simulation, project file saving, compiling, pin assignments, bill of material (BOM) display, PSoC programming, and powering the target.

PSoC Express "Drag-and-Drop Components"

In the lower left hand corner are the visual tools that form the backbone of PSoC Express. These are the icons for Input, Output, Valuator, and Interface components. These are top-level icons, as we begin development, you will see that different types of Input, Outputs, Valuators, and Communications Interfaces have their own icons as well.

Running PSoC Express

When PSoC Express starts, it displays an assistant to aid in building and organizing projects. Officially named the "PSoC Express Helper" it contains information on how to use PSoC Express, manage projects, and other useful information. Figure 2-2 shows the PSoC Express Assistant as it is displayed the first time PSoC Express is used.

Chapter 2

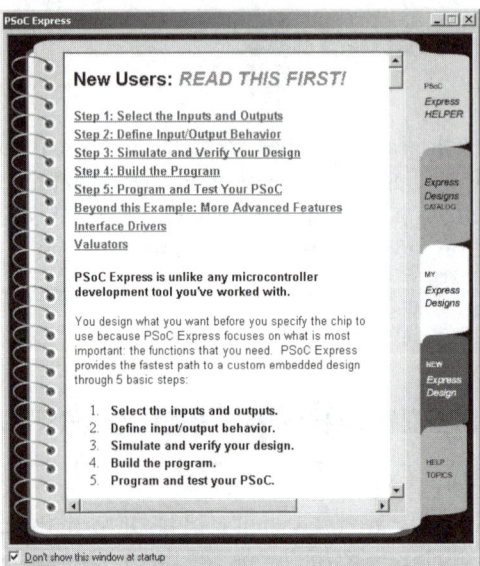

Figure 2-2 – PSoC Express Assistant

PSoC Express in the Development Process

Before we get any deeper into PSoC Express, let's step back and see how PSoC Express fits into the development scheme for the PSoC. Figure 2-3 illustrates a typical microcontroller development flowchart.

The development cycle begins on track, but typically the original design proves to be a starting point for features instead of a point of feature definition. Once that transition is made, the entire product definition begins to change and the schedule begins to slide, missing target deadlines. Another factor that comes into play is that as firmware projects progress, more code is written. The more code that needs to be changed, the longer the change and test cycles take.

These two seemingly simple scenarios have forced multi-million dollar companies into bankruptcy. Put simply, these two scenarios combined are deadly because they signal the beginning of an infinite development cycle.

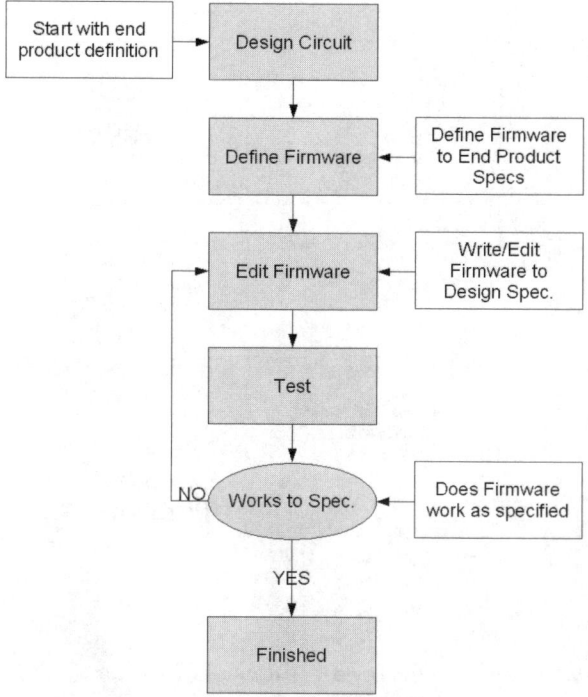

Figure 2-3 – Typical microcontroller flowchart

PSoC Express allows the early stages of product definition to also serve as the proof-of-concept stage for firmware development. While things like interrupt handlers cannot be directly written in PSoC Express, they may be created and maintained transparently by PSoC Express. This allows for an always current working "proof-of-concept" in firmware which is easily created, manipulated, and maintained. This approach solidifies the "pre-development" stage where product marketing and engineering are tightly integrated in the design process. This leads to a more concrete design that results in fewer changes as product development proceeds. Using PSoC Express, the starting design has been fully proven using the features that can be handled in the final design. In the normal development cycle, the feature list remains open until proof-of-concept can be written by a programmer. Let's take a look at how the development cycle changes with PSoC Express. Figure 2-4 illustrates how a typical PSoC development process cycle works when PSoC Express is used in early stage development.

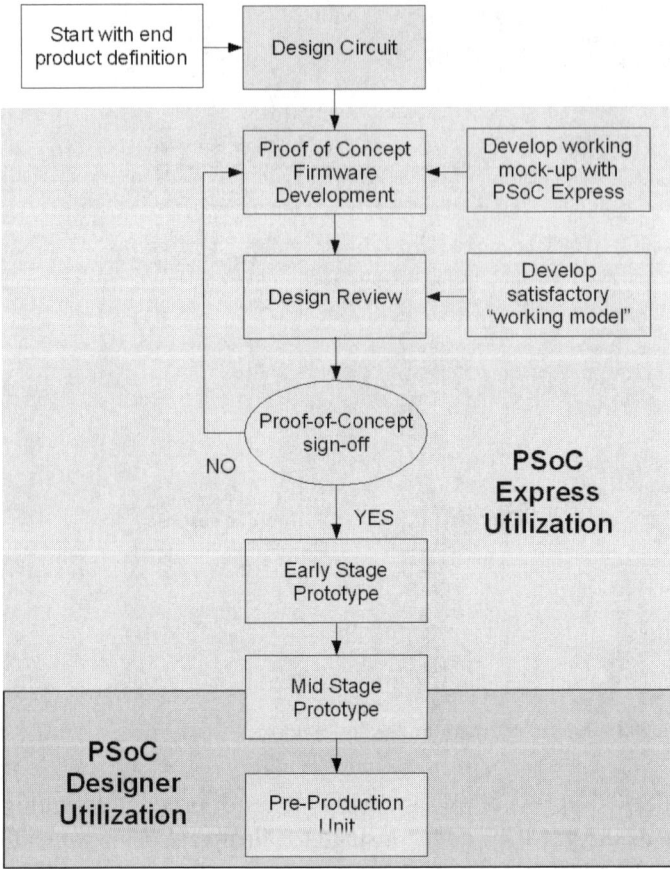

Figure 2-4

Because PSoC Express is a complete visual design and development environment, an engineer or firmware developer and a marketing person can sit down together and visually develop the "proof-of-concept" prototype, then build, program, test, and repeat the process until a satisfactory "working model" has been created. In mechanical engineering we call this "experimental engineering" and it is one of most sought after jobs because of its creative aspect. Referring again to figure 2-4, you will notice that PSoC Express can be used well into the mid-stage prototype, but remember this is dependent on the types of applications you will be developing. In some types of designs PSoC Express can be used for the entire project, while on other designs it may only be feasible to use PSoC Express during the proof-of-concept stage. In either case, you will still save time in the early stages of development because the manual creation of code in the early to mid stages has been completely eliminated.

Learning PSoC Express

So you may be thinking that the tools, skills, or software needed to develop PSoC Express projects are too expensive or complicated to learn, and too resource intensive to get started. You would be wrong, wrong, and wrong. PSoC Express is freely downloadable from the Cypress web site (www.cypress.com/psocexpress) or PSoC Developer web site (www.psocdeveloper.com), or at the author's web site (www.psoc.time-lines.com) along with additional links to resources. PSoC Express requires only the computing resources as outlined by Cypress at the PSoC Express page, and requires 2-4 hours of quiet time to grasp the concepts and start developing sample applications. How long it takes to become an expert will depend on you. So get the software and let's start using PSoC Express!

PSoC Express Hardware

Ah, I saved the best for last, the hardware. In order to use PSoC Express you'll need a MiniProg for programming the PSoC Device, and a board to build your circuits with. There are several options available for development hardware. First, there is the Cypress MiniProg1 as shown in photo 2-1.

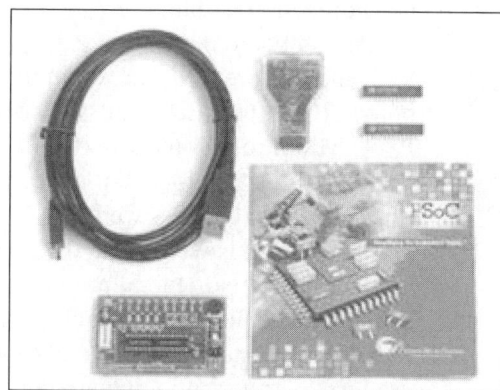

Photo 2-1

The MiniProg1 kit includes a CD with applications, notes, and other goodies; a small programming and development board; several PSoC devices; USB cable; and USB Programmer. Next we have the CY3210 PSoCEval1 kit. The MiniEval1 kit is shown in photo 2-2.

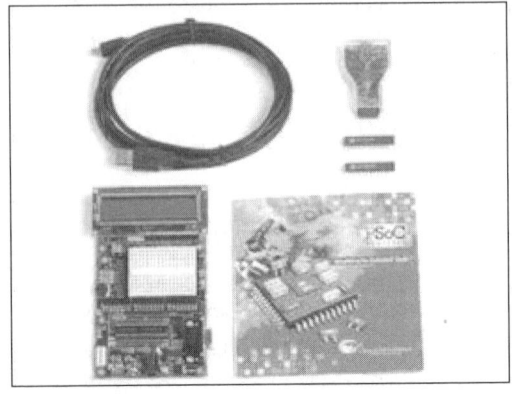

Photo 2-2

The PSoCEval1 kit has buttons, LEDs, Potentiometer, PSoC device, LCD, and solderless breadboard area. It also contains a USB MiniProg Programmer, and wire kit. The final development kit currently available from Cypress as of this writing is the CY3210 Express DK. The Express DK is shown in photo 2-3.

The CY3210 PSoC Express DK includes a development board that contain on board moni-

Photo 2-3

tor, generous prototype area, fan modules, prototype modules, serial ports, I2C ports, LEDs, buttons, switches, USB cable, serial cable, PSoC Mini Programmer, assorted PSoC parts, power supply, and getting started instructions. For a more detailed list of the contents and kit prices visit the Cypress web site. If you are doing professional development this kit is well worth the investment.

There are also several products available for the hobbyist, student, and educators available at (www.psoc.time-lines.com), (www.psoctraining.com), and at (www.embeddedbooks.com). Two products worth mentioning are the Timelines PSoC Explorer SoCsicle and the Timelines USB-Explorer boards. The PSoC Explorer SoCsicle board has an assortment of inputs and outputs, and fits nicely into a solderless bread board. Both kits also include an instructional DVD and all components for the included experiments and projects. To check availability and current pricing please visit www.psoc.time-lines.com, www.psoctraining.com, www.embeddedbooks.com or www.time-lines.com.

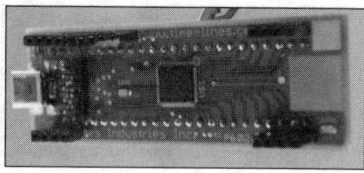

Photo 2-4

PSoC Express Concepts

We are getting close to developing with PSoC Express, but before we start let's look at the components of PSoC Express and the syntax we will be using to create projects. It doesn't matter if you're new to microcontroller development or an experienced developer, you should read the remainder of this chapter since it outlines the steps in developing PSoC Express projects and valid syntax used in expression evaluation.

The PSoC Express Development Cycle

Earlier in this chapter we learned where PSoC Express fits in the PSoC development cycle and how it changes the approach to microcontroller development. Now it's time to take a closer look at the development process and the steps needed to create a PSoC Express project from start to finish. By now you're aware that PSoC Express is a visual tool. That being said, there is little in the development cycle when using PSoC Express that doesn't require a mouse. Figure 2-5 illustrates the PSoC Express Development Process.

Chapter 2

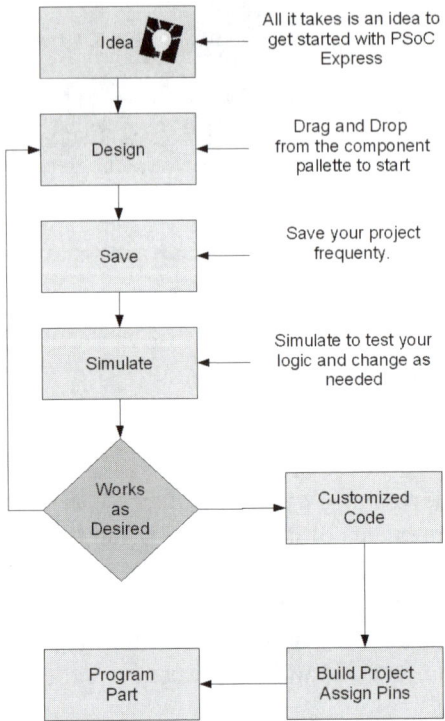

Figure 2-5

It all begins with an idea. Once you've refined your idea or design to a point where you want to test it, you're ready to start designing in PSoC Express. Everything needed is located in the component palette at the lower left bottom of the design screen. Let's take a closer look at the available components. Four components make up the PSoC Express visual component palette. The available components are:

 Input – This symbol defines all of the input types available to PSoC Express.

 Output – This symbol defines all output types available to PSoC Express.

 Valuator – This symbol defines local variables and expression analyzers, truth tables, and state machine components for PSoC Express.

 Interface – This symbol defines external communications interfaces.

Once a PSoC Express project is started, begin in the order the visual components are displayed above and start developing your application. Define your Inputs, your Outputs, then add the glue logic in Transfer Functions, and finally define your external Communications Interfaces.

PSoC Express Expression Syntax

PSoC Express uses the same logical expression tokens as the C language. For those of you who have never used C, the syntax table follows:

Operator	Expression	Definition
>>	SHIFT BIT RIGHT	Shifts all bits to the right by one bit
<<	SHIFT BIT LEFT	Shifts all bits to the left by one bit
&&	LOGICAL AND	TRUE if Left and Right values both equate to one.
||	LOGICAL OR	TRUE if either Left and/or Right values are not equal to zero
<=	LESS THAN, EQUAL TO	Equates to TRUE if left side is less or equal to right side.
>=	GREATER THAN EQUAL TO	Equates to TRUE if left side is greater or equal to the right side.
!=	INEQUALITY TEST	Equates to TRUE if either side does not equal the other side.
(	LEFT PARENS	Encloses Left Side of Equation
)	RIGHT PARENS	Encloses Right Side of Equation
!Value	LOGICAL NOT	True if Value is equal to Zero, otherwise FALSE
-	MINUS	Subtract Right Value from Left Value
+	PLUS	Add Left and Right Values
*	MULTIPLY	Multiply Left times Right Value
/	DIVIDE	Divide Left Value by Right Value
%	MODULO DIVISION	Equals the Remainder of Left Value divided by Right Value
<	LESS THAN TEST	True if Left Value is less than Right Value
>	GREATER THAN TEST	True if Left Value is greater than Right Value
&	BITWISE AND	1 if 1 in both Left and Right Values
~Value	BITWISE NOT	1 if Zero in Value
^	BITWISE XOR	1 if a 1 in either the Left or Right Value, but not both, otherwise 0
==	EQUALITY TEST	1 if Left Value is Equal to Right Value
|	BITWISE OR	1, if 1 in Left, Right, or Both Values

▲ Table 2-1

Math Expressions

If your unfamiliar with C expressions, don't worry, I'll show some examples. Let's start with math examples. Any formula in parentheses "( )" is evaluated from left to right within the parentheses so the following formula: (2 * 3) * (2 * 2) would equate to 6 * 4 or 24 is the answer. Any valid math expression can be evaluated in PSoC Express. Addition (+), Multiplication (*), Division (/), and Subtraction (–) operators can be used in PSoC Express, just as they are in C.

Logical Expressions

Logical AND (&&), Logical OR (||), and Logical NOT (!) can all be used exactly as in the C language. It's always good practice to enclose your evaluation expression in parentheses to avoid confusing the language analyzer. It's also a good practice since PSoC Express encloses the expressions in the outer parentheses. In the following expression the user input is highlighted in bold.

```
If ( (A && B) == False ) then do_something
```

In the above expression we are doing a logical comparison of variables A and B. If the two are logically not equal the above statement would evaluate to true and do_something would be executed.

Bitwise Comparisons

Now, let's look at bitwise expressions. Unlike comparing numbers bitwise operators look at the actual bits of a value to compare and set result bit(s). Depending on the expression valuator used (there's that "v" word again), the result bit may be 0 or 1. Or'ing, And'ing, and XOR'ing all produce different results because they all compare the expression bits differently. Let's look at an example of each to illustrate how bitwise operations are used. First, let's see an example of how a bitwise AND is evaluated, 10 & 20 would equate to 00001010 as decimal 10 and 00010100 for decimal 20. The result of a bitwise AND on these values would be 00000000 since each bit only equates to 1 if it is set to 1 in both values being AND'd. Since our two values do not have any bits that are set to one in both values, it will equate to a zero in every bit position. The PSoC Express evaluation of 10 & 20 follows:

```
If ((10 & 20) == 0)) then do_something
```

Next, let's look at how a bitwise OR works. Let's use our same two values, 10 | 20 (or 00010100 OR'd with 00001010). Bitwise OR'ing differs from a bitwise AND. Using a bitwise OR, only one of the compared bits need to be 1 to be set to a 1. So the result of OR'ing these two values is: 00011110 or 30 decimal. The PSoC Express evaluation of 10 | 20 follows:

```
If ((10 | 20) == 30) then do_something
```

Finally, let's look at the XOR expression. Using the XOR (which stands for Exclusive OR) with the values of decimal values 10 ^ 12 (00001010 and 00001100). So by XOR'ing these values the result would be 00000110 or decimal 6. When using the bitwise exclusive OR (XOR) only those bits that are a 1 in either value but not both values, will remain 1. Since both values contain a 1 in bit value 3 (8), that bit is set to zero leaving only the 1st and 2nd bits set to 1, for a total of 6 as shown in the following PSoC Express expression.

```
If ((10 ^ 20) == 6) then do_something
```

Boolean Expressions

Last, let's examine how the Boolean values of True and False are handled:

```
If (Input1 != True)  then Value = (Value + 1)
```

Again our input is highlighted in bold. In the C language False is always a zero but True can be defined either as a One or as NOT Zero. In the above expression Value will have one added to it only if Input1 is equal to False or zero. The reason for True equating to NOT Zero is so the input value of zero will always equate to False whereas a value greater than Zero will always equate to True. Let's look at the following expression as true example:

> *If* **(Input2 == True)** *then* **LED1 = LED1_ON**

This time we are evaluating Input2 for a True condition. So if Input2 is NOT EQUAL to ZERO then Input2 is considered True and LED1 would be turned on in this case.

We will get into the use of these and other expressions as we start building projects. If you want more information on how expression evaluation works in the C language, pick up a copy of *The C Programming Language* (ISBN: 0131101633), or you can download the PSoC Designer C Language Compiler User Guide available from the Cypress web site.

PSoC Express Valuators

PSoC Express Valuators is where the "glue" that binds inputs and outputs happens. Before we move on to using PSoC Express, let's examine each method of evaluating inputs.

Loop Delay

A Loop Delay stores the last value update loop's value of an input. Consider this example. We have an input that will provide a reading of 0-2600 millivolts. The first read is 330, the second is 1960, and the third is 500. We assign a valuator to this input and define it as a LoopDelay that has an initial value of 0. The first read will be zero, the second time the LoopDelay is read it will be 330, the third read will be 1960, and the fourth read will be 500. The LoopDelay is reading the value of the input one update loop late, hence the name LoopDelay. It Delays by one update loop the value read from an input in the main program Loop.

Priority Encoder

A priority encoder evaluates logically for a "True" input value or state in a top to bottom order of priority. Up to 63 expressions can be acted upon within the expression analyzer. A Priority encoder looks for an input condition and sets an output state based on that expression. The expressions are presented as C language if-then-else-if-then statements.

Set Point Region

When a continuous value like voltages are used as inputs, this technique allows multiple regions to be set with different hysteresis levels for each region. A SetPointRegion valuator can allow easy monitoring of voltage ranges for temperature inputs, and other types of inputs that have staged or variable inputs of any value using the correct voltage divider.

State Machine

The state machine is the heart of every microcontroller. When you need state changes based on transitions, this type of valuator is preferred due to its flexibility. The StateMachine Valuator allows the developer to define all the possible states and conditions that affect transitioning from one state to another. State machines are very flexible and allow one or more conditions to make a single state transition to another state.

Status Encoder

From the surface the Status Encoder looks identical to the Priority Encoder but there are differences. While both share the if-then-pattern rules, the Status Encoder evaluates inputs in sequential order to affect outputs, compared to the Priority Encoder which applies the rules in a prioritized fashion instead.

Table Lookup

Truth tables have been used in electronic logic before the microcontroller was conceived. Truth tables are available in PSoC Express under the name of TableLookup. A Table Lookup Valuator assigns outputs based on input conditions via a drag-and-drop interface. By simply dragging an input condition to an output state the developer can set the status of an LED, motor, or just any other type of output device they choose.

Valuator Summary

We've only covered the definition of valuator types in this section. I wanted you to have a brief understanding of these logic tools before we begin to use them in the next chapter. I know that much of what I have explained here will not make sense if you're new to micro-controller development. Don't worry, it's not you. As we begin to use valuators and gain firsthand experience, the information presented here will begin to make sense.

Valuators are the glue that make PSoC Express work and there can be multiple valuators that work together. I didn't cover that topic because it is easier to explain by example. As you will see in the next chapter, valuators are very powerful and provide endless ways to use PSoC Express. I'm certain that those of you who have never used a microcontroller before will find new and creative ways to use valuators us old-timers never thought of.

Interfaces

The final visual component we will discuss is the Interface. Interfaces allow PSoC Express to communicate with the outside world. Currently the I2C, USB, and WirelessUSB interfaces are implemented. The possibilities of Interfaces are limited only by the imagination and available interface components. We will see firsthand how interfaces play a very important role in PSoC Express in upcoming chapters.

PSoC Program Execution

Before we move on, let's examine how a PSoC program created with PSoC Express executes. As mentioned earlier, interrupts are managed entirely by PSoC Express and are totally transparent to the PSoC Express developer. So to conclude this chapter, let's look at how a PSoC Express program is structured. Figure 2-6 illustrates how a PSoC Express generated program executes.

The Inputs in figure 2-6 could easily be interrupt driven. If that is the case, then the Valuators and associated Transfer Functions would also be handled from the Interrupt Service Routine. We will examine this more closely under advanced topics chapter where we add custom code. If you're designing using the visual components only, figure 2-6 shows everything you need to know. When the PSoC is powered up it goes through an initialization sequence. This sequence prepares it to run the program in memory. In the final stage of initialization, control is passed to the main program loop and variables are initialized. Once the variables are initialized the program goes into a continuous loop of reading Inputs, executing Valuators, and setting outputs through Transfer Functions. This infinite loop continues to execute as long as power is applied to the chip.

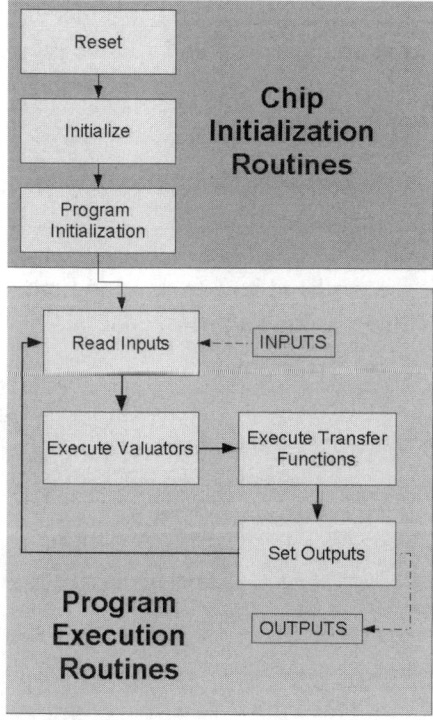

Figure 2-6

The time it takes to execute this loop depends on several factors. Number of inputs, number of valuators, and the number of outputs all contribute to changes in processing time. To allow for flexibility, the PSoC can use either an internal or external clock source. The clock is the heart of the PSoC. Just as a human heart beats so too does the PSoC clock, but with one difference. The accuracy and speed at which the PSoC clock runs depends on the speed of the clock and type of clock used. These two factors determine both the clock rate and accuracy of the clock, hence the accuracy of the PSoC in general. As we get into the project chapters, we will see how to add an external time clock and crystal as well.

Chapter Summary

This chapter outlined the PSoC Express design software and the PSoC processor at a high level. While much of what you learned in this chapter may not make sense, it will begin to come together are we start to move through the remaining chapters and into the project section.

Looking Ahead

In the next chapter we will see firsthand how to develop Embedded Microcontroller Systems without writing a line of code.

Embedded Development without Programming

Now I know there are skeptics out there who are saying "there is no visual tool around that can allow a developer to create microcontroller firmware without any programming." I was skeptical myself at first. In fact, it took a CYPros seminar session on PSoC Express to get my attention. Today, well I'm writing this book because I firmly believe that PSoC Express is such a useful tool that it belongs in the toolbox of anyone who uses microcontrollers and it's a great reason to get familiar with the PSoC. In this chapter we are going to test drive PSoC Express before we start developing actual hardware projects. We can do this because PSoC Express has a very nice simulation mode that allows us to see the results of our efforts before we program a part.

Connect the Components

Once the needed Inputs, Outputs, Valuators, and Interfaces have been added to the design desktop, they are connected by a line as the logic is plugged-in. I call it "connect the components." At a glance the developer can see the logic flow and which inputs, outputs, and valuators are connected to each other (Communication Interfaces are Implicit so connectors are not visible).

This allows for very rapid development since everything is done via a visual interface. Start PSoC Express to gain some firsthand experience with the tool. If you haven't done so already, download and install PSoC Express 2.2 (or later) or install PSoC Express from the accompanying CD. Installing the product is a simple matter of running the install program that comes with it. If you have an earlier version, you should uninstall that version completely through the Add/Remove Programs selection in control panel. When PSoC Express starts, close the startup assistant since we are just going to go through some very basic exercises.

Exercise 1 – Flashing an LED

While it may seem like a simple project, our first experience with PSoC Express will be a single push button input that flashes an LED output when it is pressed. This simple project will give you a hands-on understanding of how easy PSoC Express is to use.

Start PSoC Express and choose File → New. Then single-click or drag the input component at the lower left hand side of the design desktop and a popup window will appear listing the available input types. Scroll down the list to Button → Normally Open → Internal Pulldown N_O. When you select this choice a detailed description will appear in the area to the right and any available start-up parameters will appear below the description. At the very top is an edit box with the Input name. Let's change the input name to Button. Your screen will look like figure 3-1.

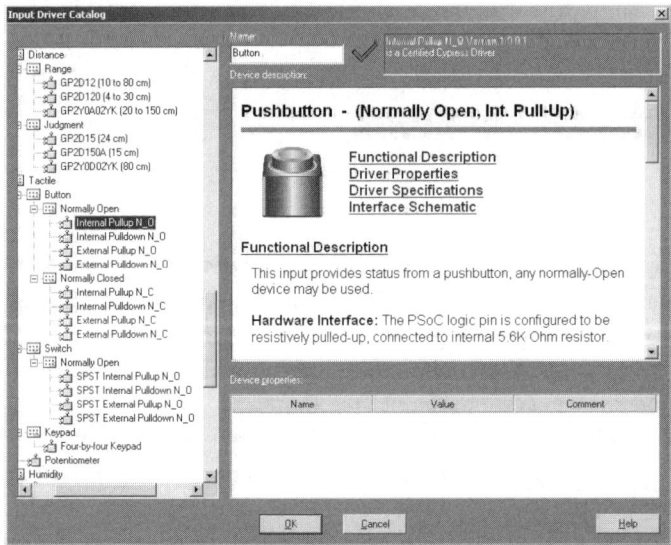

Figure 3-1

The Device Properties area is blank since a button has no configurable parameters to associate with this component. Press the OK button and an Input icon with the name Button now resides on the desktop.

Next, single-click on the output component on the palette. The display is identical to the input component dialog box except the choices are all output types. Scroll down the list to the LED category and select LED, Single Color, ON/OFF as the output type. Change the name to LED1, leaving the Initial Value set to Off. Since the LED can be on or off, we can initialize it to either state. Your display should look like figure 3-2.

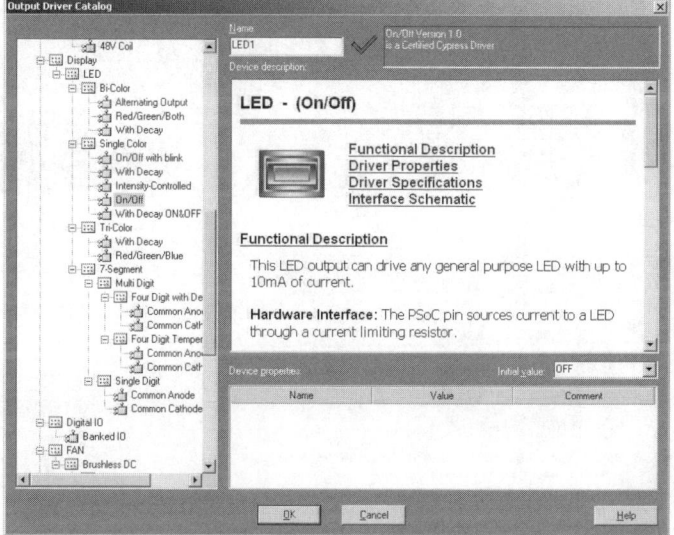

Figure 3-2

Press the OK button and the window will close. Now your design desktop should look like the screen in figure 3-3 on the following page.

In Chapter 2 we discussed Valuators and what their purpose and capabilities are. What I didn't tell you is that Transfer Functions are also available in outputs. Since we simply want to turn the LED on when the button is pressed, we can use the LED's built-in Transfer Function. Highlight the LED1 component, right-click and select "Transfer Function" and the screen in figure 3-4 will be shown.

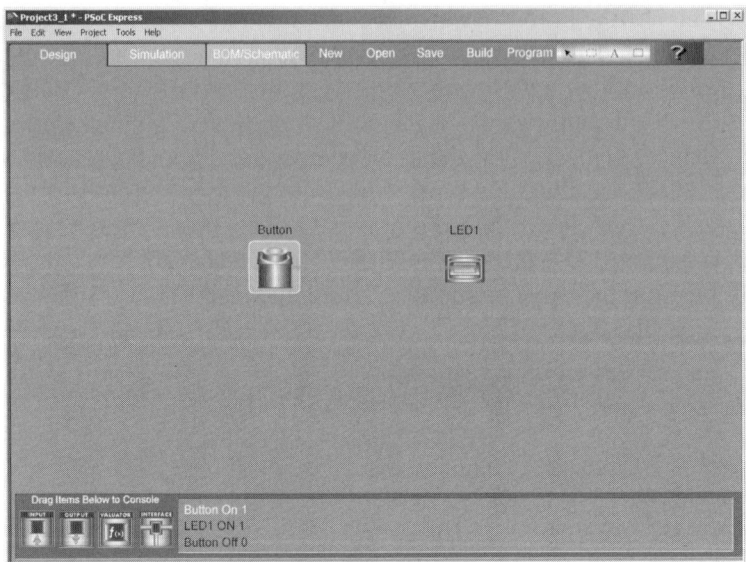

Figure 3-3

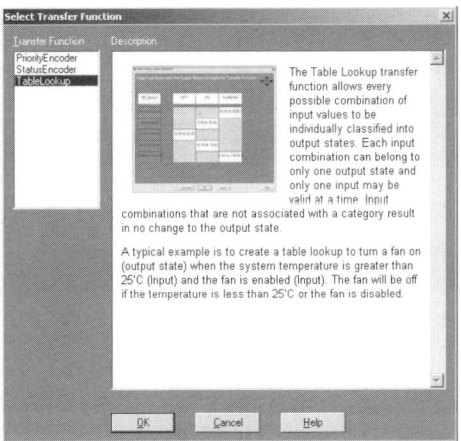

Figure 3-4

Priority Encoder, Status Encoder, and
Table Lookup are the only Valuator types
allowed for the LED component. Choose the
Table Lookup Valuator and press the OK button. The Input Select window will pop up.
Choose the Button as the input selection and
then press the Next>> button as shown in
figure 3-5.

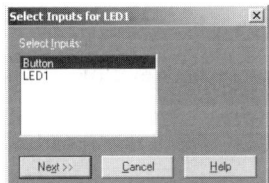

Figure 3-5

Note: You will notice that the LED1 Transfer Function allows LED1 to select itself as an input. You may be asking why would you want to do this. One reason would be to set an external variable if the condition of LED1 were to change. In that case it would be to signal the main program of a change that would be monitored by the output itself.

The next window allows you to modify or delete the defined values, states, and expressions, or add new values, states, and expressions. Figure 3-6 shows the Add Values window.

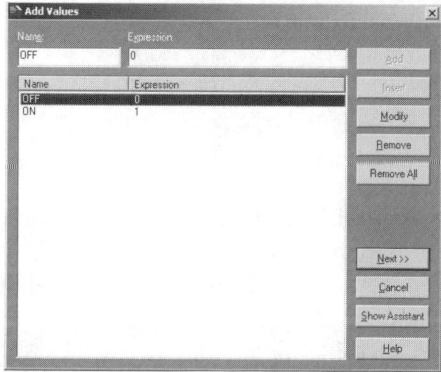

Figure 3-6

Notice that the OFF value is highlighted. Here is where we add local output values, states, and their values or evaluation expressions. For this demonstration we have two states that have permanent values assigned to them. But we could just as easily have an expression associated with an input that controls an output value. In the next demonstration we will use this feature to add more than two states, but for now just press the Next>> button which brings us to our final window for the Table Lookup Transfer Function.

Figure 3-7 (see the following page) shows the default Table Lookup window before any assignments have been made. I wanted you to see how easy it is to use the Table Lookup Transfer Function before finishing this exercise.

At the top the message says "Drag Input Rows onto the Output States to create the Transfer Function." Below the left and right columns I added two pieces of text and they are running different directions on purpose. The left column contains "Input Conditions,"

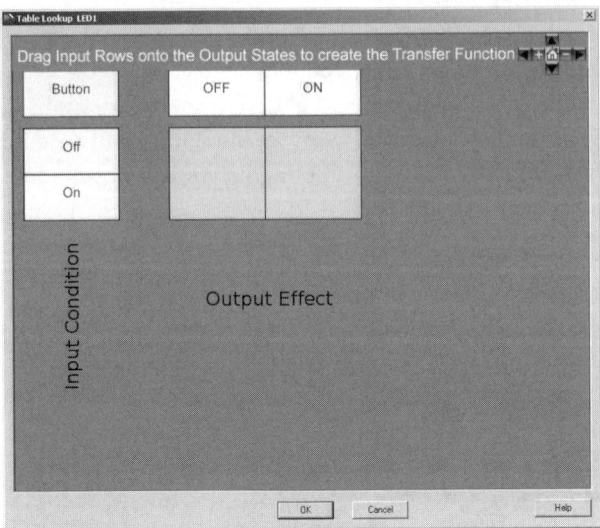

Figure 3-7

which in this case is the On or Off condition of the Button object. In the right column written horizontally is "Output Effect." We want to drag the Input Condition to the desired Output Effect. When the Button object is On, LED1 should be On, and when the Button is Off, the LED1 object should also be off. Figure 3-8 shows how the finished screen should look.

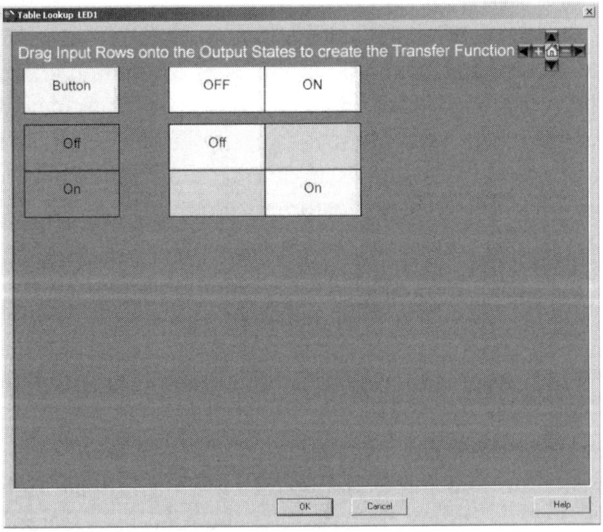

Figure 3-8

This example illustrates just how easy using the TableLookup Transfer Function can be. We drag the Off condition of Button to the Off column of LED1. We then drag the On condition of Button to the On column of LED1. There are a couple of items to note about the TableLookup window. The inputs are each marked on the left column(s) and yes there can be more than a single input. The output in this case is the window itself and if you look at the title bar of the window it clearly states this is the Table Lookup for LED1. So, if you get confused while in a Transfer Function for an Output or Valuator component, simply look at the title bar to see where you are.

> **Note:** About the definition of a Transfer Function. A Transfer Function could be considered equivalent to a C or assembler subroutine where the Input value affects the Output condition.

After pressing the OK button you are returned to the design desktop where there is now a line drawn between the Button and LED1 objects, indicating these objects are now connected logically. Now we are ready to test the logic of this system.

The PSoC Express Simulator

Now we are ready to see if our logic works in simulation. Before we can run a simulation the project must first be saved. This is done by selecting File → Save As or clicking the Save tab on the design desktop. A Save is also done automatically when the Simulation tab is chosen, if the project has not been saved, a path and filename will be prompted. Whichever method you choose, save the project as Chapter3_1. We will be using this project as a starting point for the next exercise. Once the project is saved you can run the simulation by pressing the Simulation tab at the top. Go ahead and run a simulation now.

You'll notice the screen looks exactly as before except there are now boxes next to the Button and LED1 objects that are titled Current Value, Cypress documents refer to these as widgets where this book refers to them as components. For input components using the mouse cursor and left mouse button allows the input value to be changed. Note that the Button and LED1 components are Off. To change the state of the Button object, move the mouse cursor over the On value and click the left mouse button. The On value should now be dark green in color indicating your change was successful. Note the value of the LED1 object is now On. Click the mouse button on the Off value of the Button and notice how LED1 changes to Off. Figure 3-9 shows how the screen looks after running the simulation, but before any values are changed.

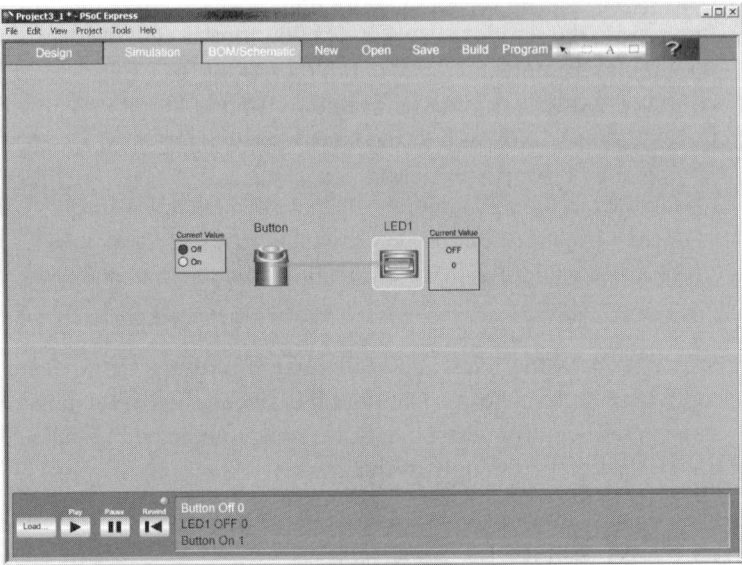

Figure 3-9

In this example, we have taken the input of a Button directly into the Transfer Function of LED1 to be changed. This is the simplest PSoC Express project we can create. Transfer Functions and Valuators are two terms you will hear over and over again. So before we go any further, let's take a brief look at the definition of these terms.

Valuators

What exactly is a Valuator? Think of a Valuator as the glue that binds input logic to output control. If you look at all of our projects you will find Valuators are the heart and soul of expression analysis, input evaluations, evaluation prioritization, output type, and state management. Without Valuators, PSoC Express would not be able to do much at all. Throughout the remainder of this book you will hear the word Valuator used frequently. Each time the term is used, think of how you would glue your input values to output control or states. Would you use a status encoder, where you run through a list of if..then..else statements, each with equal priority, or would you prioritize a list of if..then..else statements to manage your logic. Maybe you would prefer a state machine to handle your I/O logic or a Set Point Region where you input values may cause different actions based on hysteresis. You could also assign a lookup table to handle your logic or use the Loop Delay to keep track of the last state value of a triggered input, or assign a byte or word variable using the Interface Valuator.

Transfer Functions

So what exactly is a transfer function. Even if you're an experienced programmer you may never have heard this term before. A transfer function can be thought of as a function or subroutine that contains the logic to transfer input data into output control storing the input data in memory. In this example we are taking the state of the button input and setting the state of the led in the transfer function. Transfer functions are just as important as Valuators and are at the heart of a Valuator.

Chapter 3

Codeless PSoC Development

You've just developed your first circuit with the PSoC Express program. If you're new to microcontrollers, then congratulations are in order. If you've never used PSoC Express before but have written code for other microcontrollers congratulations, you just developed your first program without writing a line of code. That was easy, wasn't it. For the remainder of this chapter we will explore the additional Valuator and transfer Function techniques. I will not be showing all of the screenshots, only those that illustrate how the different techniques work.

WYSIWYG Microcontroller Development

What you've just witnessed is the world's first What-You-See-Is-What-You-Get (WYSIWYG) microcontroller development package. It's great to be able to reuse an acronym from so long ago (WYSIWYG) pronounced whis-ee-wig. This term was first coined for the desktop publishing packages over 20 years ago.

Will PSoC Express code perform the same when programmed into a PSoC part, installed in a circuit. The answer is yes, but the question will have to remain unproven until we reach the project section. For the remainder of this chapter we will be using the simulator to prove our results. The reason for this is twofold. First, you need to be confident that you can use PSoC Express effectively and second, you need to have confidence in the simulator so you can debug before ever burning your first chip and save a lot of time in the development process. So, with that in mind we will move on to exercise 2.

Exercise 2 – A Simple Voltage Input

For our second exercise, we are going to simulate a voltage input monitor. Before we change the design from our first exercise, let's draw a simple flowchart that outlines the objective. This way, we will have a guide to describe the end result. In the real world you would (hopefully) have a complete design document that would serve this purpose.

> **Note:** You may have heard the term GIGO or Garbage In, Garbage Out. This refers to poorly designed systems that evolved rather than designed. No visual design tool in the world is a substitute for good design practices. If you fail to design your system and rely on PSoC Express as your design tool, you will be very disappointed, and rightfully so. PSoC Express is not a substitute for design but a tool to expedite the delivery of a design.

In flowchart 3-1, the do-forever loop is handled by PSoC Express and the default variable setting will occur at the time the input is defined. For this example we will use a Set-Point-Region Valuator with transfer Function. This allows us to set multiple threshold values. Both the Potentiometer and Set-Point-Region controls use percentages so we need to only set three threshold values. Since we have a 5 volt system, 100% is 5 volts, 1.25 volts would be 25%, 2.0 volts would be 40% and 2.25 volts would be 45%. So by setting three threshold values to 25, 40, and 45 we will in effect be setting the proper voltage thresholds. This in turn will set our LED to Off if less than 25%, low between 25% and 40%, medium 40% to 45%, and high if above 45%.

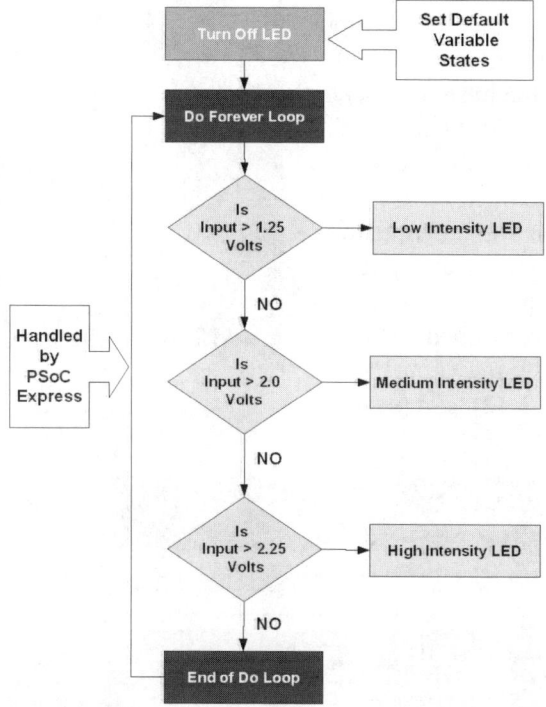

Flowchart 3-1

Let's begin by single-clicking an Input or dragging an Input on to the design desktop, choosing a Potentiometer, and leave the default name of Input1 as shown in figure 3-10.

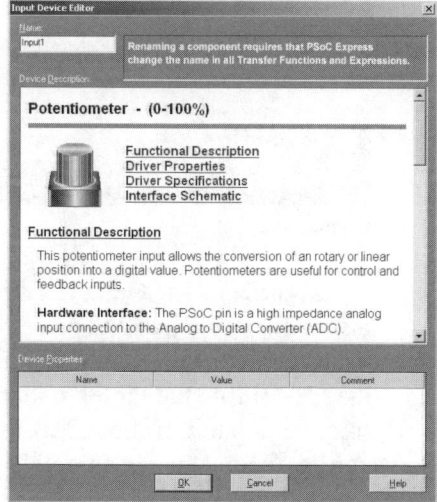

Figure 3-10

Next, click or drag a Valuator, choose Set-Point-Region, leave the default name of Valuator1 and click Next>>. Choose Input1 as the Input and add three thresholds at 25, 40, and 45, leaving the hysteresis set to 0. When you're done, your Threshold points should look like the screen in figure 3-11.

After completing the Valuator's Transfer Function, add an output by clicking the output component, select Intensity controlled LED, leave the name set to Output1 (as shown in figure 3-12), and press OK.

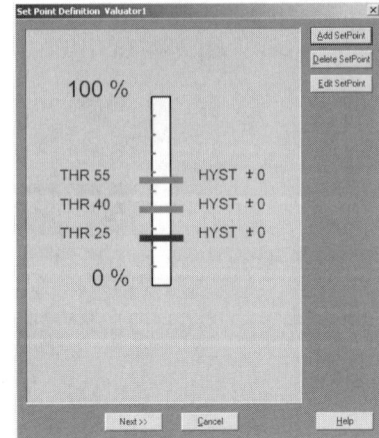

Figure 3-11

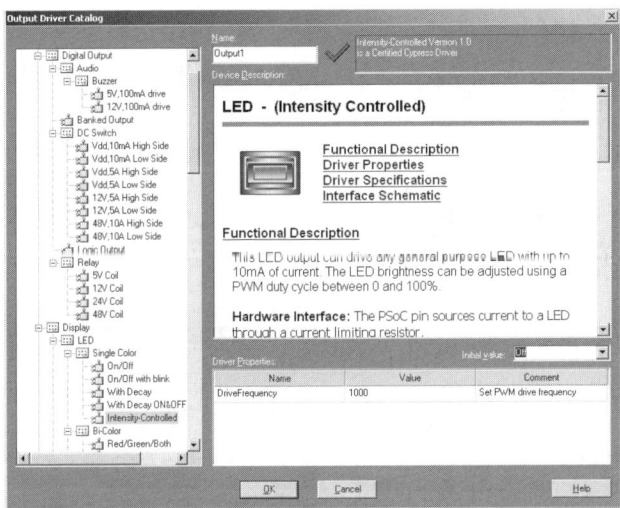

Figure 3-12

Right-click the Output1 component and choose Transfer Function. Select Table Lookup and press Next>> twice. Now you're looking at the screen where we will map the threshold points to the intensity of the LED. From the far left column, drag-and-drop each box starting from the top to Off, Low, Medium, and High respectively. When you're done, your screen will look like the one in figure 3-13.

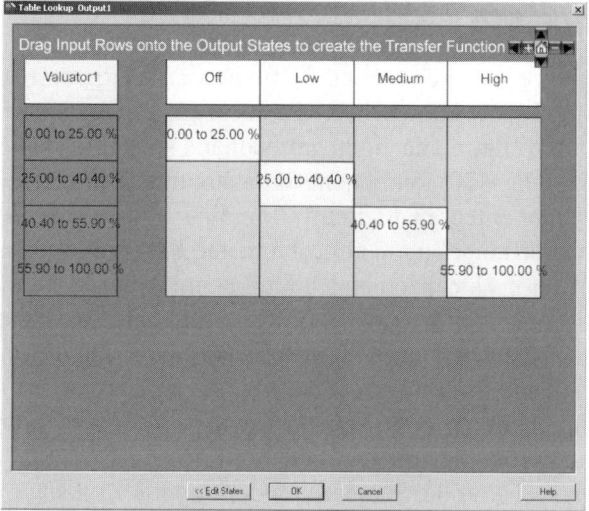

Figure 3-13

Once again, we are ready to test our logic with the simulator. If you haven't done so already, save the current project and press the Simulate tab at the top. Change the position of the slider and watch the intensity of the LED change. Figure 3-14 will look similar to your simulation display.

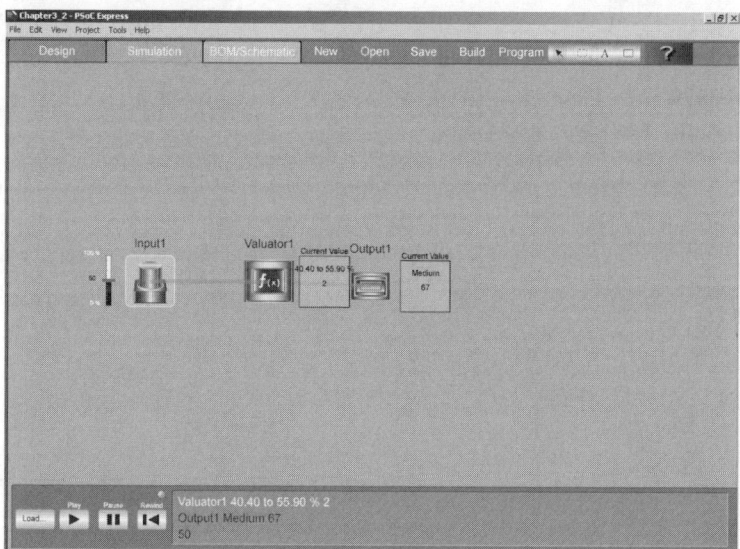

Figure 3-14

The I2C Interface

The I2C interface has been around for many years. Originally developed by Phillips (now known as NXP), its original purpose was to provide a simple communications protocol and serial bus that could be shared among other I2C components on a circuit board. I2C is an acronym for Inter-Integrated-Circuit Communications. I've used I2C successfully in distances up to almost a meter, but it's really designed for communications localized on a circuit board or across short distances. I2C is a master-slave protocol which can have one master to a maximum of 127 slave devices. It utilizes two wires and a common ground wire. Aside from the ground wire, one wire provides the data clock and the other provides a path for the data. The bus supports three data rates, 100Kbps for standard, 400Kbps for Fast and 3.4 Mbps in high speed mode. Standard mode supports 7 bit slave addressing while fast and high speed modes support 7 or 1 bit slave addressing.

PSoC Express supports standard-mode speed for I2C command and slave modes, and fast-mode speed for PSoC based slave-only devices built using PSoC Express. Since I2C is address based, communicating with an I2C device is a simple matter of setting the proper address, assigning the proper command and reading or writing slave data. PSoC Express handles all protocol packetizing and depacketizing at both the master and slave device side when developed with PSoC Express. Let's put PSoC Express I2C to a test drive in the next two exercises.

Exercise 3 – Creating the I2C Master

In the last exercise a simple circuit was built using a potentiometer to adjust the intensity of an LED. This exercise will begin by opening exercise 2, adding an I2C command register that will hold the LED intensity control value. Then a new project will be created, using an I2C Slave component to update the remote LED with the value of the local potentiometer. When this exercise is completed, a better understanding of I2C communications should be gained and the ease at which I2C can be implemented in PSoC Express.

Adding the I2C Slave Command

The first step in adding remote I2C capabilities is to add the slave command register which contains the slave address and slave data bytes. Since I2C is master controlled let's begin by opening our last project, then adding a new output component. This component will be an I2C Slave Command component in the Remote Devices category. Choose the first parameter and change the variable type to Byte. Since the LED intensity is expressed in percent from the Potentiometer, the maximum value will be 100, which is well within the range limit of a byte which is 255. Your screen should look like figure 3-15.

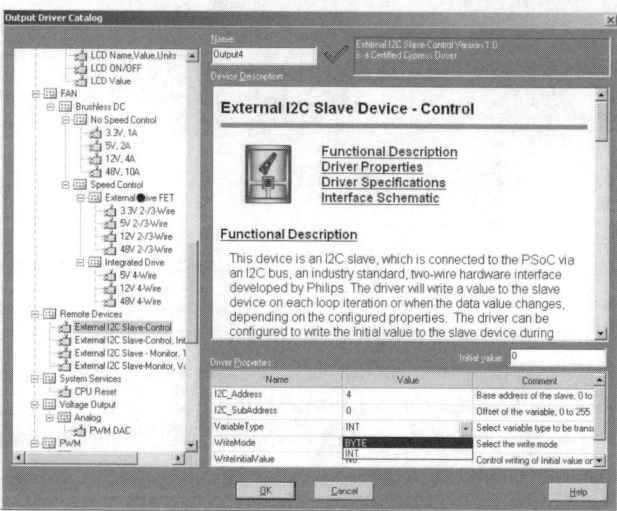

Figure 3-15

Chapter 3

After pressing the OK button, right-click and select Transfer Function, choosing a Table Lookup as we did for the LED. After Pressing Next>>, add the values for the lookup table that will match the LED. Add values to make the display look like figure 3-16.

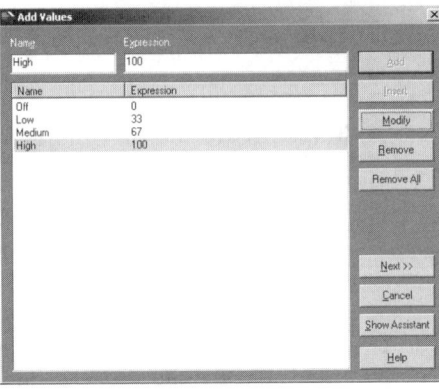

Figure 3-16

Now, press Next>> and let's set our table values as shown in figure 3-17, which are identical to the LED table lookup function.

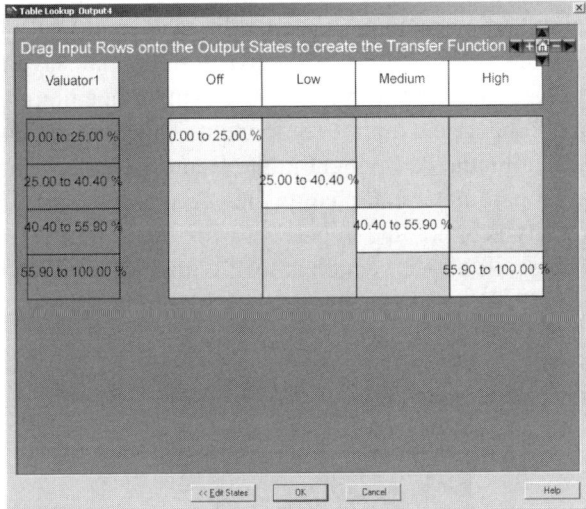

Figure 3-17

After pressing OK once more, the design desktop will look like figure 3-18.

Let's simulate to see if our new output works as designed. As you adjust the slider, the value for the I2C output should be identical to the value of the LED as shown in figure 3-19.

Now save the project and start a new project. Name the new project Example3_3s (the S is for slave).

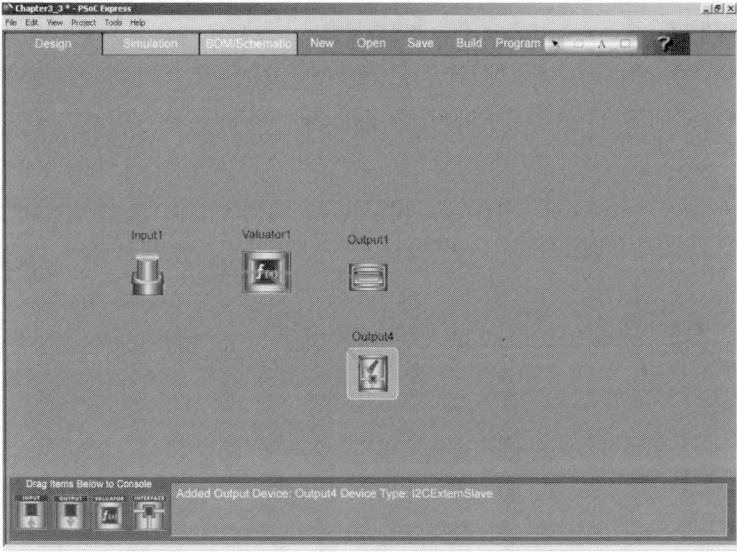

Figure 3-18

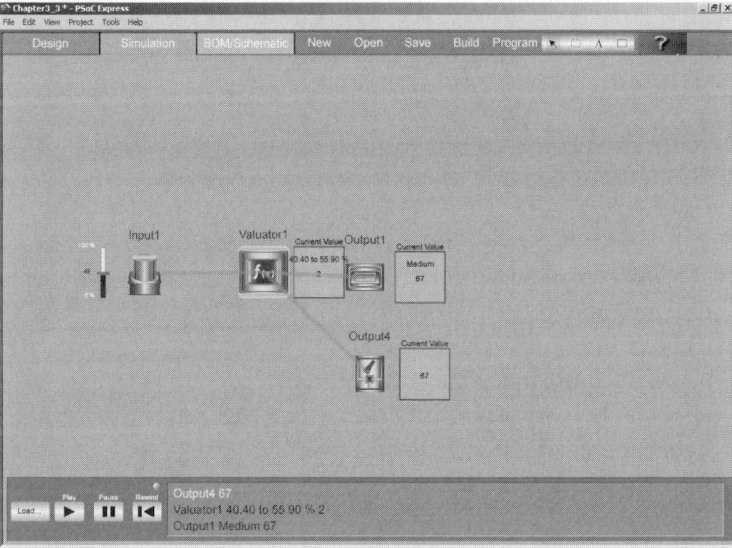

Figure 3-19

Chapter 3

Exercise 4 – The I2C Slave

This new project will be the I2C slave that sets the light intensity of the remote LED. Click the Interface icon at the bottom left area of the design desktop. Choose Communications → I2C → Slave component. This will act as the connection between the master and slave devices. Choose the I2C address of 4 as shown in figure 3-20.

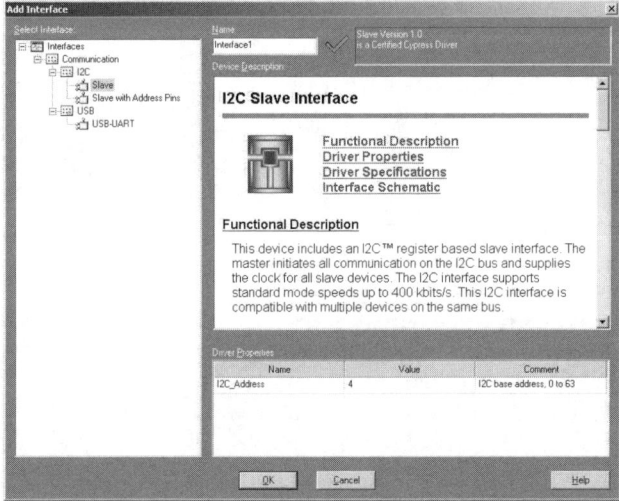

Figure 3-20

Next, drag-and-drop a Valuator component on the desktop. Choose Interface Valuator and name it Command. This will allocate memory storage for the byte data received from the interface. Figure 3-21 shows how the first screen of the Valuator will look.

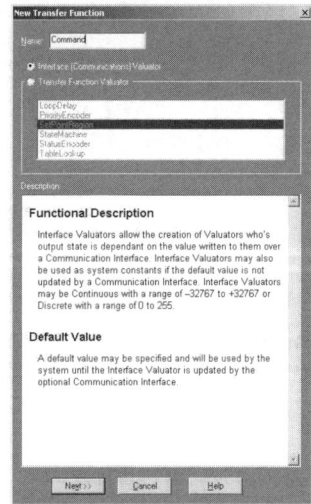

Figure 3-21

Press Next>> and you will see a window like figure 3-22.

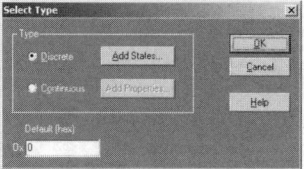

The screen in figure 3-22 is very important as it determines if the declared variable is a byte (Discrete) or signed integer (Continuous). A Discrete type can contain a value between 0 and

Figure 3-22

255. A signed integer that can hold a value between –32767 and +32767. It's important to note that PSoC Express will cast a single byte value (Discrete) to the lower 8 bits of a signed integer value, so keep this in mind when designing PSoC Express projects.

For the final step in this project, click the Output component icon on the design desktop, select LED → Intensity Controlled. Name the component RemoteLED then right-click and select Transfer Function. Select Status Encoder. This will be a single expression that gets executed each time through the main program loop. The expression is:

If **1** *then* **Command**

To enter this expression select the first field and enter the number 1, then select the next field and type Command. When you're finished the Status Encoder window will look like figure 3-23.

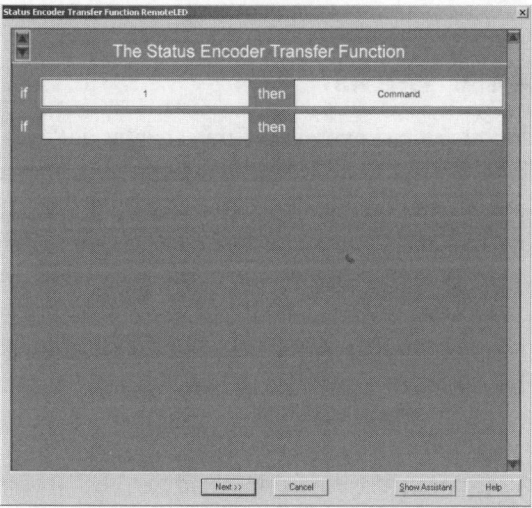

Figure 3-23

Chapter 3

Press Next>> to return to the desktop and your design desktop will look like figure 3-24.

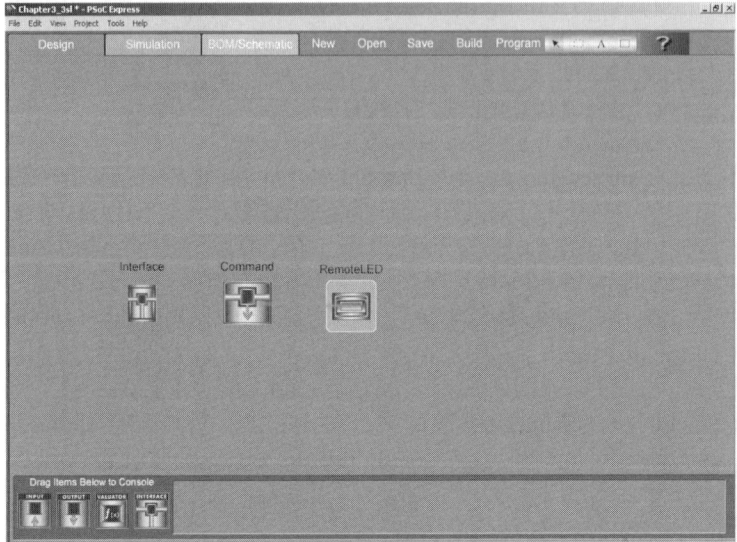

Figure 3-24

Now, press the Simulate tab and change the value of the Interface value. Each time the Interface value changes, so does the intensity of the LED.

How the I2C Slave Works

Before we move on to the last exercise of this chapter, let's take a look at how the I2C slave works. Since we only have three components on the desktop, this is a simple enough project to examine. The Interface component sets up the logic that listens to the I2C bus at the selected address. The Interface Valuator reserves a memory variable for the data received from the I2C Master. The RemoteLED component provides the connection for the Intensity Controlled LED through the PSoC Register Map.

The If 1 then Command statement is very simple. Each time through the execution loop this expression is evaluated. The If 1 is always True so the Command value is read and the LED intensity is updated. When the Master was created and the I2C Slave Control added, the default value of "Update on Change" causes the slave to be updated whenever the potentiometer on the master is changed. This means that when the potentiometer is changed on the master, the I2C value is written immediately to the I2C bus and the I2C Slave updates the intensity of the LED each time through the loop. This will cause an immediate change at the remote.

Exercise 5 – The State Machine

Our final exercise for this chapter will introduce you to the PSoC Express State Machine. State machines are a big part of embedded development with the PSoC, so we will cover them here, to show you in practice how a state machine is implemented. Let's get started!

This exercise will implement a simple push button that will transition from off-to-on and on-to-off each time it is pressed. While this is a simple exercise, it covers both the State and State Transitions in an easy-to-follow fashion. Start by creating a new project. First add an Input → Button → Normally Open, and Name it Button1 as shown in figure 3-25.

Next, add an Output, choose LED, On/Off, and Name it LED1 as shown in figure 3-26.

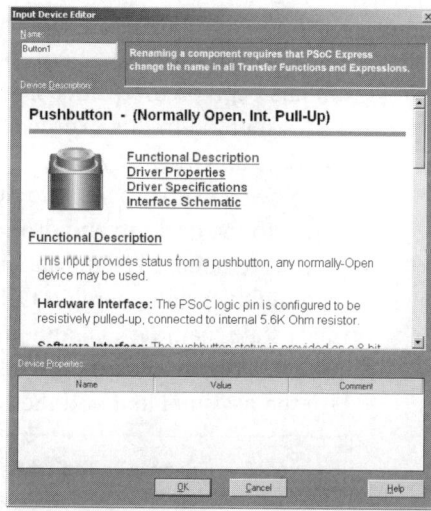

Figure 3-25

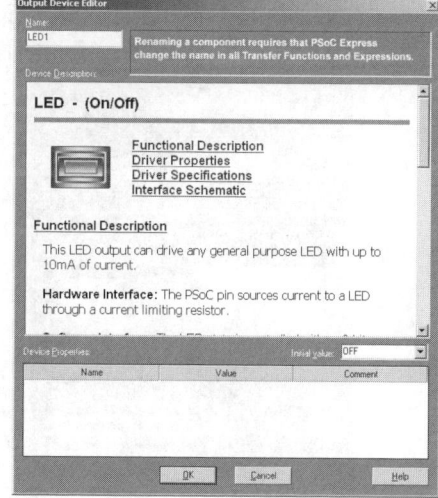

Figure 3-26

Next, drag a valuator onto the design desktop. Name it LoopDelay1, choose type of LoopDelay, press Next>> and accept the default value of 0 as shown in figure 3-27.

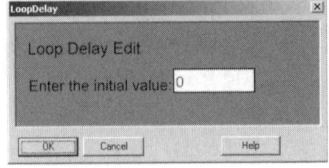

Figure 3-27

What is the purpose of a LoopDelay component? Each time the button is pressed, LoopDelay toggles between 0 and 1. It starts at Zero, goes to One, and then back to Zero to start the process all over again. Since LoopDelay starts at 0, the first time Button1 is pressed and released the associated LoopDelay will be 1. It tells us if the button has been pressed since LoopDelay was last set to 0. It provides us with a method in this exercise to use a momentary contact button to simulate an On/Off switch.

Now it's time to add the State Machine. Drag another valuator object to the desktop and drop it. Select StateMachine as the type and give it the name of StateMachine1, press Next>>. Let's add the first (and default) state, name it Off, and press OK. Let's add our next (and final) state, name it On. and press OK. Now we will add our state transitions. Double-click on the Off state, select Transitions, then Add. Use the assistant and add the following expression:

```
(Button1 == Button1__Off) && (LoopDelay1 == LoopDelay1__On)
```

Select Off as the From Transition and On as the To Transition. The display should look like figure 3-28.

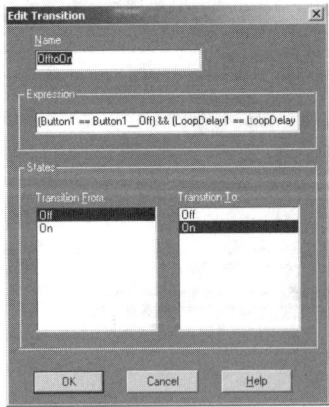

Note: The expression in figure 3-28 does not show the complete expression. That is why the complete expression appears above.

Figure 3-28

The logic of the LoopDelay and how it relates to the StateMachine should now begin to make sense. The expression just entered explains it all: If the button is released (Off) and the button has been pressed since our last evaluation (LoopDelay1 == On) then the State changes from Off to On. Click OK and let's add the final state transition. Double-click the On state and add a new Transition. Name this transition OntoOff and add the same expression again as shown below.

```
(Button1 == Button1__Off) && (LoopDelay1 == LoopDelay1__On)
```

Select On as the From transition and Off as the To transition and press OK. The display will now look like figure 3-29.

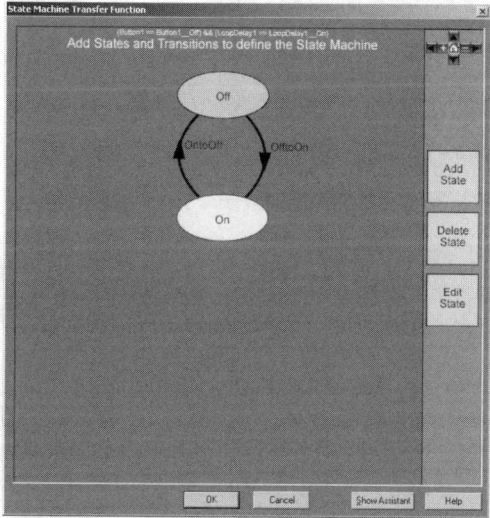

Figure 3-29

There is one more step to complete this exercise. Select the LED1 object and right-click, selecting Transfer Function. For this exercise select Priority Encoder and press Next>>. Click the first expression field and enter the number 1, then press OK. Click the second field and enter the following expression:

Chapter 3

```
LED1 = StateMachine1__State
```

Again clicking OK when finished. The screen will now look like the one in figure 3-30.

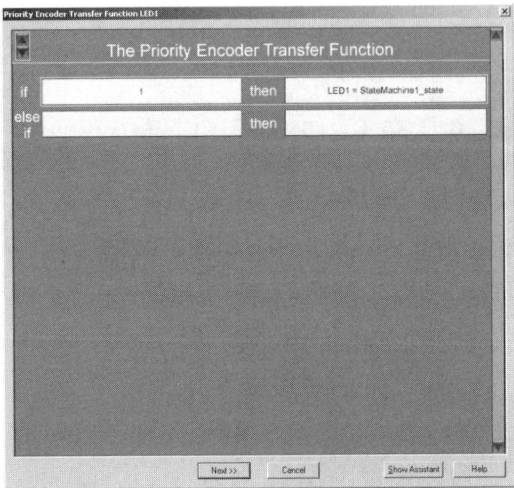

Figure 3-30

Save this project (if you haven't done so already) and press the Simulation tab. Note the StateMachine1 Valuator is set to "No Transition" and LED1 is set to "0" or "Off." You will also note that LoopDelay1 is initialized to "0" and our Button1 object is "Off." Toggle the Button1 object from Off to On and back to Off. Your display should look like the one in figure 3-31.

If you were watching the changes when you pressed the button from Off to On you would have seen that LoopDelay1 changed to a 1. When Button1 was released it satisfied the transition requirement and changed the state of LED1 to ON before setting LoopDelay back to 0 and setting StateMachine1 back to No transition. If you cycle the button from off to on and on to off again, LED1 will turn off.

If you wish to build this project, go ahead, otherwise we will get into more depth about part selection, building, and programming in the next chapter.

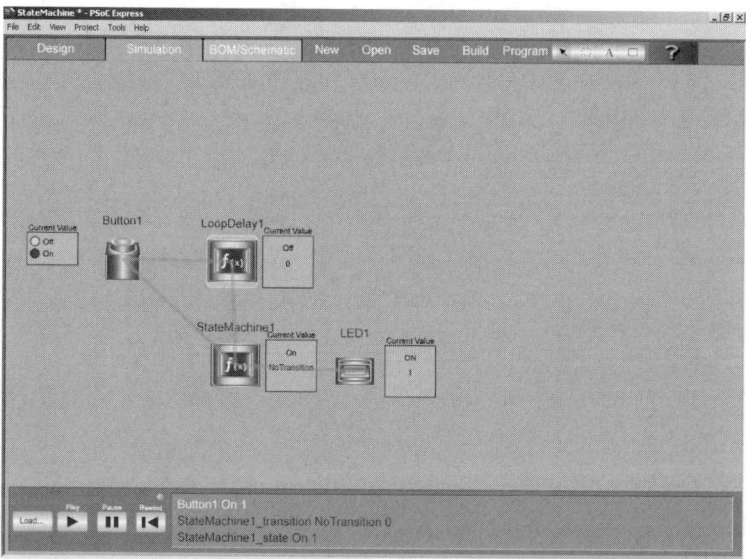

Figure 3-31

Chapter Summary

The intent of this chapter was to get you familiar with the PSoC Express IDE, and Simulator. Hopefully you have a better understanding of how PSoC Express components, expressions, and communications work. You can learn a lot without ever programming a part using the PSoC Express simulator. I encourage you to use the simulator to test the boundaries of PSoC Express, visualizing your own ideas, and testing program logic before programming a chip.

Looking Ahead

By now you should have confidence both in PSoC Express and your skills in making it work for you. In the next chapter, we will go from concept to prototype in 15 minutes. That's right, a quarter of an hour to implement a new product prototype.

From Concept to Prototype in 15 Minutes

Chapter Overview

In my book *Embedded Systems Desktop Integration* (ISBN 1-55622-994-1) many types of communications (RS232, USB, Ethernet, I2C) are covered as a thermostat is built using various microcontrollers. At the end of that book I cover the PSoC using PSoC Designer. That book is 472 pages long. Implementing the thermostat took 2-4 weeks per microcontroller due to the amount of coding that was necessary.

While we aren't going to implement a thermostat in this chapter, we are going to implement a complete working product prototype in 15 minutes from start to finish. The project files and components are on the CD if you want to build this project on your own.

A Real PSoC Express Based Product

Among other things, I'm also a photographer. I do all of my own photographs for my books and articles, and love taking pictures. If you are also a photography buff, then you know the importance of lighting to make your subject look its best. Whether it's a circuit board or a family photo, lighting makes the image, period.

In the next 15 minutes we are going to fully implement a light meter. This is no cheap light meter but one that has the following functions:

1. Measures a wide range of lighting conditions.
2. Has a switch to snapshot and store a light reading.
3. Has a low and high thresholds that can be adjusted by a potentiometer.

That may seem like a lot of features to implement but as you will see PSoC Express is more than up to this task.

This project will use the following components:

▶ 3 LEDs

▶ 1 Momentary Push Button

▶ 2 Potentiometers

▶ 1 CDS Photocell

You're probably saying that we can't do this in 15 minutes and it's understandable why you would believe that. I went to a seminar a few days ago and the presenter touted advanced tools that could be installed in less than 20 minutes and sure enough 20 minutes later he had an empty main.c file on the screen. So developing a working project in 15 minutes is 5 minutes less than it took to install the toolset a week ago

The CDS Photocell

The CDS Photocell is the component we will use to determine light levels. These come in various sizes and values. As the amount of light shed on the photocell increases the amount of resistance decreases, so the higher the resistive value, the darker the surrounding light. There are two different inputs that can be used in PSoC Express for a photocell. The first is a resistive input that allows assorted resistive values to be input directly or we can use a potentiometer. Whichever you choose, pick a photocell with the matching resistive properties.

Starting the Prototype

Start a new project in PSoC Express. Drag an Input component on to the desktop, select Push Button → Normally Open → Internal-Pullup and name it TriggerButton. Your display will look like figure 4-1.

TriggerButton will be used to turn the circuit on when pressed and off when released. Next, drag-and-drop another Input component to the desktop, this time choosing a Potentiometer, and name it Photocell. Repeat this process adding two more Potentiometer Inputs named LightThreshold and LightHysteresis. Add the Output objects. First, choose Output → LED → ON/OFF, and name it HighThreshold. Repeat this procedure once more this time naming the LED LowThreshold.

Separating Logic and Control

We have one more component to add, but before we do, let's briefly talk about a problem that can crop up if you're not made aware of it, and can cause serious problems if it occurs.

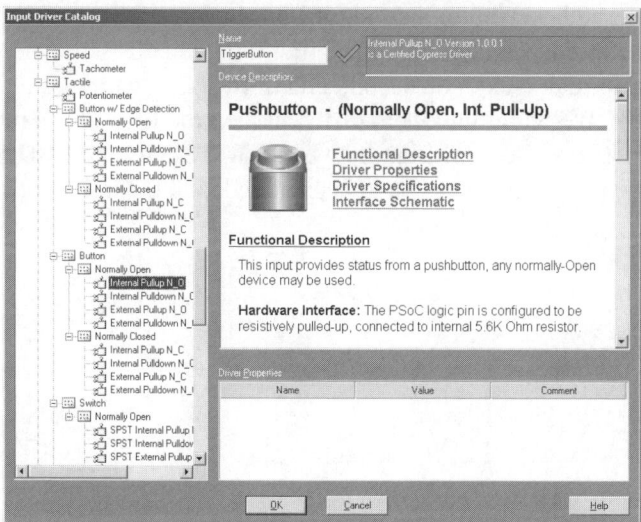

Figure 4-1

Chapter 4

Visual design tools like PSoC Express are wonderful tools for helping us be more productive and reducing time-to-market, but they don't replace our thought process, they supplement it. When hand coding a system in C or assembler, we separate out logic from control during the course of designing code. Since PSoC Express is generating all of the code, it would be very easy to attempt combining our logic and control. Attempting to do that would make a valuator or transfer function that would not behave as expected.

To avoid this from happening, make the project easier to implement, and future enhancements easier we will add a State Machine Valuator to measure and act on the amount of light being provided and set the light level settings accordingly. That will set the corresponding LED based on the amount of light provided with minimal logic.

This approach separates logic and control while providing maximum capability with minimal effort. The end result will be the proper light setting LED when the button is pressed, leaving the LEDs off when released. Now your first comment to this will be, "Why should I care about the button state if I kill power when the button is released?" and that is a very valid question. In truth however, by separating the logic states and control of the LEDs, we can add an On/Off button, and still use the existing push button to provide current light level readings without making any further changes to the PSoC Express project.

Now, add a Valuator, naming it LightLevel and choose State Machine as the Valuator type. The first (and default) state will be named Normal. Next, add second and third states, naming them Bright and Dark. We're naming them different than the LEDs for a reason, and that is to avoid confusion between Logic States and LED names. Once the remaining states have been added, add the transitions.

Setting the Light Threshold and Hysteresis

By now you may be asking, "How are we going to set the proper transition expressions?" because it seems complicated in taking adjustments from two potentiometers to set threshold and hysteresis settings, but in truth these expressions are very simple both to work out logically and to implement in PSoC Express expression syntax.

The Light Threshold Potentiometer

This is a simple potentiometer that will read 0-100 percent of the light level in the middle of what the "Normal" light level should be. Let's say we want 50% light to be a normal light level with 5% hysteresis giving us a normal reading from 45% (50 – 5) to 55% (50 + 5). We would set the Light Threshold Potentiometer to its midpoint, 50 percent. Now keep in mind this is just the prototype, so this can be refined later.

The Light Hysteresis Potentiometer

This potentiometer will set the hysteresis level of Light Threshold. Instead of reading 0 to 100 percent, we will divide the read value by 10, allow this potentiometer to set the hysteresis to a value between 0 and 10 percent for light threshold. If we were to connect this to a sliding variable resistor, this value would be our "fine tuning" or "overlap" value.

Chapter 4

The Valuator Logic

Bringing this all together is fairly simple. To go from Normal to Bright. A single line expression would be as follows:

```
Photocell > (LightThreshold + (LightHysteresis / 10))
```

If the Photocell reading is greater than the value of Light-Threshold plus LightHysteresis divided by 10 then transition from Normal to Bright. To go from Bright to Normal would simply mean changing the greater-than sign (>) to a less-than sign (<) as follows:

```
Photocell < (LightThreshold + (LightHysteresis / 10))
```

Going from Normal to Dark is a simple matter of subtracting LightHysteresis / 10 from LightThreshold instead of adding as shown below:

```
Photocell < (LightThreshold - (LightHysteresis / 10))
```

The above equation would transition from Normal to Dark. Going from Dark to Normal would be a simple matter of changing the less-than sign to a greater-than sign as shown below:

```
Photocell > (LightThreshold - (LightHysteresis / 10))
```

This example illustrates how a simple one-line expression can be used for some powerful state transitions in PSoC Express. Now, add the transition logic to the light meter.

Double-click on the Normal state and select Transition, Add. Let's name the transition NormaltoLighter and add the expression as shown in figure 4-2.

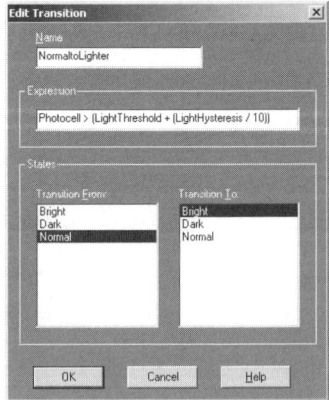

Figure 4-2

Next, add the transition back to normal. Double-click on the Bright State, select Transition, Add, and name the Transition LightertoNormal. Your display will look like figure 4-3.

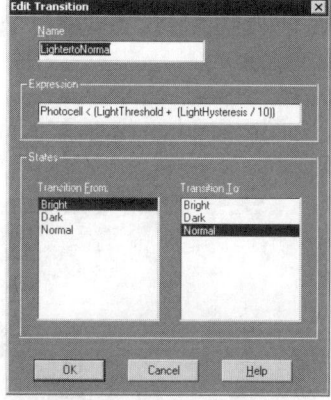

Figure 4-3

The State Machine is not half completed. Double-click on Normal state, select Transition, Add, and name the next transition NormaltoDarker and match the remainder of the display to that of figure 4-4.

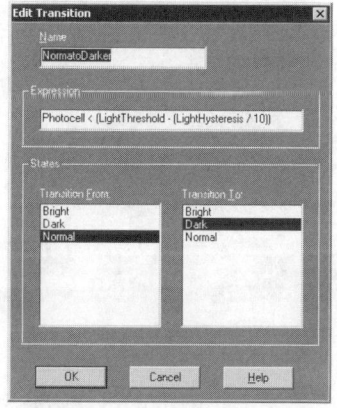

Figure 4-4

For the last state transition, double-click the Dark state, choose Transition, and Add. The final transition will be named DarkertoNormal. When completed, the transition window will look like figure 4-5.

Press OK to return to the State Machine diagram.

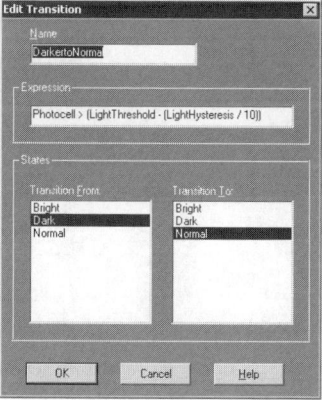

Figure 4-5

Chapter 4

The Finished State Machine

The finished State Machine should now be complete and look like figure 4-6.

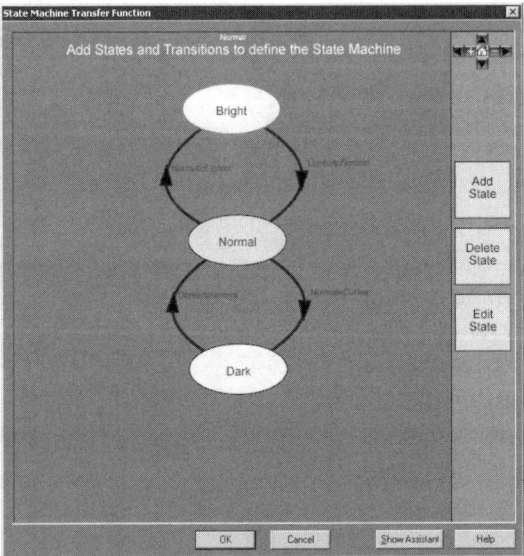

Figure 4-6

Now that all of the States and State Transitions have been added, press OK to return to the main design desktop screen. This State Machine controls all the logic in the four lines of expressions that have been declared.

Controlling the LEDs in the Transfer Functions

To complete the prototype the final step will be to control the LEDs.

First, select the LED named Bright, right-click, choosing Transfer Function. Select Lookup Table, click Next>>, and click Next>> again. Now you should be at the screen in figure 4-7.

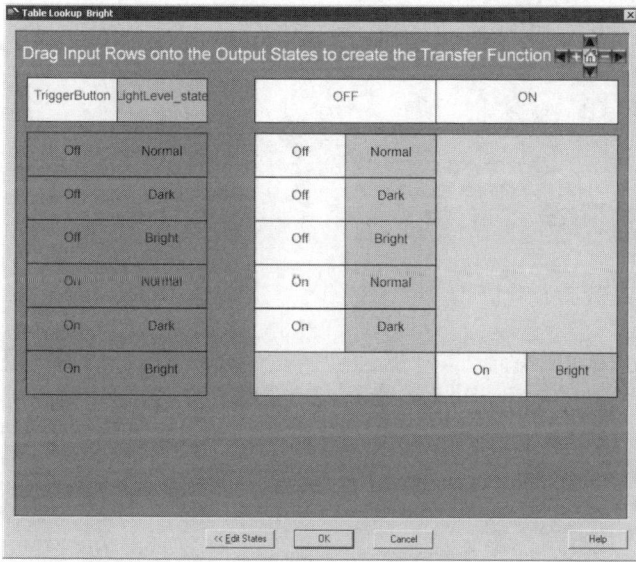

Figure 4-7

Figure 4-7 is a simple Lookup Table. When the button states are off, so are the LEDs. In this case when the TriggerButton is On and the State Machine is Bright, the Bright LED is turned on. The same logic applies to Normal and Dark named LEDs. Figure 4-8 shows the display after the Normal LED Transfer Function is created.

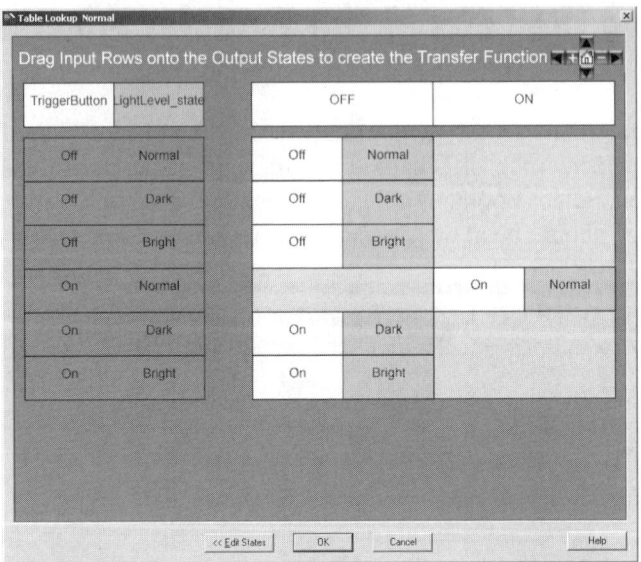

Figure 4-8

And finally, figure 4-9 illustrates how the Dark named LED Transfer Function will look after completion.

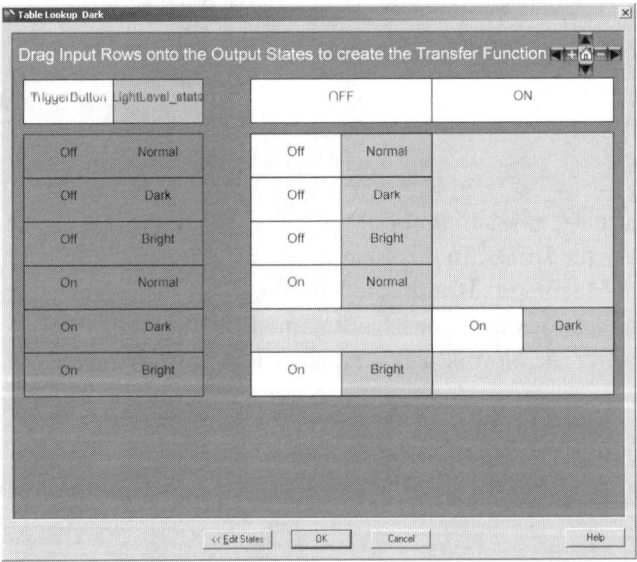

Figure 4-9

Finishing the Design

Before simulating, do a sanity check on the prototype design. The main design desktop should look similar to figure 4-10 when the last LED transfer function has been completed.

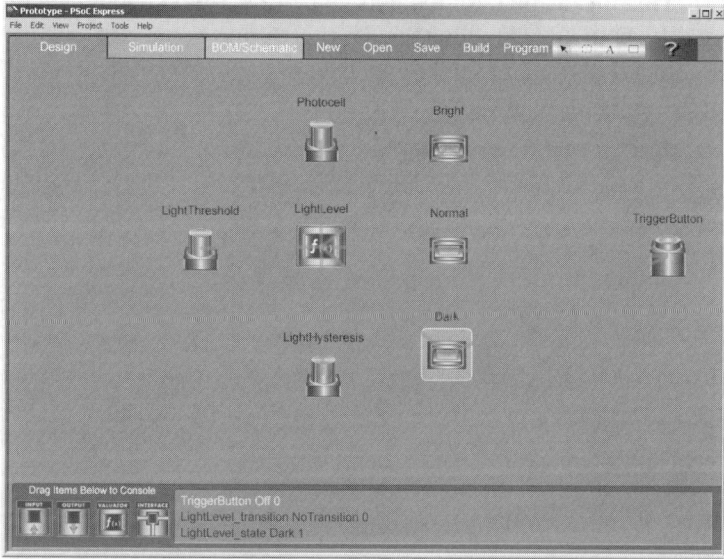

Figure 4-10

Look at this image very carefully and note the lines connecting TriggerButton to the Bright, Normal, and Dark LED components. Also note that Photocell, LightThreshold, and LightHysteresis are all connected to the LightLevel Valuator on the left and the Bright, Normal, and Dark LED components on the right. As shown in figure 4-10, LightLevel is the control point for the program Logic while the Bright, Normal, and Dark LED Transfer Functions are each are in control of their respective On/Off function by combining the State of LightLevel to the state of TriggerButton.

Chapter 4

Chapter 4

Prototype Simulation Time

Will it work you ask! Let's find out. If you haven't done so already, lets save this project as Chapter 4_1, then press the Simulation tab. Start by setting the LightThreshold to 49, next set LightHysteresis to 51. This means that a Photocell value of 45 to 55 should set the Normal LED to ON (1) when the TriggerButton is pressed. Set the Photocell to 48, and set TriggerButton to On. Your display will look like the window in figure 4-11.

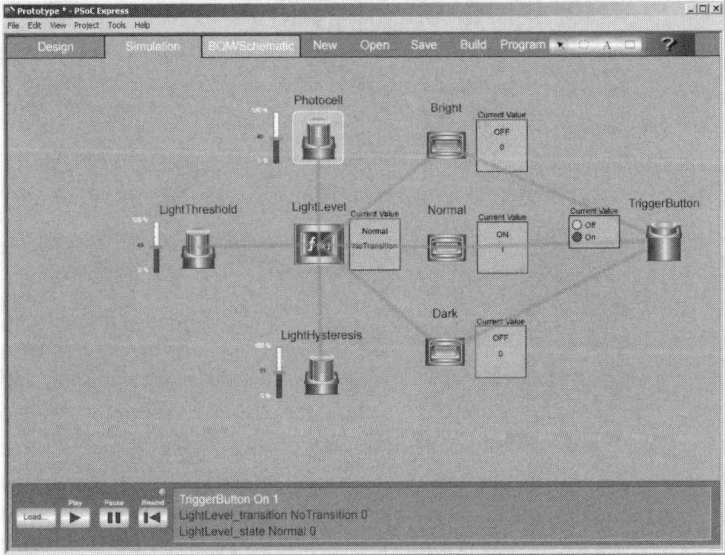

Figure 4-11

The Normal LED is lit when TriggerButton is pressed. Next, set the Photocell value to 43 and again turn on TriggerButton. Your display will look like figure 4-12.

<footer>

64

</footer>

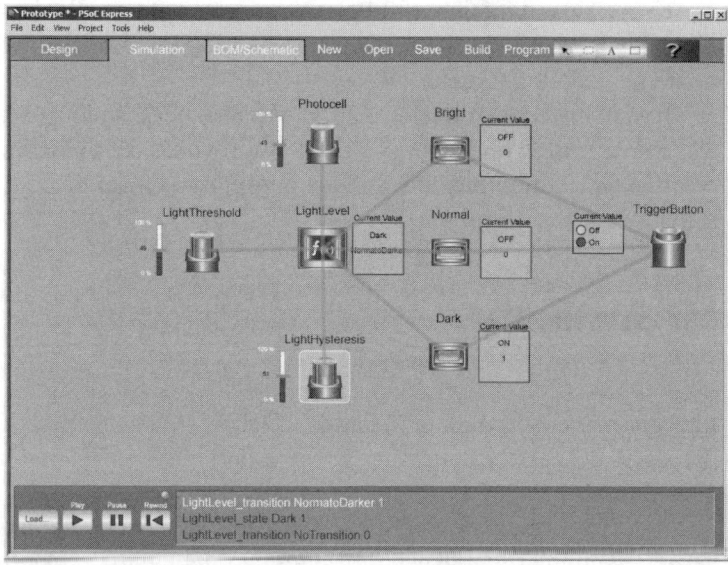

Figure 4-12

Note the Dark LED is now lit. For our final test, set the Photocell to 56 and again, turn on the TriggerButton. Note that the Bright LED is now lit as shown in figure 4-13.

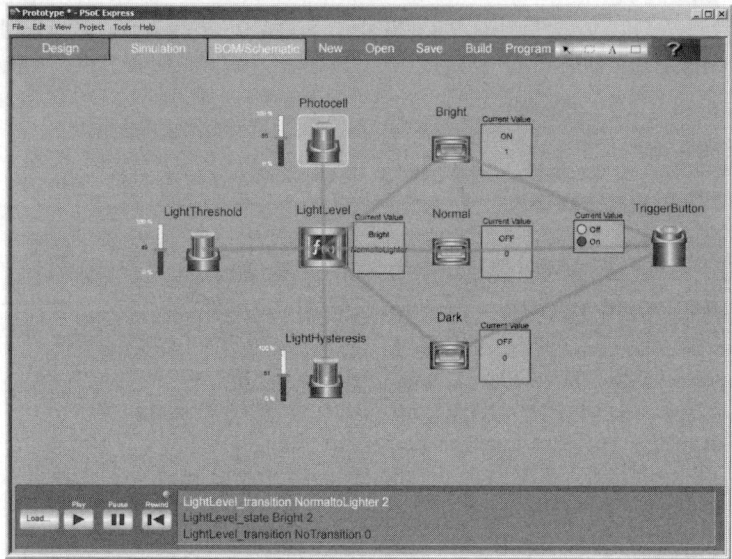

Figure 4-13

Chapter 4

Using a combination of 2 Potentiometers, 1 Photocell, 3 LEDs, and 1 Push Button (plus a resistor), and PSoC Express we have fully implemented a light meter.

It may have taken longer than 15 minutes because this exercise was implemented one-step-at-a-time. But I would bet that with a little practice, you can implement an idea in prototype form, from start-to-finish in 15 minutes or less.

Chapter Summary

This chapter covered State Machines, Design Practices, Look Up Tables, and Transfer Functions. Most importantly, real experience was gained in how to build a complete project from start-to-finish in PSoC Express. The simulator can be an invaluable tool in developing projects and eliminating the need for in-circuit debugging under the right conditions as demonstrated in this chapter. Remember, this was only a prototype, not a finished product.

Now ask yourself, how many products do you use that allow a fully functional prototype to be built in C, from start-to-finish in 15 minutes or less? How about 30 minutes or less? Or even an hour or less? The point is that PSoC Express really does work, and really does shave considerable time off the development process. Yes, there is a learning curve, but that's what this book is all about.

Looking Ahead

Beginning in Chapter 5, we'll roll up our sleeves and start building hands-on projects. Until now we've done practice exercises to gain an understanding of how PSoC Express works, to gain confidence in the PSoC Express Simulator, and your abilities to create working PSoC Express projects through hands-on exercises. Even if you don't completely understand how PSoC Express works and how Valuators, Transfer Functions, and Communications Interfaces work, don't despair. Work through the projects section and you will find that with each project your level of understanding will increase. By the time you get through the projects section, you'll have no problems implementing your own unique ideas in PSoC Express.

Your First PSoC Express Project

Chapter Overview

It's time to start developing some real projects with PSoC Express. In this chapter we will begin the first of several PSoC Express projects using the World Tour board. When finished, a working hour meter will have been completed.

This is by far not only the biggest chapter but also the most extensive in content. While it may appear that some of the content has been covered previously, remember that in previous chapters we have only worked through example projects in simulation. Topics covered in this and future chapters are topics covered in the actual practice of using PSoC Express. We will also look at the ways that PSoC Express shouldn't be used. In the course of writing this book I've found some dead-ends that you should be made aware of.

> **Note:** You may notice that from time-to-time I re-emphasize information already covered in a prior chapter. This is not accidental. The fact is, the more you know about Valuators and Transfer Functions, the easier PSoC Express will be to use. The importance of these two topics are often overlooked by the developer. If these topics are not completely understood, serious logic problems may exist in working PSoC Express programs. I would rather repeat myself more than once to have you learn the critical pieces needed to have quicker success.

Topics Covered in This Chapter

The following topics will be covered in this chapter:

▶ Button Input
▶ Timer Input
▶ LED Output
▶ Logical AND (&&)
▶ Bitwise AND (&)
▶ Logical OR (||)
▶ State Machine
▶ Addition
▶ Multiplication
▶ Creating Variables
▶ Variable Assignment
▶ Loop Delays
▶ Valuators
▶ Transfer Functions

Remember these topics are being covered for the first time in the practice of using PSoC Express in an actual project.

The First PSoC Example

Now it's time to get started with a real PSoC example project. So let's see what the requirements are for this first project. To develop on actual hardware requires the following:

▶ PSoC Express Software 2.2 (or later)

▶ A PSoC "World Tour" board or PSoC Explorer SoCsicle Board

▶ PSoC MiniProg Programmer

▶ PSoC Programming Software

▶ 9-Volt Battery or USB connected directly to a PC (no hub connection please!)

▶ USB Cable with USB mini connector on one end.

If you don't have these components remember to check the web sites in the reference chapter for information on how to obtain them. PSoC Express, Express Packs, Updates, and the MiniProg software are all available as free downloads from www.cypress.com/psocecpress.

The World Tour Board

The World Tour board has four different sections each driven by a different PSoC. These four sections are connected via an I2C bus so that communications between each PSoC can take place. So, let's take a look at each section of the board, starting with the lower right section and moving in a clockwise direction. The full World Tour board is shown in photo 5-1.

Photo 5-1

Section 1 – The CY8C29666 and Seven Segment Display

This section contains a four
digit seven segment display,
six LEDs (four green, two
red), one push button (normally open – with pull down
resistor), 10K potentiometer,
expansion header, programming header, and a
CY8C29666 PSoC at the core.
A close-up of section 1 is
shown in photo 5-2.

Photo 5-2

Section 2 – The CY8C27643 and Accelerometer

This portion of the board contains the Analog Devices
ADXL322 accelerometer,
eight LEDs (four red, four
green), one push button (normally open, with pull-down
resistor), one 10K potentiometer, one LCD Interface, one
LCD brightness adjustment
pot, expansion header, programming header, and a
CY8C27643 PSoC device. A
close-up of section 2 is shown
in photo 5-3.

Photo 5-3

Section 3 – The CY8C21434 and CapSense

This section includes a PSoC CY8C21434, one push button (normally open with pull-down resistor), six LEDs (four green, two red), 10K potentiometer, four CapSense pads, expansion header, and a programming header. A close-up of section 3 is shown in photo 5-4.

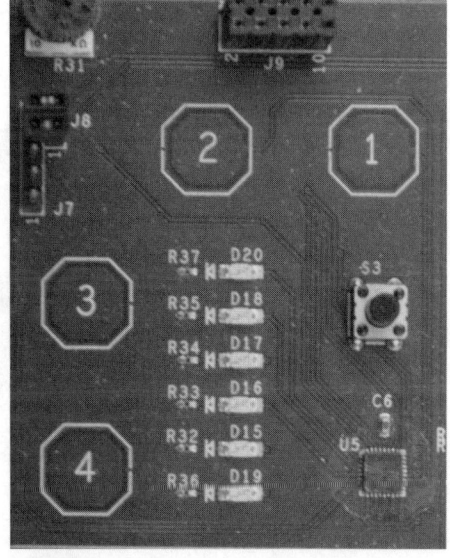

Photo 5-4

Section 4 – The CY8C24894 and USB

This section includes a PSoC CY8C24894, USB interface with mini USB connector, one push button (normally open with pull-down resistor), six LEDs (four green, two red), 10K potentiometer, expansion header, and programming header. A close-up of section 4 is shown in photo 5-5.

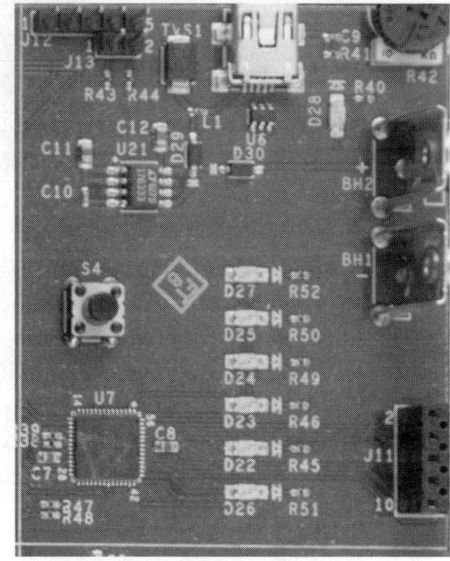

Photo 5-5

Chapter 5

71

Expansion Headers

There is an expansion board adapter that changes the pin out of the expansion header. The adapter makes the header compatible with the WirelessUSB modules. Photo 5-6 shows the expansion header adapter.

The WirelessUSB modules allow wireless data to be sent or received. Two WirelessUSB modules will allow you to send and receive data to a remote device. The WirelessUSB module is shown in photo 5-7.

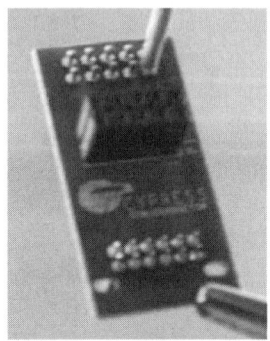
Photo 5-6

Photo 5-7

And finally, photo 5-8 shows the fully assembled expansion header adapter and wireless module attached to each other.

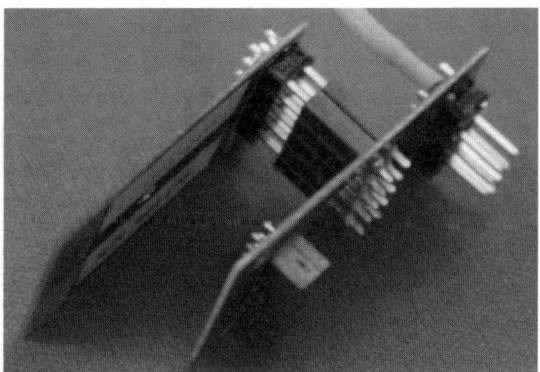
Photo 5-8

Note: If you have the WirelessUSB module(s), plug them into the header adapter and not directly into the World Tour board. The adapter header pins are different than header pins on the World Tour board. Plugging the WirelessUSB modules into the World Tour board will damage or destroy the WirelessUSB module(s), the World Tour board, or both.

The MiniProg Header

The MiniProg device is used to program the hex files into the PSoC part. Since it is for programming only, debugging capabilities are left entirely to simulation mode. The MiniProg fits the 5 pin header in each of the four quadrants of the World Tour board. Two jumpers need to be removed to program the parts and can be restored once the programming is completed. The MiniProg's five pins are:

VDD	+5 Volts
GND	Signal Ground
SRES	Reset Line
SCLK	Data Clock
SDATA	Data

The MiniProg attaches to a Windows system with a USB cable that has a mini-USB connector at one end. The MiniProg header pins are spaced 0.100" apart making it easy to add ISSP programming to your own projects. Photo 5-9 shows the MiniProg from the end of the MiniProg that connects to the board.

Photo 5-9

The Design

As stated earlier, PSoC Express helps you develop faster, but it is not a substitute for a good design. In keeping with that spirit, let's spend a few minutes designing this first project.

The Objective

The first objective will be to create a simple counter that will count from one to sixty in increments of one. This project will use a timer input combined with an Interface Valuator to increment and reset the counter. Next, there will be the addition of a seven segment display used as a visual output for the seconds counter. And finally, a button will be used to reset the clock back to zero. Figure 5-11 is a simple flowchart that shows how this project works.

Chapter 5

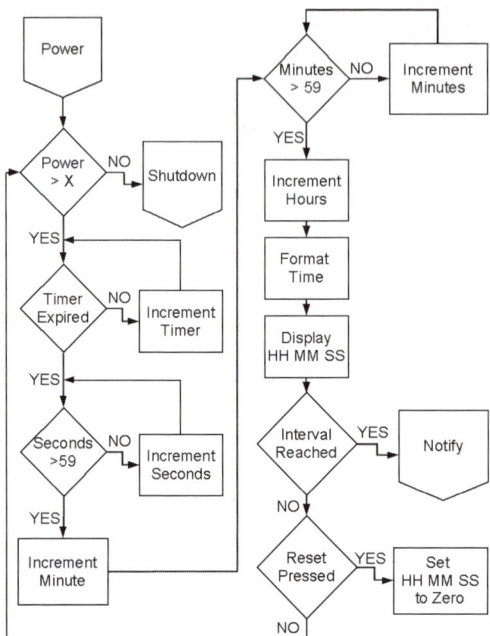

Figure 5-11

The Power, Notify, and Shutdown design details are not on this flowchart and will not be addressed in this book. So, let's begin the journey of understanding real-world development with PSoC Express and how to move this design from the flowchart to PSoC Express implementation.

BIT Testing

In order to see if a bit is zero or one, we test the bit position by using the BITWISE AND operator, this operator is represented in C by the ampersand (&) character. If either of the tested bits are one, the result will be one, otherwise it will be a zero. For example to test BIT four we would write the following:

```
if (Value & 16) == 16    ' BIT 4 is equal to 1
```

Or to test if bit 4 is zero, we would write:

```
if (Value & 16) == 0     ' BIT 4 is equal to 0
```

That's all there is to it! Remember that a single ampersand (&) represents a BITWISE AND while a double ampersand (&&) signifies a LOGICAL AND, as mentioned earlier. To change which BIT position is being tested, simply change the value that is being AND'd to the value of the bit position to be tested. To test position five, change the value from 16 to 32. To test position three, change the value from 16 to 8. And remember, the bit positions are numbered 0 through 7 starting from the left. The same bit values are numbered 1, 2, 4, 8, 16, 32, 64, and 128 (each position moving right is doubled in value from the prior position. Totaled up this equals 255.

Implicit versus Explicit Assignment Operators

As an old C and Assembler programmer, it's all too easy to use brute-force programming techniques when it comes to variable assignments. I urge you to not fall prey to this programming practice. Instead, PSoC Express provides alternative methods to variable assignment which should be used. The easiest way to realize PSoC Express isn't doing the work, is when Priority and Status Encoders are loaded with direct assignment statements using the single equal (=) sign. That's a dead giveaway trouble is nearby.

Thinking and doing are separate processes and worlds apart when writing in C, versus designing in PSoC Express. Old habits are hard to break and the same will be true when it comes to letting PSoC Express do the work. One of the goals is to teach how to think in PSoC Express so the reader can avoid the pitfalls of applying old methods to new thought processes. That's why it's important to work through the examples in this and following chapters. That will assure an understanding of the new concepts and techniques that are used in PSoC Express.

Almost any valid C operator can be used in PSoC Express, but remember the "if," "then," and "else" statements are handled by PSoC Express. Only the actual expression is entered by the developer. If a complete expression is accidentally entered, PSoC Express will generate an error as the Valuator screen is exited with the OK button.

Chapter 5

Direct Assignments in PSoC Express

As noted earlier, direct assignments in PSoC Express don't require the use of the single equal (=) sign. Instead, direct assignments are done by simply entering the value or calculation in the Valuator or Transfer Function. It's also a good idea to use Interface Valuators for calculated fields as this physically separates your logic, control, and variables. There is nothing to lose taking this approach and all of the same math and logic expressions can be used. This means the use of addition, subtraction, multiplication, division, and many other C math symbols are still useable. A table of valid operators is listed in Chapter 2.

Byte and Integer values are defined through Valuators, but not Strings. Strings must be defined manually. Defining strings and string manipulation are advanced topics not covered in this book. If you are not familiar with C or customizing PSoC Express applications, using string or character values in PSoC Express Valuator Expressions is not recommended.

Once again revisiting the BITWISE AND, to modify the expressions assigning a 1 or 0 to bit testing bit 4 would look like the following:

```
if (Value & 16) == 16 then 1      ' BIT equals 1
```

The above expression would assign the value 1 to a Transfer function that has bit position 4 set to a 1. Following is the expression that would set the Transfer Function to 0 if bit position 4 were set to a 0.

```
if (Value & 16) != 16 then  0     ' BIT equals 0
```

In the above expressions the items in *italics* are inserted by PSoC Express. There is no direct assignment operator in the use of either of these assignment statements. These assignments are accomplished through PSoC Express components and their associated Transfer Functions. To make this process is fully understood, we'll begin by building a timer triggered binary counter that is started by a button press.

Building the Hour Meter

Modular Development Methodology

> **Note:** When developing real-world projects, use PSoC Express to implement the design in a modular "building block" fashion. When completed this approach will lead to several completed "cells," "blocks," or "projects" that make up a completed product.

An hour meter can display seconds, minutes, hours, days, weeks, or a combination of these to use as a gauge for service or other triggered event. At the foundation is the second timer. Since this design will use the seven segment display component as the output means, each counter will need to be validated to be certain of clock accuracy. A state machine will be used to determine start and stop conditions. A second state machine will also be used to determine display mode. So, it is with the state machine this project will begin.

Starting, Ending, and Display States

The counter will start by a simple press of a button. To make this design flexible, the button will set a simple On or Off state for the counter. The state value will determine if the interval clock should be On or Off. Actually, it will determine if the timer that triggers each second will update the second counter.

Display States

In addition to the On/Off state, the push button will also be used to toggle between display states. In this way the single button will have a dual purpose and implement the following state transitions in the following order.

> Off → On → Seconds → Minutes → Minutes & Seconds →
> Hours → Hours & Minutes → Off

This could go on to Days, Weeks, and Months, and beyond, but this example will stick to the above states. A Push Button Input and

Chapter 5

LoopDelay Valuator will be used together to form a logical toggle switch that will toggle each time an On-Off cycle has been completed.

The Heartbeat of the Hour Meter, the Seconds Counter

The "heart" of this design is a timer that will take a State input, and output the results visually using LEDs as the first proof-of-concept. Then the design will be modified to show the elapsed seconds, using the LEDs to show the heartbeat.

The Output Display

The end result of this project will be a timer display that shows elapsed seconds in binary format using LEDs. There are three components to this simple design. They are: State Input, Timer Control, and LED Output. Figure 5-11a shows a block diagram of the first prototype.

The first flowchart has been broken down to three separate tasks in PSoC Express. Next, overlay the PSoC Express tasks over the original flowchart as shown in figure 5-11b.

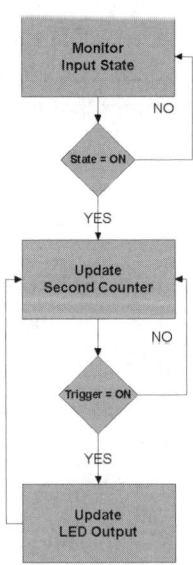

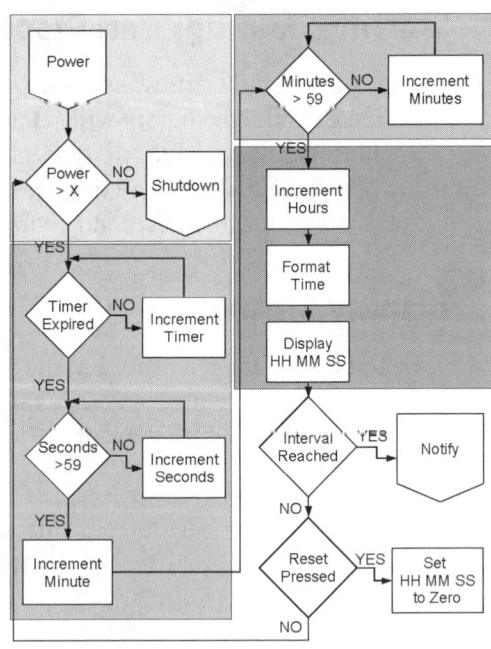

Figure 5-11a   Figure 5-11b

Notice that minutes and hours have been highlighted using the seconds counter logic. The seconds counter can be used to manage all timing for the minute and hour counters as well. Figure 5-11b doesn't cover the alarms, as the initial goal is to provide the actual metering of time.

Step 1 – The State Machine

The state machine consists of four components. They are 1) Push Button Input, 2) LoopDelay Counter, 3) State Machine Valuator, and 4) LED Output. Each time the Push Button is pressed and released the state machine will transition to the next state until it ends up back at the Off state. Start PSoC Express or select File – New to begin a new project. Add a button by choosing Tactile → Push Button → Normally Open Internal Pulldown and name the component Start_Stop as shown in figure 5-12.

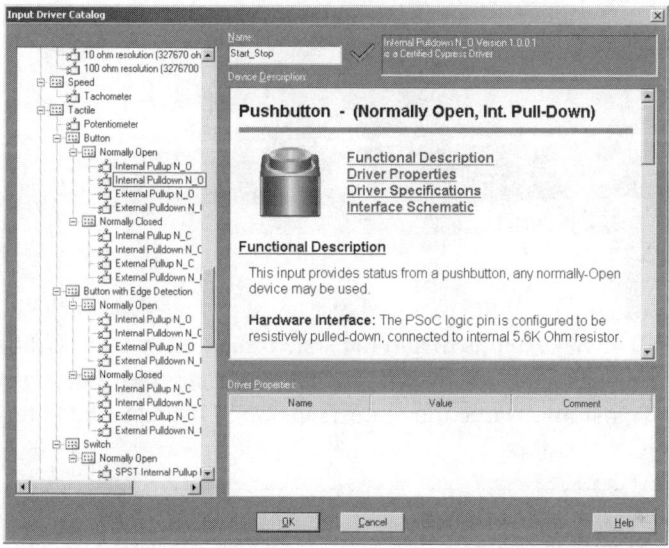

Figure 5-12

This will be the only source of state and display management at this time. Next, add a Valuator choosing LoopDelay as the type, and naming the Valuator Last_StartStop, then press the Next button. On the next screen, choose Start_Stop as the input and press the Next button again. Now, press the OK button.

Click the Valuator component again to add a second component, and name it Run_State, choosing StateMachine as the Valuator type, then press the Next button. There are seven states in this State Machine. The first state is always the default state, so press the Add State button and name the first state Off. Now, add the following states: On, Seconds, Minutes, MinutesSeconds, Hours, and HoursMinutes. The State window should look like figure 5-13.

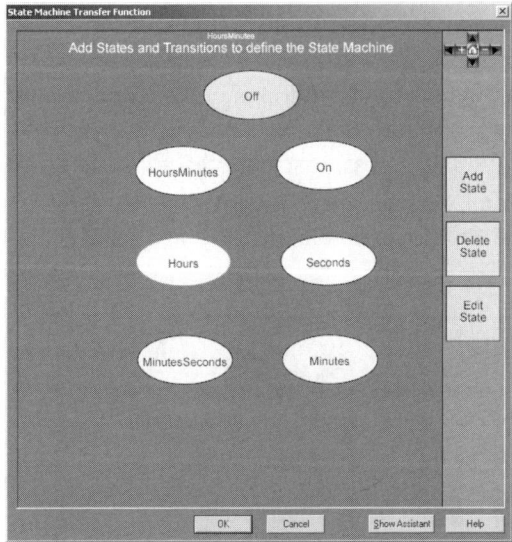

Figure 5-13

This covers all the required display states needed for the hour meter. The next step is to add the state transitions which will toggle between each state. Begin with the Off state, double-click, select Add State Transition. Name the State Transition OfftoOn, and enter the following expression:

```
(Start_Stop == Start_Stop__Off) && (Last_StartStop ==
Last_StartStop__On)
```

This statement will transition to the next state if the current button state is off and the last button state is on. Change the button state transition to On as shown in figure 5-14.

Press the OK button twice to return to the main State Machine window. Each time the Push Button component is pressed, Last_StartStop will transition from 0 to 1, then back to 0 when released. By using the same expression in OfftoOn, a transition to the next state will occur each time the button is pressed and released. Add the named Transitions below to the corresponding state, and enter the same expression used in the OfftoOn transition.

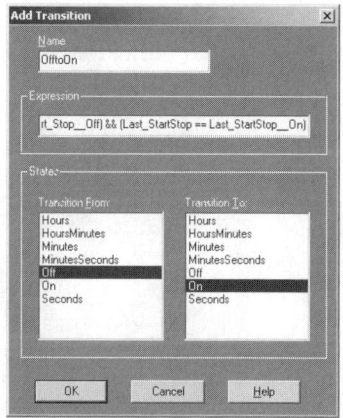

Figure 5-14

State:	Transition
Seconds	SecondstoMinutes
On	OntoSeconds
Minutes	MinstoMinutesSecs
MinutesSeconds	MinSecstoHours
Hours	HourstoHrsMinutes
HoursMinutes	HoursMinstoOff

When finished the StateMachine window will look like figure 5-15.

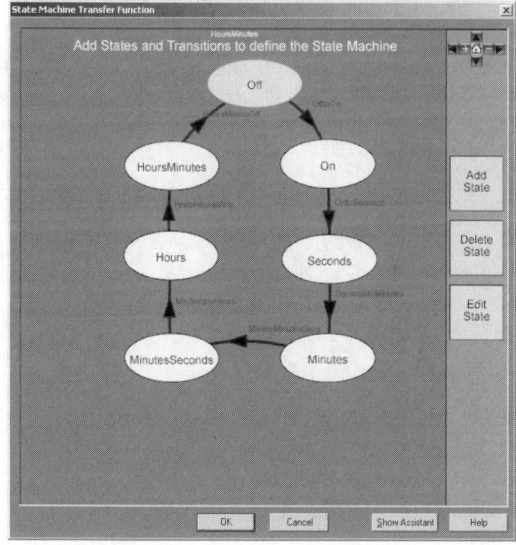

Figure 5-15

Pressing the OK button will return to the design desktop. Add a visual indicator to acknowledge the State Machine has worked properly. For this task choose an LED. Choose Output → Display → LED → Single Color → Intensity Controlled and name it Running as shown in figure 5-16.

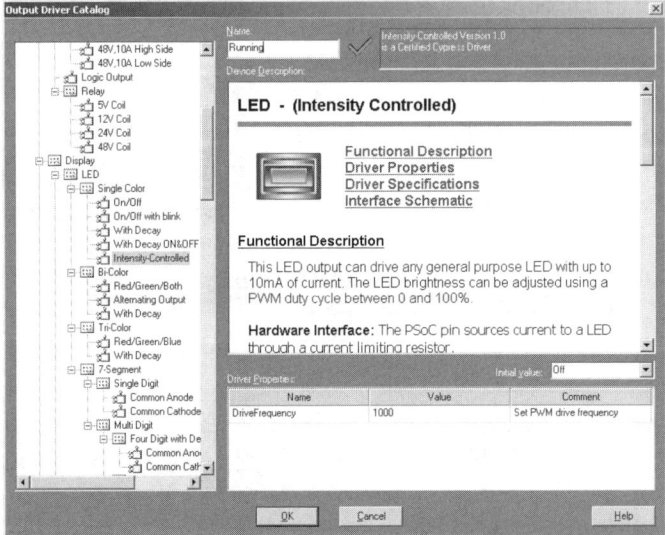

Figure 5-16

Press the OK button, then right-click, choose Transfer Function, Table Lookup, and choose Run_State_state as the input. Press the Next>> button. Click the Remove All button, then add the names and values as shown in figure 5-17.

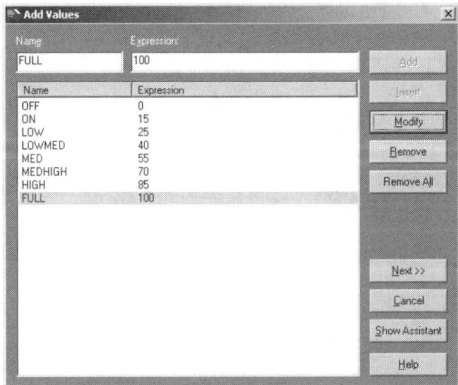

Figure 5-17

Press the Next>> button again and assign the expressions to states as shown in figure 5-18 and in the following table.

Run_state__state Value	LED Values
Off	OFF
On	ON
Seconds	LOW
Minutes	LOWMED
MinutestoSeconds	MED
Hours	MEDHIGH
HourstoMinutes	HIGH

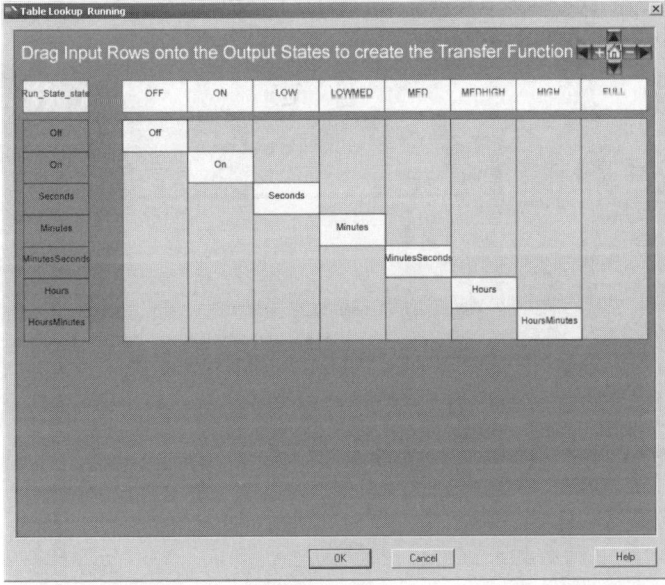

Figure 5-18

Press OK to return to the design desktop which will now look like figure 5-19.

These four components make up the state machine input for the clock. Running in simulation mode will prove the logic works. With each transition of the button the intensity of the LED changes. Before continuing, save this project as Chapter5_StateMach.

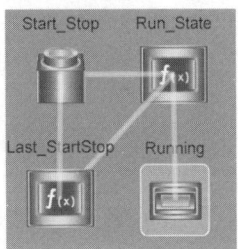

Figure 5-19

Step 2 – The Interval Timer, our Seconds Counter

With the Input State machine now working, it's time to focus on the timekeeping function of this project. At the heart of the timekeeping function is a single Interval Generator component that keeps track of seconds. Using a single time object allows the time hierarchy to always be synchronized. Getting the next phase of this project working correctly will mean the difference between success and failure. If the timekeeping portion is wrong, then everything else relating to time will also be wrong.

The next part of the project requires three objects, they are: 1) Interval Generator, 2) Interface Valuator, and 3) Status Encoder Valuator. With the prior design desktop still open select Input → Timing → Interval Generator, name it Seconds_Timer, and set the IntervalTime to 1000 as shown in figure 5-20.

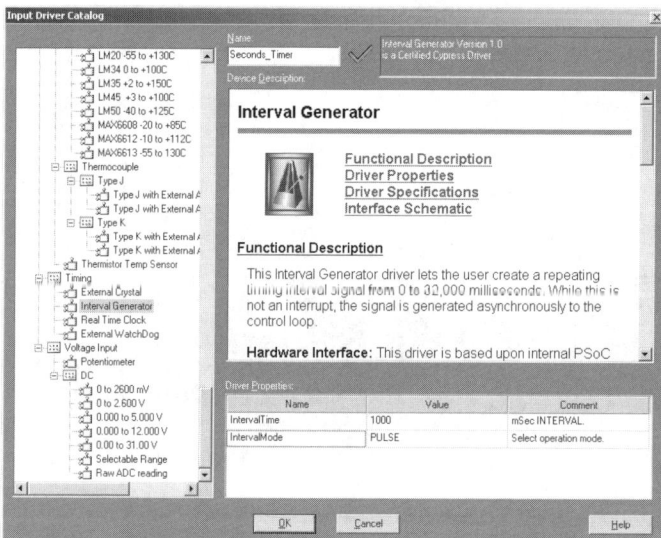

Figure 5-20

The value of 1000 milliseconds is equal to one second and each time one second has passed, a trigger pulse will be generated. Press the OK button to continue. Next, a reference is needed to which time can be measured. So the next object to add is a Valuator → Interface Valuator, and name this component SecondsinMinute, leaving it a discrete counter, set to a value of 0x3C (60 Decimal). This Interface Valuator is a holder for the number of seconds in a minute.

Now there is a trigger and time reference, logic is required to bind this all together. Click on a Valuator component, this time choosing a Status Encoder, naming it Elapsed_Seconds. There will be three lines of expressions to enter.

The first expression will increment the seconds counter. This counter should only be incremented if the Run_State is not Off, the Timer has triggered, and Elapsed_Seconds is less than or equal to SecondsinMinute. The expression follows:

```
(Run_State_state != Run_State_state__Off) &&
(Seconds_Timer == Seconds_Timer__Triggered) && (Elapsed_Seconds
 <= SecondsinMinute)
```

If the above expression is true, the action statement would increment Elapsed_Seconds by one as shown in the following expression.

```
(Elapsed_Seconds + 1)
```

Next, the SecondsinMinute Interface Valuator is compared to Elapsed_Seconds to reset the Elapsed_Seconds counter when Elapsed_Seconds has reached SecondsinMinute. That expression is:

```
(Run_State_state != Run_State_state__Off) &&
(Seconds_Timer == Seconds_Timer__Triggered) &&
(Elapsed_Seconds >= SecondsinMinute)
```

When this statement is true, the action sets Elapsed_Seconds to zero. The Status Encoder window will look like figure 5-21 after completing this expression.

Chapter 5

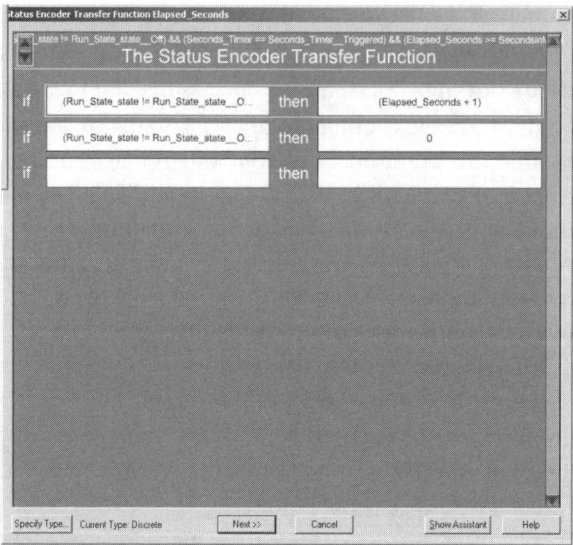

Figure 5-21

A visual display that shows the seconds counter working would help in assuring the counter is working properly. An output display is needed to compare our timer value with. Next, add an Output → Display → LED → Seven Segment → Multi-Digit → Common Cathode, and name this component Display. Keeping Display selected, right-click, select Transfer Function, Priority Encoder and add the following expression.

> *If* **(Run_State_state == Run_State_state__Seconds)** *then* **Elapsed_Seconds**

This expression first checks the value of the state machine. If the value is equal to Run_State_state__Seconds then the seven-segment display will display the value of Elapsed_Seconds. If the counter is working as it should this will show a value between 0 and 59 on the seven-segment display. When 59 is reached, the value should rollover to 0. Before building this project save it as Chapter5_SecTimer. Next, build the project before adding any more logic to see if the counter and values are correct. Your design desktop will look similar to figure 5-22.

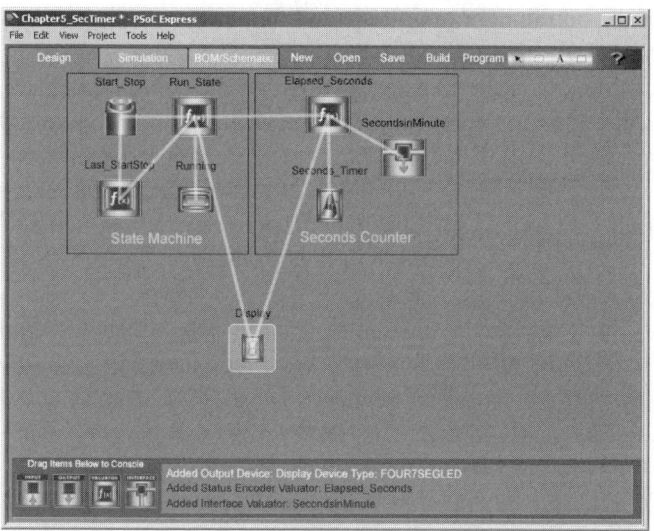

Figure 5-22

The drawing box and text commands at the top-right of the menu bar can be used to identify different "blocks" or "cells" of this project. After the Build tab has been clicked, a window similar to figure 5-23 will be displayed.

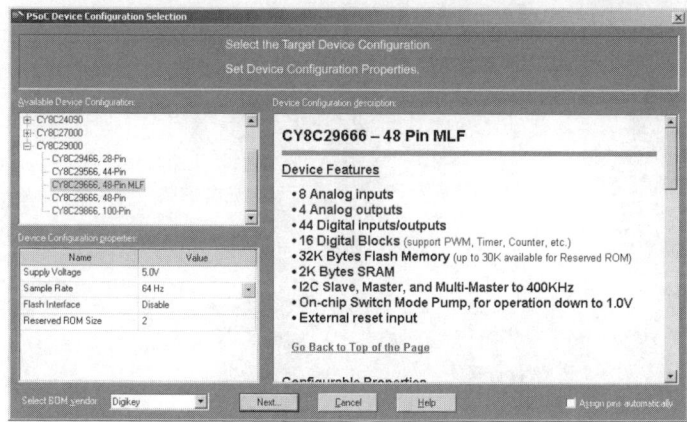

Figure 5-23

Choose the CY8C29666 part. Note the four configuration parameters. Supply Voltage can be either 5.0 or 3.3 volts DC for this part. Setting this to 3.3 volts will allow the part to continue running when the supply voltage drops below 5.0 volts. If the circuit were battery powered, this could extend the life of the batteries by a large margin,

Chapter 5

depending on the battery voltage and amperage. For this project you can leave 5.0V selected.

Sample rate is the frequency at which the PSoC goes back to the start of the loop to perform tasks. The setting of 64Hz means the main program loop will execute 64 times per second. This can be slowed down by selecting 8Hz or it can be set to free Running which means the number of loops will vary depending on the components and logic. Selecting 8 or 64 Hz provides a known time base for the PSoC application, 8 or 64 times per second

The next parameter flash interface enables or disables the flash interface. By default this feature is disabled. There are two other selections, Enable and Enable with no Timeout. Accept the default of Disable. The final parameter is Reserved ROM size. This should also set to the default size. If flash memory or additional ROM were required, these values would be changed accordingly, but for now accept the defaults. The Bill Of Materials vendor that has been selected is Digikey, but any other vendor from the pull-down list may be selected. Press the Next button to see the pin assignment screen as shown in figure 5-24.

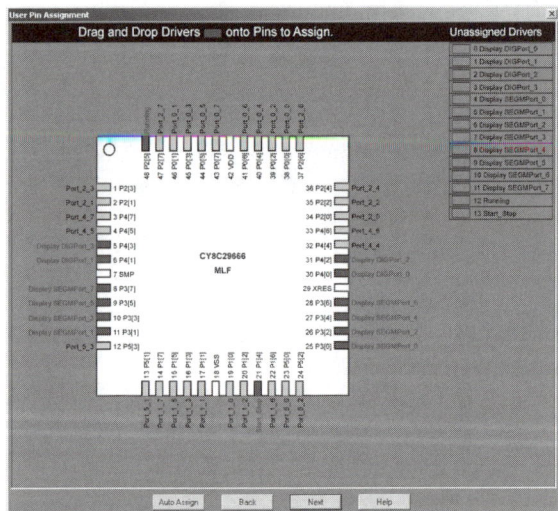

Figure 5-24

It doesn't matter which section of the PSoC World Tour board is used, there is always an LED connected to P1[5] and a Button connected to P1[4]. The seven-segment display takes a total of 12 pins. The pins are connected to P4[0] through P4[3] with each pin turning one digit on or off. Pins P3[0] through P3[7] control which of the seven segments of each digit are on or off. Set the pins as assigned in figure 5-24 and press the Next button again.

> **Note:** When designing from scratch, moving the mouse over the input or output, left clicking and holding the mouse button will highlight the available pins for the selected input or output. This point should be noted to assure the pins are always connected to the proper port and pin. In many cases multiple choices are available. PSoC Express does not always connect the proper device pins to the proper port and pin. The developer is always responsible for being certain the pin assignments are correct.

The build process is now running and will display a build status window. If the build fails, an Error window will be displayed, allowing the developer to scroll through the build report and locate the source of the error. If the build succeeds, a window will appear with the pin out map, BOM (Bill of Materials), schematic, and datasheet as shown in figure 5-25.

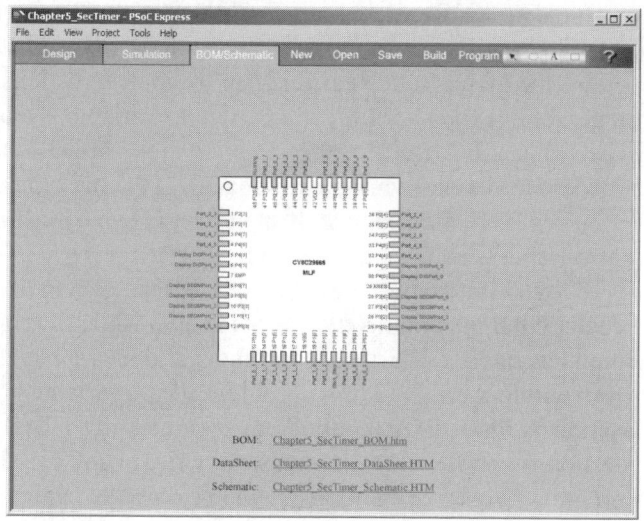

Figure 5-25

At first glance figures 5-24 and 5-25 look very similar but at a closer examination figure 5-25 has the Bill of Materials, Datasheet, and Schematics available for viewing where figure 5-24 does not. This

Chapter 5

indicates a successful build. Before programming the part, the Datasheet will be displayed.

The Datasheet

The data sheet contains all of the information about drivers, logic, and storage variables. Scroll down to Table 2, the interface register map which is shown in figure 5-26.

Table 2: Chapter5_SecTimer Interface Register Map		
OFFSET	NAME	READ/WRITE ACCESS
0	SecondsinMinute	RW
1	Last_StartStop	RO
2	Run_State_state	RO
3	Run_State_transition	RO
4	Start_Stop	RO
5	Running	RO
6	Display	RO
7	Elapsed_Seconds	RO
8	Seconds_Timer	RO

Figure 5-26

This is being brought to your attention to highlight some not so obvious features of this Register Map. Each item in the Register Map is a variable. So each line in figure 5-26 is a variable item. The left column shows the offset from Register Map location zero. This allows the developer to quickly determine if a particular variable is a byte or integer. The size can be determined by looking at the offset of the next variable (except for the last variable in the list). If the offset is one higher the current variable is a byte, if the offset is two bytes higher, the current variable is an unsigned integer.

In figure 5-26 all variables are defined as bytes.

The center column contains the variable name while the right hand column has the Read/Write access status of the variable as viewed from within a PSoC Express program. If the variable is Read Only, then how is PSoC Express assigning a value to it?". The answer to that question is simple, PSoC Express can write to any variable where a program accessing the Register Map externally cannot write to a Read-Only Register variable. The only way to write to a Read-Only Register Map variable is through custom code. Attempting to change a read-only register variable using any other means will result in the change being ignored.

Taking a second look at the Transfer Function for Value, the developer can see the indirect assignment to the LED values. When a value is assigned through a Transfer Function it is important to note the Transfer Function is a part of the Output object. This means that Transfer Function values are bound to the component and any values or action statements are also part of the target component.

The Read-Only status for the register variables in figure 5-26 indicate these variables values can only be assigned through PSoC Express Valuators, Transfer Functions, or the use of custom code in custom.c. Again, if an attempt is made to alter a Read-Only register variable via remote communications such as USB, WirelessUSB, or I2C, PSoC Express will simply ignore the request to alter the register variable.

Programming the PSoC Part

If the datasheet is still open, close it and press the Program tab. Make certain the MiniProg is attached as shown in figure 5-27.

Figure 5-27

While the programming software is invoked from PSoC Express, it is an external program. When it is first started, the device type, and programming file name are passed to the software. It will attempt to connect to the MiniProg and if successful the window as shown in figure 5-28 (on the following page) will be displayed.

Note the top line indicating a successful connection has been made. Also note the MiniProg Firmware version is displayed on the second line, which in this case is version 1.71. The device type and amount of program flash is displayed on line four. Click the Program button to program the part. When programming has completed the window in figure 5-29 will be displayed if the programming was successful.

Chapter 5

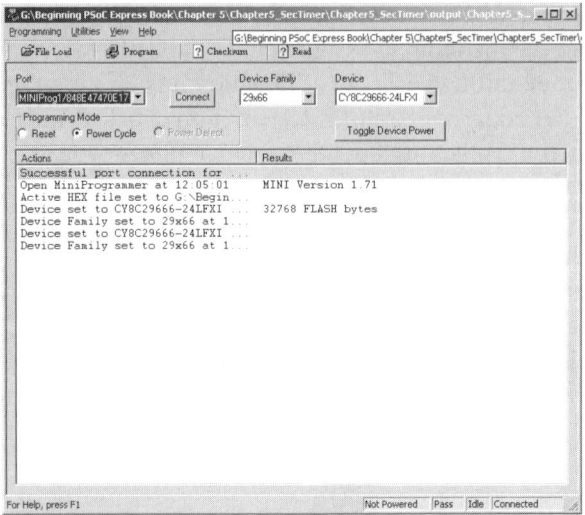

Figure 5-28

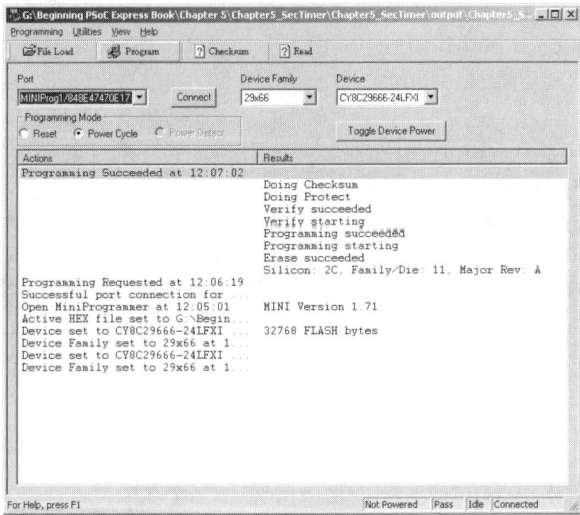

Figure 5-29

Status messages will appear in the right column after the programming process starts. First, the part is erased. Next, the programming started and finished successfully. After programming a Verify was started and successfully completed. The final step is to apply read/write protection followed by a final checksum. When the process completes successfully, a "Programming Succeeded" message is displayed at the top left of the programmer software display.

When programming the World Tour board, the programming mode should be set to "Power Cycle" if power is being supplied by the MiniProg, otherwise the" Reset" option should be checked.

Powering the Target Device

Using the World Tour board we have three methods of powering the device. They are:

1. 9-volt battery

2. USB

3. MiniProg

Using a 9-volt battery or USB are the preferred methods of powering this board. These methods both use the onboard regulator and provide adequate power. Apply power to the board, then press the button, and the seven-segment display will show zero and the cycle LED will be off. Pressing the button once will dimly light the LED but the seven segment display will still remain set to zero. Now that the button has been cycled once, the system has gone from the Off state to the On state, which starts the counter. Pressing the button a second time will display and update the seconds counter on the seven segment display. The seconds go from 0 to 59, then roll over to zero again, for a total of 60 seconds. This proves that the SecondsinMinute compare is working. The next step is to add a minute counter.

Step 3 – Add the Minute Counter

Before continuing save the existing project as Chapter5_MinTimer. With that step completed, it's time to add the minute counter. The minute counter requires the addition of two components, and changes to the Display Transfer Function. The components added are A) Interface Valuator to hold the minute rollover status, B) Interface Valuator to hold the value of Elapsed_Minutes, and C) Status Encoder to handle these new variables. The first Interface Valuator will be named MinuteRollover and will have two values. They are: False which is 0, and True which is 1. This Interface Valuator is used to flag the minute rollover. The second Interface Valuator will be named Elapsed_Minutes, and is similar to Elapsed_Seconds. This component will hold the current number of minutes that have elapsed since the last Rollover.

Chapter 5

Timers within Loops

Going back to figure 5-23, note once again the sample rate setting in the first screen of the build process. This is the outer loop or control loop timer. 64 times each second or once every 15.625 milliseconds the outer loop execution starts. Everything else is timed within the outer loop. That means in theory that once every 64 loop iterations the Interval Generator is triggered and the associated events are executed.

The seconds counter has already been proven to work. Can the same logic be applied to the minute counter? To find out add a Valuator to the project, name it MinutesinHour, select a type of Discrete, and set the initial value to 0x3C (60 decimal). Add a second Valuator, name it Elapsed_Minutes, and select Status Encoder as the type. Then, add the following expression:

```
If (Seconds_Timer == Seconds_Timer__Triggered) && (Elapsed_Seconds
>= SecondsinMinute)  then (Elapsed_Minutes + 1)
```

This expression states that when the one-second Interval Generator triggers and Elapsed_Seconds is equal to or greater than SecondsinMinute and Elapsed_Minutes is less than or equal to MinutesinHour, then 1 is added to Elapsed_Minutes. Double-click the Display object and edit the existing Transfer Function, adding the following two expressions:

```
If (Run_State_state == Run_State_state__Minutes)  then Elapsed_Seconds
```

and

```
If (Run_State_state == Run_State_state__MinutesSeconds)
then ((Elapsed_Minutes * 100) + Elapsed_Seconds)
```

The first statement will display the Minutes when the Run_State state machine is set to the state of Minutes. The second statement displays Hours and Minutes when the Run_State state machine is equal to MinutesSeconds. After entering these statements the Display Transfer Function will look like figure 5-30.

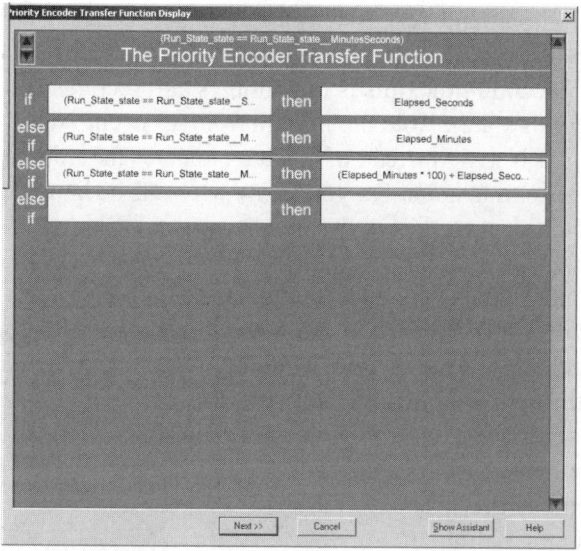

Figure 5-30

Click the Next>> button and your design desktop will look similar to figure 5-31.

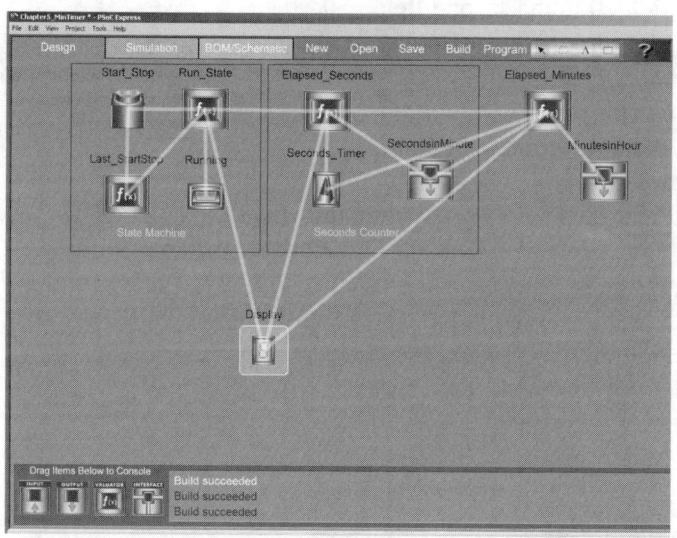

Figure 5-31

Build, Program, and Test this project, and see the results. Program the part, then apply power. Press the button until the seconds counter is displayed a second time, this is the minutes and seconds counter (MinutesSeconds state). Note the minute rollover occurs when the seconds counter is at 59 instead of 0. This indicates the minute display updates one second to soon. Do you know why this be happening?

The key to this error lies in the first expression, ElapsedMinutes. ElapsedMinutes increments when the Interval Generator triggers. ElapsedSeconds equals SecondsinMinute and ElapsedMinutes is equal to or greater than MinutesinHour. So when the number of seconds in a minute is reached, and the number of minutes in an hour is reached, a roll over to the next hour occurs. How can this problem be fixed? There are several ways, but for this project simply creating an Interface Valuator named Hours_Rollover that has the values True and False will remedy this problem. Select a Valuator, naming it Hour_Rollover, click the Interface Valuator type, followed by the Next>> button. Next, click Add States. Enter False in the first field, 0 in the second field, and press Add. Next, enter True in field one, 1 in field two, and again press the Add button. You window will now look like figure 5-32.

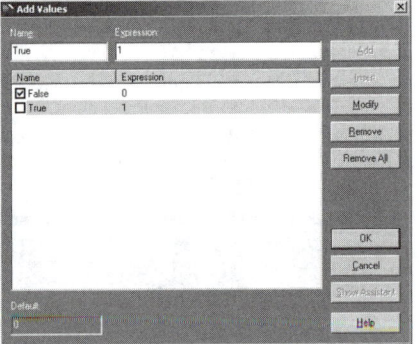

Figure 5-32

Press the OK button to complete this step. Now the Elapsed_Minutes Status Encoder Transfer Function needs to be modified. The first expression in Elapsed_Minutes currently adds 1 to Elapsed_Minutes so change the assignment expression from:

```
(Elapsed_Minutes + 1)
```

To:

```
(Hour_Rollover = Hour_Rollover__True)
```

Next, add a new expression to this Status Encoder. Before changing the logic in Elapsed_Minutes, the name of Hour_Rollover needs to be changed to Minute_Rollover. PSoC Express makes it easy to change the name of an object. Select the Hour_Rollover component, right-click selecting RENAME, then change the name from Hour_Rollover to Minute_Rollover and press the OK button. Every-where Hour_Rollover appeared, is now changed to Minute_Rollover. This includes all logic expressions as well.

To complete the Minute counter some additional changes to Elapsed_Seconds and Elapsed_Minutes Status Encoders are needed. First, the Minute_Rollover flag needs to be set. That is done by adding a new expression to the Elapsed_Seconds transfer Function and plac-ing the expression correctly within that Transfer Function. First, double-click the Elapsed_Seconds component, select Edit the Current Transfer Function selection, then add the following expression:

```
If (Run_State_state != Run_State_state__Off) && (Seconds_Timer ==
Seconds_Timer__Triggered) && (Elapsed_Seconds >= SecondsinMinute)
then (Minute_Rollover = Minute_Rollover__True)
```

After entering this new expression, use the Up Arrow key in the upper-left of the current window to move the expression up one posi-tion as shown in figure 5-33.

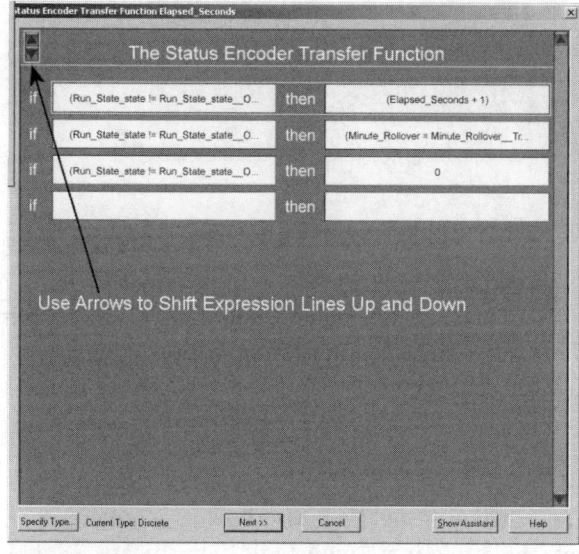

Figure 5-33

Click the Next>> button to complete the changes to Elapsed_Sec-onds. The next and final changes will be made to Elapsed_Minutes.

Chapter 5

Double-click Elapsed_Minute, choose Edit current Transfer Function reorganizing the logic and order of logic to be as follows:

> *If* (Seconds_Timer == Seconds_Timer__Triggered) && (Elapsed_Seconds == 0) && (Minute_Rollover == Minute_Rollover__True) *then* (Elapsed_Minutes + 1)

The Elapsed_Minutes Transfer Function will now look like figure 5-34.

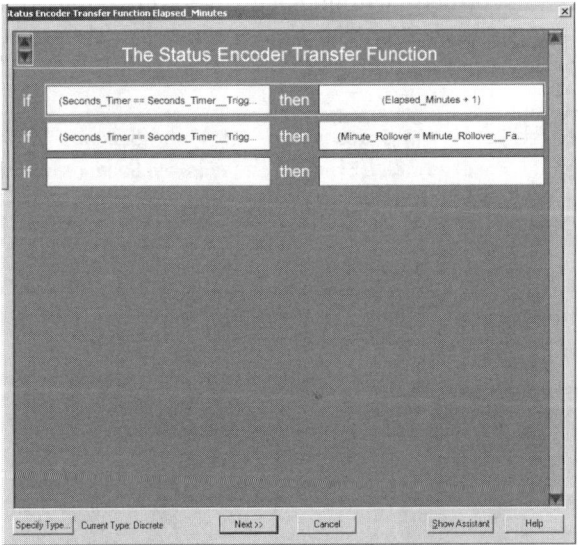

Figure 5-34

Click the Next>> button to return to the Design Desktop, Build, and Program this project. To test the new logic, press the button until the seconds display is reached a second time. After the first minute has elapsed, note the minute counter properly rolls over when the second counter is reset to 0.

Step 4 – Adding the Hour Counter

As demonstrated earlier, PSoC Express allows the renaming of existing components while retaining their logic. This means PSoC Express automatically does a global rename search and replace throughout the project without altering existing expressions. Just as components can be renamed, components and their associated logic can be copied.

This comes in handy when new components with similar functionality to existing components are needed. In this next step existing components and their logic will be duplicated with the copy function. First, select the dashed box in the upper-right corner of the design desktop and click. This puts the cursor into copy mode. Next, click Elapsed_Minutes and Minute_Rollover, noting that each should now be surrounded with a light green dashed line (this indicates the component has been included). Next, right click the chosen components and choose Duplicate. This will create copies of both selected components so click on the desktop to de-select the components. Once the components have been de-selected, the dashed lines will disappear. Move the duplicated components to the lower portion of the design desktop, renaming Elapsed_Minutes to Elapsed_Hours, and Minute_Rollover to Hour_Rollover. Next, add another Interface Valuator, naming it MinutesinHour, set it as a discrete (Byte) type with a default value of 0x3C (60 decimal).

To finish the hour counter a couple of changes are needed to the Elapsed_Hours Valuator. Double-click Elapsed_Hours, and choose Edit Transfer Function. At the lower left corner of the Status Encoder screen click the Specify Type button, changing from Discrete to Continuous (this will change the type from a Byte to an Unsigned Integer). Next, click the Properties button, changing minimum to 0 and maximum to 10000, clicking the OK button until the main Status Encoder window is displayed.

Now a couple of changes are needed to existing logic by adding new expressions. To complete the hour meter, change the current Status Encoder to have the following expressions in the following order:

If (Hour_Rollover == Hour_Rollover__True) *then* (Elapsed_Hours + 1)

And

If (Hour_Rollover == Hour_Rollover__True) *then* (Elapsed_Minutes = 0)

And finally

If (Hour_Rollover == Hour_Rollover__True) *then* (Hour_Rollover = False)

Chapter 5

When finished the display will look like figure 5-35.

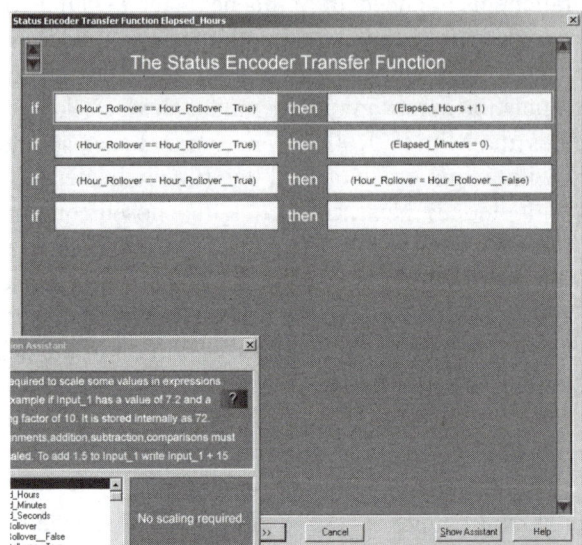

Figure 5-35

Finally, one new expression needs to be added to the Elapsed_Minutes Status Encoder. If you haven't done so already, click the Next>> button to return to the design desktop. Next, double-click on Elapsed_Minutes, choosing edit existing Transfer Function. Then, add the following expression:

```
If (Seconds_Timer == Seconds_Timer__Triggered) && (Elapsed_Minutes
>= MinutesinHour) then (Hour_Rollover = Hour_Rollover__True)
```

Now, the Elapsed_Minutes Status Encoder window will look like figure 5-36.

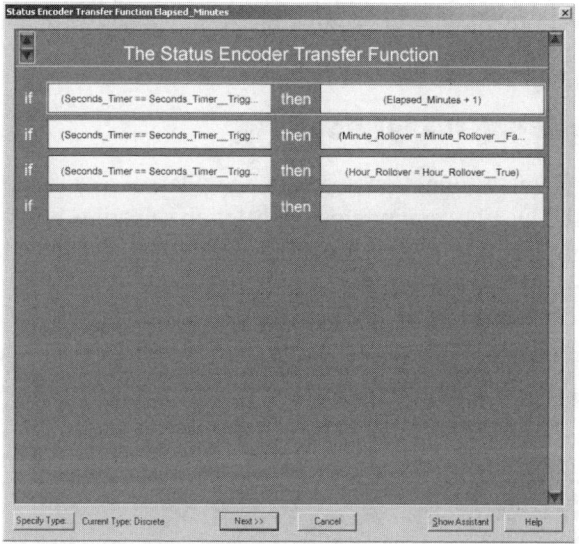

Figure 5-36

Again, press the Next >> button to return to the design desktop. The design desktop should now look like figure 5-37.

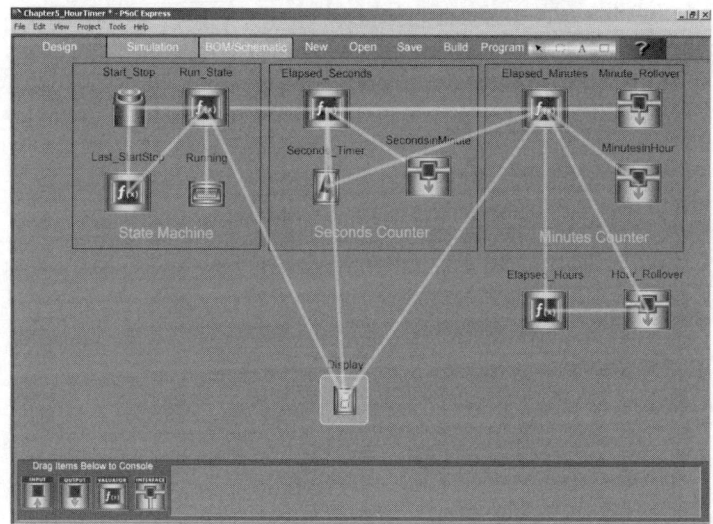

Figure 5-37

Select File → Save As and name this project Chapter5_ HourTimer. Then, press the Build tab. Even though logic has been added and changed, the pin configuration hasn't changed. Go ahead and build this project, then Program and run the newly generated application.

Step 5 – Updating the Display

The Display Transfer Function needs to be updated, so let's do that now. Select the Display component, right-click selecting Edit existing Transfer Function. Two new expressions need to be added to this transfer function. They are:

if **(Run_State_state == Run_State_state__Hours)** *then* **Elapsed_Hours**

And

if **(Run_State_state == Run_State_state__HoursMinutes)** *then* **(Elapsed_Hours * 100) + Elapsed_Minutes**

The first expression displays the value of Elapsed_Hours when Run_State equals Hours. The second expression displays the hours and minutes when Run_State equals HoursMinutes. The later expression displays a maximum of 99 hours 59 minutes.

Both HourMinutes and MinutesSeconds have been added for test purposes. When these changes have been successfully made the Display Transfer Function will look like figure 5-38.

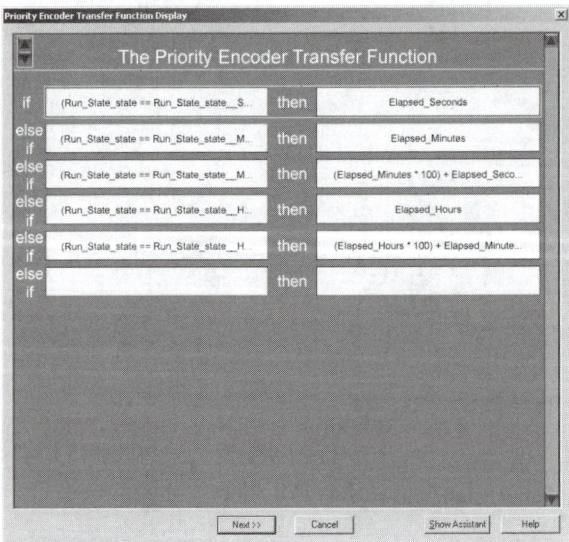

Figure 5-38

And the design desktop will look like figure 5-39.

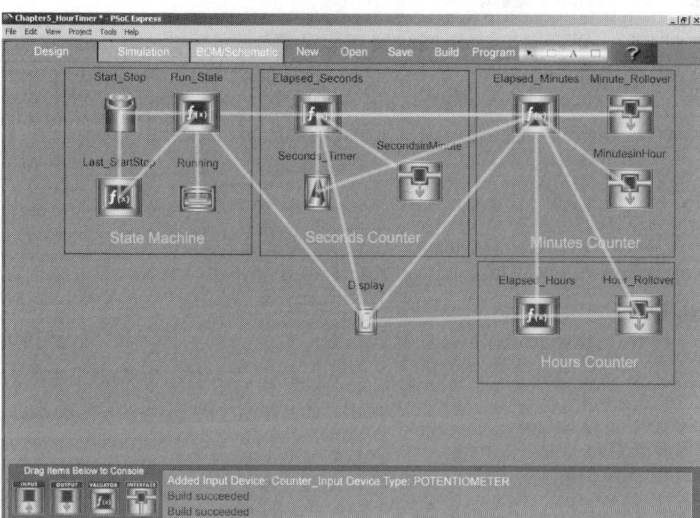

Figure 5-39

Save and Build the project, then program the board. To test the logic run the project on the World Tour board. Change display states by pressing the button to cycle between the display of: seconds, min-utes, minutes & seconds, hours, hours & minutes, then back to Off.

On Your Own

A lot of topics have been covered in this chapter. Can you figure out how to add a Days counter? Try adding counter that keeps track of the number of days that have elapsed and adding a new state to display the number of elapsed days. I'll give you a couple of hints. It requires a new Interface Valuator (maybe named HoursinDays) and a Status Encoder (named Elapsed_Days?). Set HoursinDays to the number of hours each day the hour meter would normally run. Then increment the Elapsed_Days counter on each roll over. Then, add one final Inter-face Valuator named Expired that contains the number of days before maintenance is due. Then when Elapsed_Days == Expired, assign the value of 10000 to Elapsed_Days and the display will flash until the hour meter is reset.

Chapter 5

Chapter Summary

This has been a very long chapter but has covered the basics of PSoC Express. Valuators, Transfer Functions, Status Encoders, Priority Encoders, Button Inputs, LED Outputs, Timer Inputs, and State Machines have all been addressed and used. Logical AND statements, Logical OR statements, and Bitwise OR statements have also been used as have the State Machine. The build process, component renaming, and component copy have also been used.

If the fundamentals of PSoC Express are still not completely understood, then please review this chapter again. And finally, don't be afraid to experiment. Try using different expressions to see what effect it has on the outcome of the final result. By experimenting, you'll gain valuable knowledge, and find out exactly what the best practices are for your style of development.

And remember when developing real-world applications with PSoC Express, always use a written design or a flow chart as your roadmap. That will prevent you from getting lost, and provide guidance on your path of PSoC Express development.

What's Ahead

In the next chapter a closer look will be taken at the thought process needed to develop successful PSoC Express applications. Precision timing will also be a covered topic so the hour meter can be accurate as possible. The Watchdog timer will also be discussed and new uses for LoopDelays will be explored. Alternate techniques for Valuator assignments will also be discussed to provide additional insight into proper design techniques for PSoC Express.

Chapter 6

How to Make Life Easier with PSoC Express

Chapter Overview

In the last chapter a complete hour meter was built from start to finish using the CY8C29666, Input Button, and the 7 Segment Display. A lot of ground was covered in understanding how PSoC Express works and how to build a project using techniques already learned.

But what if I said that allowing PSoC Express to handle even more of the program logic, the number of desktop components could be reduced even further, more code could be eliminated, all direct assignments could be removed. The truth is, changing the thought process just slightly and trusting that PSoC Express generates solid code will reduce the development process even more.

This chapter examines alternate development methods, alternate ways of assigning values to valuators (the preferred method), and how a slight change in the thought process when using PSoC Express will yield better results.

> **Author's Note:** I once again encourage you to read through the chapter before opening the associated projects. In the last chapter I used a method that is familiar to existing assembler and C programmers to do variable assignments directly within the Status and Priority Encoder framework. If you're an existing programmer taking this approach eases you into using PSoC Express to its fullest potential.

Topics Covered in This Chapter

The topics covered in this chapter include:

▶ PSoC Precision Timing Methods

▶ Watchdog Timer Techniques

▶ Alternate Uses for LoopDelay

▶ Variable Assignment Methods

▶ The PSoC Express Design Process

Changing Existing PSoC Express Projects

Adapting to a tool like PSoC Express can be easy or difficult depending on many factors. Many people like to maintain absolute control over their code. For PSoC Express to be used effectively, a developer must trust the backend code generator to create high quality code. Once this level of confidence is gained in the code generator, the developer also needs to feel confident in the proper use of PSoC Express. To gain more confidence in your PSoC Express skills and the code it produces, a closer look how PSoC Express creates and maintains logic will be taken.

Timing Techniques and Accuracy

For the purpose of this book, the internal oscillator in the PSoC itself is being used. So first let's examine the accuracy of the internal clock.

Internal oscillators are fine if a high degree of timing accuracy is not required. Internal oscillators can vary as much as 25%, depending on a number of factors (environmental, voltage, etc.). If using external communications where a clock is used to synchronize data transfer, timing inaccuracies can be dealt with through the use of the communications clock. But if non-clock based communications such as RS232, RS422, or RS485 are in use, then a higher degree of accuracy will be required. This is also true if maintaining accurate timing loops are required.

It will only be a matter of time (no pun intended) before accurate timing loops or accurate communications are needed. To address this issue, PSoC Express provides several types of Timer and Clock Inputs. Each technique uses a different clock or crystal source that has varying degrees of accuracy. Each technique also has a different purpose in the overall system design picture, providing the developer with a choice based on requirements.

In the last chapter an Interval Generator component was used, because it required no change to the existing circuit, no additional PSoC Express components, and is more than suitable for educational purposes. This chapter will begin by examining alternate ways of both keeping and tracking time.

External Crystals

This method of timekeeping requires a clock crystal and two capacitors. Some crystals have the capacitors built in while other require external capacitors. In either case this method involves using a 32,768 Hz crystal on pins P1[0] and P1[1]. A 22pf cap is attached between each pin to VDD to provide a smooth accurate heartbeat. These same components are also required for many of the accurate time chips on the market. This is a very accurate timing technique used for providing a heartbeat to the timekeeping chips used in PCs and other devices that require a high degree of timing accuracy. Using this method of timing also leaves the option of using the PSoC as an independent clock source, or using it in PLL (Phase-Lock-Loop) mode, which synchronizes all of the PSoC clocks to the crystal, making the PSoC a very accurately timed device.

Interval Generator

This was covered in Chapter 5. This Input provides an Interval that can be programmed to trigger every 0 to 32,000 milliseconds (32 seconds). If you aren't using an external crystal for input, then the accuracy of this timer is based on the accuracy of the clock in the PSoC device and environmental conditions. Variance in temperature, humidity, other environmental conditions can cause this clock to vary widely in its accuracy. Look at the data sheet for the PSoC you are using (in this case CY8C29666) to see what the accuracy of the internal clock is for your project. You may want to attach an external crystal if you need more precision timing capability of the PSoC in use.

Real Time Clock

This is an internal clock that keeps track of time and date through the use of six byte variables. If used alone its accuracy is dependent on the PSoC clock (discussed above). The real-time clock can (and should) be used with an external clock crystal to provide a very accurate time and date tracking mechanism.

Watchdog Timer

Also known as the "keep alive" timer, the watchdog is used as an input from an external source to keep the PSoC from going into a reset state. In PSoC Express the watchdog timeout can be between 32 milliseconds and eight full seconds. The watchdog timer uses a Reset Delay variable to set the number of periods the watchdog must be properly read to keep it alive, or to transition it back to alive.

Watchdog timers are traditionally used to prevent the processor from a hang condition. While it's a great tool to have, caution must be used to allow the watchdog enough time for the outer loop to complete one full cycle. This means you should time your loops and then add some time for padding in a worst-case situation. If the watchdog expires before the loop is completed, the watchdog will reset the processor before the cycle has completed.

It should also be stressed that if a watchdog timer is used, a clock crystal should be used as well. This will avoid a condition where the processor goes into a reset condition due to a simple environmental change such as temperature. So if your project requires a watchdog, also add a crystal to have accurate timing loops.

Internal Oscillator Accuracy

Be certain to check the data sheets for the PSoC part you are using to determine accuracy of the internal oscillator. Currently the PSoC documentation states that internal oscillator accuracy is 2.5 to 4.0%. Always check the latest data sheet in case part specifications change, and they do change.

Letting PSoC Express do the Work!

Just as PSoC Express components can be renamed and replaced with similar components, there are also choices in how PSoC Express can be used to develop a logic flow. In the last chapter, Interface Valuators were used to create SecondsinMinute and MinutesinHour variables. Figure 6-1 shows how the project looked at the end of chapter 5.

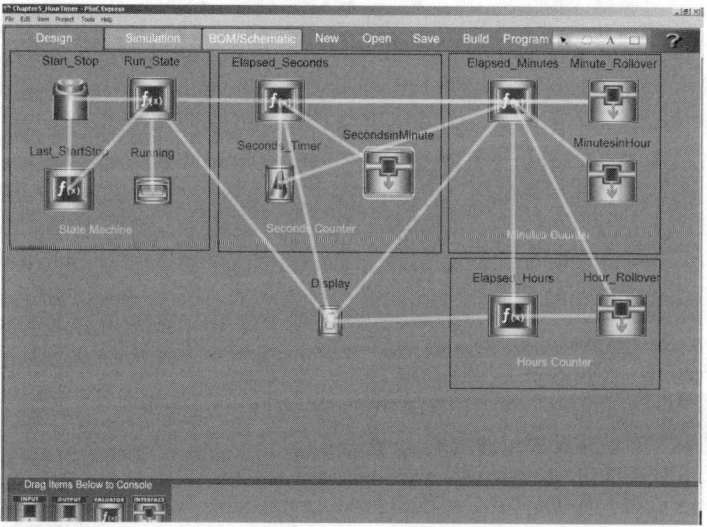

Figure 6-1

This design approach leaves both of the Interface Valuators available as Read/Write outside of the PSoC Express application. If remote accessibility to change a minute or hour from another source, then this would be an acceptable design practice, In this case however, the length of both Elapsed_Minutes and Elapsed_Hours need to remain under the control of the PSoC Express application exclusively. This means some changes to this project are required to assure these values cannot be changed outside the application but remain available outside the application as Read-Only. Load the Chapter5_HourTimer project and save it as Chapter6_1 before continuing.

Chapter 6

LoopDelays Revisited

Until now, the LoopDelay has been used to retain the last value of a variable or state. The LoopDelay also has another purpose. It can be used to keep track of a counter to determine (in this case) when the minute or hour rollover should occur. The benefit of using LoopDelays in this case, prevents the value from being altered by an outside application via a communications interface or another means. This method actually reduces the amount of logic needed and eliminates several components.

Originally the LoopDelay was used to track the state last value of the Start_Stop button. But the LoopDelay can also be used to eliminate Minute_Rollover and Hour_Rollover too. The LoopDelay will ALWAYS contain the last value of the object that has been used for the LoopDelay input. This means when Elapsed_Seconds is equal to 60, SecondsinMinute would be 59. This assumes of course, that the current Interface Valuator name SecondsinMinute is replaced with a LoopDelay of the same name.

This design change will change the SecondsinMinute variable from a comparison value to an incrementing variable, and from Read/Write to Read Only access, eliminating the possibility of the values being changed from outside sources.

Remember, this doesn't mean SecondsinMinute can no longer be changed, it means the technique that changes SecondsinMinute has changed. Since the number of seconds in a minute and the number of minutes in an hour are both the same (60), and the same method of incrementing minutes and hours are the same the same technique can be used for both. SecondsinMinute and MinutesinHour won't change once they have been set. So to implement these changes, begin by deleting the following components:

1. Minute_Rollover — This component will be permanently eliminated

2. Hour_Rollover — This component will be permanently eliminated

3. SecondsinMinute — This component will be replaced with a LoopDelay

4. MinutesinHour — This component will be replaced with a LoopDelay

Note: While PSoC Express is very flexible in allowing us to rename and replace components, replacing an existing component with a different type of component is done manually. This prevents you from accidentally selecting a different component type which may have some very bad effects on program logic.

Removing these components has invalidated some of the existing logic. Anywhere these components were used in Transfer Functions, the expressions using their names have been replaced with the expression NULL_EXPRESSION. This is a placeholder that has been inserted as shown in figure 6-2 to show which expressions have been affected. The Transfer Functions affected by the removal of the above components will be repaired shortly.

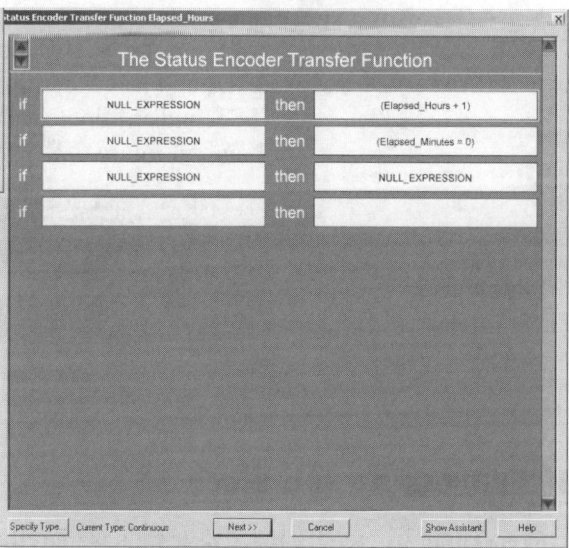

Figure 6-2

To get the project back in working order, start by adding a new Valuator, and name it SecondsinMinute, making it a LoopDelay as shown in figure 6-3.

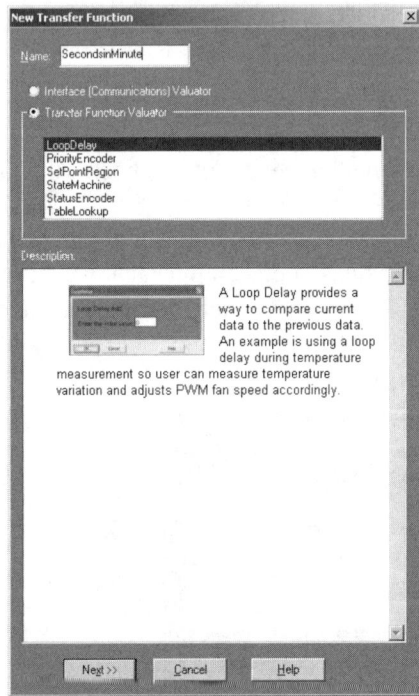

Figure 6-3

Press the Next>> button and select Elapsed_Seconds as the input to this LoopDelay as shown in figure 6-4.

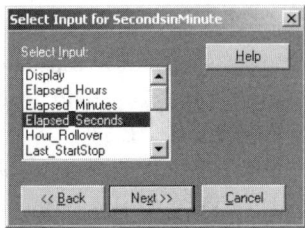

Figure 6-4

Press the Next>> button again, and leave the initial value of SecondsinMinute set to 0 as shown in figure 6-5.

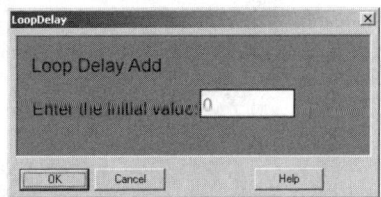

Figure 6-5

Letting PSoC Express do the Work

When the Seconds_Timer triggers Elapsed_Seconds is incremented, so the value of SecondsinMinute should be compared against a fixed value to reset the Elapsed_Seconds counter, and increment Elapsed_Minutes.

This is a much different approach then a direct assignment of Elapsed_Seconds and Elapsed_Minutes, then having Minute_Rollover and Hour_Rollover flags which also had to be set and reset. The other benefit to this technique is the elimination of the Status Encoder, replacing it instead with a Priority Encoder. This change means that only one expression in a transfer function will evaluate to true, each time through the main program cycle. This makes finding logic errors in the Transfer Functions much easier, and should a bug sneak through, it will be much easier to track down and fix. It's important to notice that the fewer expressions that evaluate each time through the main loop, the less likely the chance for hard-to-find bugs. This technique allows PSoC Express to do the bulk of the work during the development process.

In chapter 5 values were assigned in transfer functions manually. In this chapter the logic is being changed so PSoC Express has more control over the application logic, which reduces the possibility of manual coding errors in transfer functions.

Completing the Project Changes

Let's finish making the changes to this project. Now that a new Secondsin-Minute component has been added, changes need to be made to the Elapsed_Seconds Transfer Function. Double-click on Elapsed_Seconds, and check the "Select New Transfer Function" button as shown in figure 6-6.

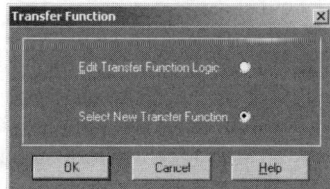

Figure 6-6

This time choose the Priority Encoder type and enter the following expressions:

```
if (Run_State_state != Run_State_state__Off) && (Seconds_Timer ==
Seconds_Timer__Triggered) then (Elapsed_Seconds + 1)
```

and

```
if (Run_State_state != Run_State_state__Off) && (SecondsinMinute ==
60) then 0
```

There are now only two lines of logic in the Priority Encoder. The first line simply states that if Run_State is not off and the Seconds_Timer has triggered, then add one to Elapsed_Seconds. The second expression sets Elapsed_Seconds to 0 if Run_State in not off and SecondsinMinute is equal to 60.

Chapter 6

Add another LoopDelay Valuator, named MinutesinHour. Next, change the Transfer Function in Elapsed_Minutes to a Priority Encoder and add the following two expressions:

```
If ((Seconds_Timer == Seconds_Timer_Triggered) && (SecondsinMinute
== 59)) then (Elapsed_Minutes + 1)
```

and

```
If (Seconds_Timer == Seconds_Timer_Triggered) && (MinutesinHour ==
60) then 0
```

Once again everything is synchronized to the Seconds_Timer trigger. Note that Run_State is not being evaluated because if Run_State were off, Elapsed_Seconds would not increment leaving SecondsinMinute unchanged. This would induce a very nasty bug.

One more change is needed before the compile and build. Select the Elapsed_Hours component, and again replace the existing Status Encoder with a Priority Encoder. Then, add the following expression:

```
if (Seconds_Timer == Seconds_Timer_Triggered) && (MinutesinHour ==
60) then (Elapsed_Hours + 1)
```

This single expression handles incrementing our Elapsed_Hours counter. Your design Desktop will now look like figure 6-7.

Build and Program the part. The goal of letting PSoC Express do all of the work has been accomplished. Now, Priority Encoders are being used for Elapsed_Seconds, Elapsed_Minutes, and Elapsed_Hours, so there is no longer a worry about these values being changed from outside the application. These three values been successfully changed to Read-Only. Replacing the Status Encoders with Priority Encoders has improved the integrity and predictability of the code, making debugging much easier should a problem arise.

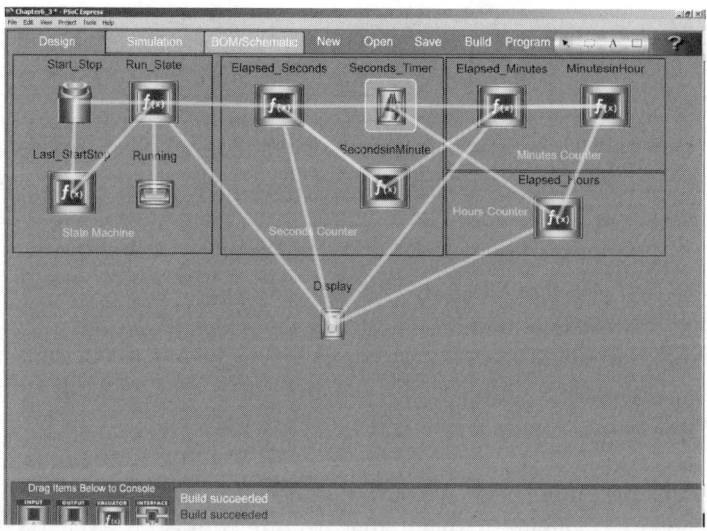

Figure 6-7

Priority Encoders vs. Status Encoders

It may appear that Priority Encoders are favored over Status Encoders from the changes made in this chapter. Both have their place in PSoC Express. Use a Priority Encoder whenever one action can be used for one set of conditions. Use Status Encoders when multiple actions are required for one set of conditions. And, remember that only one action can be taken per evaluation expression in both Status and Priority Encoders.

Save, Build, and Test

It's time to save, build, and test once again. Press the Save tab, followed by the Build tab. Since no pin assignments have been made since the last build, press the Next button twice to start the build process. Once the build process has completed successfully, click the Program tab, program the part, then toggle the power upon successfully programming the part to test these final changes.

Chapter 6

Chapter Review

Once again, quite a few changes were made to this project. Two variables were eliminated during the process making the design easier to understand. The amount of logic required was reduced while readability was improved by replacing Status Encoders with Priority Encoders. As more experience is gained with PSoC Express, the developer will gain more trust in the code generator, allowing PSoC Express to do more of the work. As this happens, productivity in PSoC Express will improve, even more new ways to work within PSoC Express will be found. This chapter has shown how much different a project can look and perform when PSoC Express handles the application flow, instead of using direct assignment statements. This chapter has shown firsthand, that as more comfort is gained with PSoC Express, developers will find better ways of application development, letting PSoC Express do the majority of the development work.

Looking Ahead

In the next chapter we will learn how to use PSoC Express to communicate with other PSoC devices and other types of external devices using I2C interface.

PSoC Express Communications using I2C

Chapter Overview

By now there should be a level of comfort in using PSoC Express. The basic hour meter will be completed in this chapter. By the end of this chapter the hour meter will be fully functional with some unique capabilities.

PSoC Express Communications Techniques

The PSoC family is composed of many parts that have a wide variety of capabilities. Before getting started, let's understand how the PSoC families of parts differ in functionality, and the capabilities of the PSoC line so the best part can be chosen for the job. Up to this point the CY8C29666 has been used on the World Tour board. To keep the design modular and to give the reader maximum exposure to the PSoC, this chapter is going to implement communications between two PSoC devices using the I2C interface.

The second reason for this approach is to give the developer experience in how I2C is properly implemented from both a Master and Slave view. By walking through the actual implementation of I2C, the reader will gain firsthand experience on how to implement this protocol. This will be very useful when developing applications requiring either PSoC-to-PSoC communications or PSoC communications with another I2C device.

The first portion of this chapter addresses I2C Master implementations on the CY8C29666, followed by I2C slave implementation on the CY8C27643 (at the lower left quadrant of the World Tour board).

PSoC Resource Usage

Before moving into the project, let's first examine a Build Report. PSoC Express creates a command file that invokes the compiler and linker, to create the executable program hex file, that is downloaded to the PSoC part. The file created is called a "make file" and upon completion creates a "Build Report." The "Build Report" contains information about the compile and build events, including any errors that may have prevented the hex file from being created. If errors occurred during the compile or link processes, the errors will be displayed instead of a successful build message. If the build was successful, a build report will contain any warning messages from the compiler and linker, along with statistics about how much memory (ROM and RAM) of the PSoC part has been used.

Up to this point, the discussion has been kept to learning PSoC Express. Now let's learn some of the less glamorous (but necessary) features of this product. Start by loading the last project from Chapter 6 (project Chapter6_3). Select File → Save As and name the new project Chapter7_1. Then select Build and press the Next button twice. When the build is complete, select Project → Show Last Build Report.

Unless this option is chosen explicitly, the developer will never see a Build Report (unless an error in the build process occurred). If a build error does occur, a window will pop up and display the error report automatically. The build report contains the compiler output from the make file used to build the project. The Make file is never seen or interacted with directly because this is all handled in the background. Scroll all the way to the bottom of the build report and to see how much of the current part's resources have been used by the PSoC Express program. Scrolling all the way to the bottom of the report will look similar to figure 7-1.

As shown in the last few lines of figure 7-1 only 14% of the flash ROM area, and 2% of the RAM area have been used. This means this project could be put into a much smaller part. Always keep in mind that one of the reasons the CY8C29666 was chosen is because of the available pin resources, digital, and analog blocks available for the type of components being used and the types of applications being

Chapter 7

```
lib/led7seg_09int.asm
lib/psocconfig.asm
lib/psocconfigtbl.asm
lib/systemtimer.asm
lib/systemtimerint.asm
./boot.asm
./calibration.c

./cmx_dio.c

./cmx_dio_chan.asm
./cmx_four7segled.c

./cmx_gswitch.c

./cmx_interval.c

./cmx_led7seg_chan.asm
./custom.c

./driverdecl.c

./functionparamdecl.c

./main.c

./systemconst.c

./systemvars.c

./transferfunction.c

Linking..
LMM info: area 'InterruptRAM' uses 16 bytes in SRAM page 0
LMM info: area 'data' item of 17 bytes allocated in SRAM page 0
LMM info: area 'virtual_registers' uses 9 bytes in SRAM page 0
LMM info: area 'data' item of 2 bytes allocated in SRAM page 0
LMM info: area 'data' item of 1 bytes allocated in SRAM page 0
LMM info: area 'data' item of 1 bytes allocated in SRAM page 0
LMM info: area 'data' item of 1 bytes allocated in SRAM page 0
LMM info: area 'data' item of 1 bytes allocated in SRAM page 0
  ROM 14% full. 4728 bytes used (does not include absolute areas).
  RAM 2% full. 48 bytes used (does not include stack usage).
idata dump at output/Chapter7_1.idata

Chapter7_1 - 0 error(s) 1 warning(s) 14:14:10
```

Figure 7-1

developed. And, PSoC Express will only display parts that have the right mix of digital and analog blocks, and enough I/O pins to support a PSoC Express application. And finally, remember that until a project is built for the first time, PSoC Express doesn't know how much memory a design will take.

Based on the memory resources consumed thus far, a much more complex project can be developed using PSoC Express before running out of memory. This also demonstrates how well the PSoC Express third generation code-generator optimizes the compiled code, reducing the size of the target executable.

There is one more less glamorous item to explore before continuing. Select the Project main menu item, then select Assign Register Map. You will see a window similar to figure 7-2.

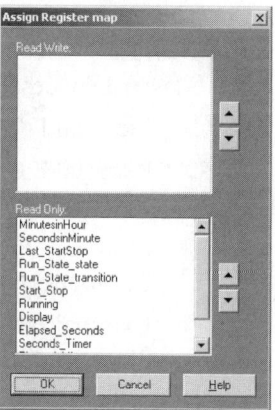

Figure 7-2

Remember that a Register in the context of PSoC Express is a variable. Looking at figure 7-2, note that Elapsed_Seconds, SecondsinMinute, and MinutesinHour are all Read-Only variables and currently no Read/Write variables exist in this project. Valuators that contain logic expressions of any type are Read-Only, while Interface Valuators (type variables) are always Read/Write.

The I2C Interface

Phillips (now known as NXP) developed the I2C Protocol as a means for Inter-Component-Communications.

The PSoC has both built in I2C Master and Slave capabilities. In I2C communications, the host initiates all communications. The host monitors data coming from the slave devices by requesting slave data. Note the use of the word devices. Many devices can be connected to the same I2C bus, and each has a different (or unique) device ID. When a device is addressed by the master, that address alone responds. While using I2C in PSoC Express is easy, it is not very intuitive. That's why this chapter will concentrate on setting up I2C Master and Slave devices, then add slave monitoring capabilities to experience I2C capabilities firsthand. So, let's get started.

Adding the I2C Master

To implement the I2C master, begin by selecting Output → Output Devices → Remote Devices. This selection offers four types of I2C Master Devices. They are:

▶ External I2C Slave-Control – Standard Slave Control Component

▶ External I2C Slave-Control, Interval – Interval Standard Slave Control Component

▶ External I2C Slave-Monitor, Triggered – Triggered Slave Monitor Component

▶ External I2C Slave-Monitor, Variable Interval – Variable Interval Slave Monitor Component

Select the first choice, External I2C Slave Device – Control. The Output widow is shown in figure 7-3.

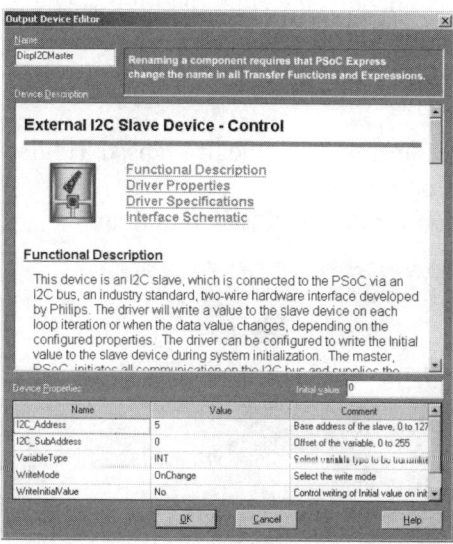

Figure 7-3

After selecting the External I2C Slave-Control, name it DispI2CMaster, and change the I2C_Address to 5. This is the channel (or address), which will send data to the slave device. The purpose of this component is to provide a channel to slave device control. This could be considered similar to a radio channel in a car. Different channels have different types of information. In this case different channels send data to different devices. The difference between a radio and I2C control is that while many radios can tune to the same channel, only one device should be listening to an I2C address.

This doesn't provide a channel for monitoring data coming from the slave device. That will be added a little later in this chapter.

Transmitting I2C Data

Now that the I2C Slave Control Interface has been added, the next step is to choose the data that will be transmitted. This component has a Transfer Function that allows it to handle the data and calculated expressions for data transmission. In the last chapter, a DisplayValue Interface Valuator was added that the hour and minute counter values is assigned to. This variable was created with the intention of using it to send data to a remote component. To send data, select the DispI2CMaster component, Right-click and choose Transfer Function. Select a Priority or Status Encoder and enter the following expression:

> *If* **1** *then* **Elapsed_Hours**

This expression will transmit the value of Elapsed_Hours, each time through the main program loop.

The Transfer Function window will look like figure 7-4.

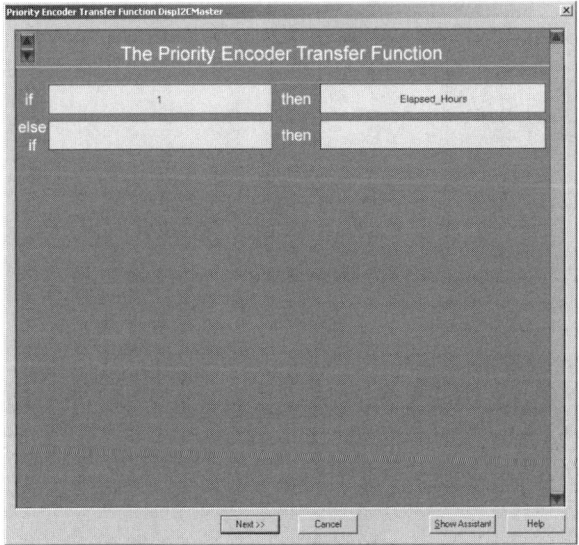

Figure 7-4

Here the Priority Encoder was used, but both the Priority or Status Encoder will work in this case. Since 1 is always True, DispI2CMaster will always be assigned the value of Elapsed_Hours immediately when Elapsed_Hours changes. Therefore, each time Elapsed_Hours is updated with a new value, the following assignment is made: **DispI2CMaster = Elapsed_Hours** and the new value of DispI2CMaster is transmitted to the I2C slave device at the pre-set address, which in this case is address 5. After clicking the OK button the design desktop should look like figure 7-5.

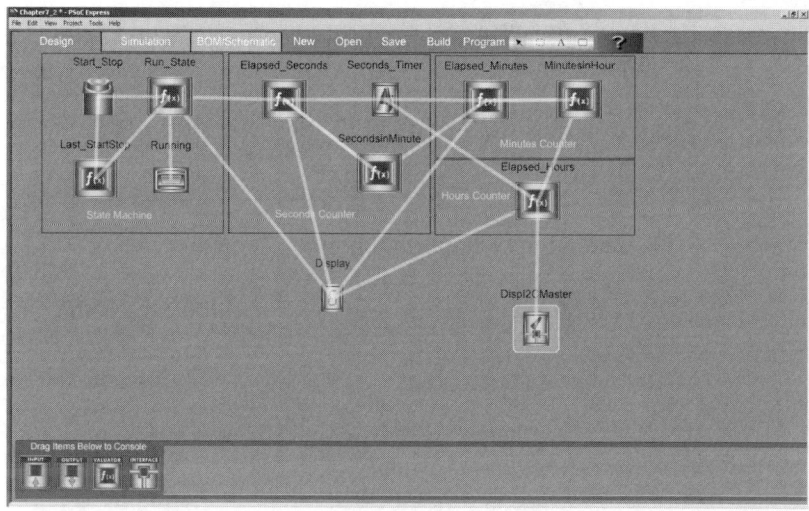

Figure 7-5

Before doing a build, select File → Save As, and name this project Chapter 7_2. Then Build and Program the CY8C29666 (Seven Segment Display) quadrant with the new code.

The I2C Slave

Next, create the I2C slave project. Aside from using a different PSoC part, developers need to be aware of other important information. There are two very important parameters that will cause this project to not work as expected if not set correctly.

The Importance of the Slave Address

The first parameter of importance is the setting of the slave address. If the slave address doesn't match the address assigned in the Master, the slave device will either not see the correct data or it will not see any data at all. To make this situation potentially worse, should another device have the address assigned in the master, that device may also work incorrectly, erratically, or not at all. So a working project can go completely awry because of an incorrect slave address setting or a Master-Slave address mismatch.

To avoid this problem some simple rules should be implemented. Rule number one is:

> **The same address assigned as the slave address in the master must also be assigned in the slave.**

The second very important point to remember is:

> **Always make certain the width of the value sent is the same as the width of the value received.**

If the width of the Register variables is not the same, byte values on the Master will differ from the values on the Slave. This has to do with byte-ordering and can be difficult to find and fix.

A Word about Power

Let's emphasize one final rule. The PSoC is both a 3.3 and 5.0-volt device. If you accidentally set it to 5.0 volts and provide 3.3 volts, it may end up in a continuous reset state. That can be fixed by simply changing the supply voltage selection to 5.0 volts.

On the other hand, some of the peripherals used in this book are 3.3-volt devices. If 5.0 volts is accidentally applied to a 3.3-volt device, the device will likely be destroyed. Powering the World Tour board with a 9-volt battery or from the USB port of a PC will pass the supplied voltage through a 3.3 volt regulator, eliminating most of the danger. There is one exception. When programming the board with the MiniProg programmer, 5.0 volts is applied during the programming cycle. So, rule number three is:

> **Always unplug any devices attached to the World Tour board headers before programming the PSoC part.**

There is one final rule, rule four. Rule four is:

> **In your own designs be certain that you use and provide the proper voltage to the PSoC, and use a voltage that is tolerable by any peripheral components.**

Let's continue with the project!

Create the Slave Project

First, Select File → New to start with a fresh design desktop. Next, select File → Save As, and name this project Chapter7_2Slave. There are only three components in this project. They are:

▶ I2C Slave Interface

▶ Interface Valuator

▶ LCD Display

Start by adding the I2C Slave Interface. Select the Interface component from the bottom of the design desktop. Choose Slave, and change the I2C address to 5, then naming the component DispI2CSlave. Your window will look like figure 7-6.

Figure 7-6

This component provides the ability to accept data from the I2C host. This is a communications Interface and nothing more. This driver listens for data bound to slave address 5, receives the data, and stores it to a buffer (Interface Valuator).

The I2C Slave Interface Valuator

Now the communications interfaces exist on both the Master and Slave devices. Next, a variable is needed to store the received information. Click on the Valuator component, checking the Interface Valuator box, name it Display_Value, select Continuous, Add Properties, and enter 0 as the minimum and 9999 as the maximum values. Press the OK button twice to return to the design Desktop. It's time to add the final component. Choose Output, add LCD Name, Value Displayed in a Column component. Name the component LCD_Display, select Row 0-1, assign the text string "Hours" to the Label String, choosing Decimal as the output type. The display should look like figure 7-7.

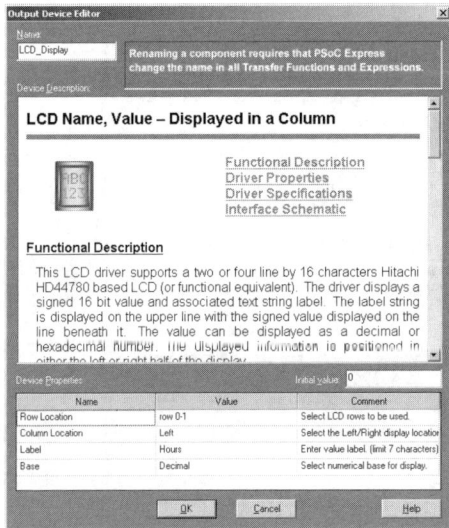

Figure 7-7

Press the OK button, then right-click the LCD component, choose Transfer Function, Priority Encoder, and enter the following expression:

```
If 1 then Display_Value
```

This expression will cause Display_Value to be updated each time through the main program loop. Remember, the value from the Master is only updated when it changes.

The display will look like figure 7-8.

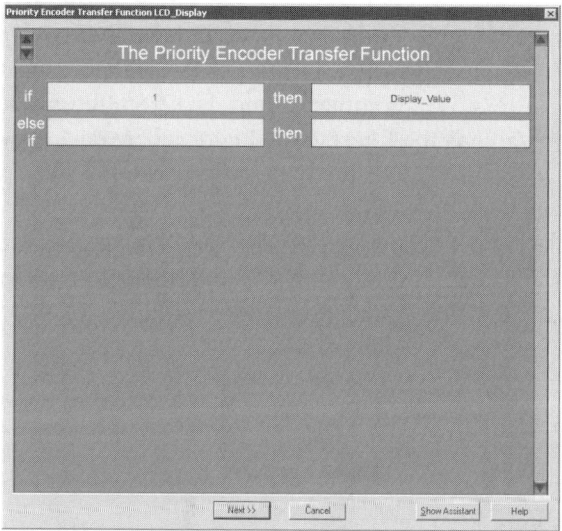

Figure 7-8

The design desktop should now look similar to figure 7-9.

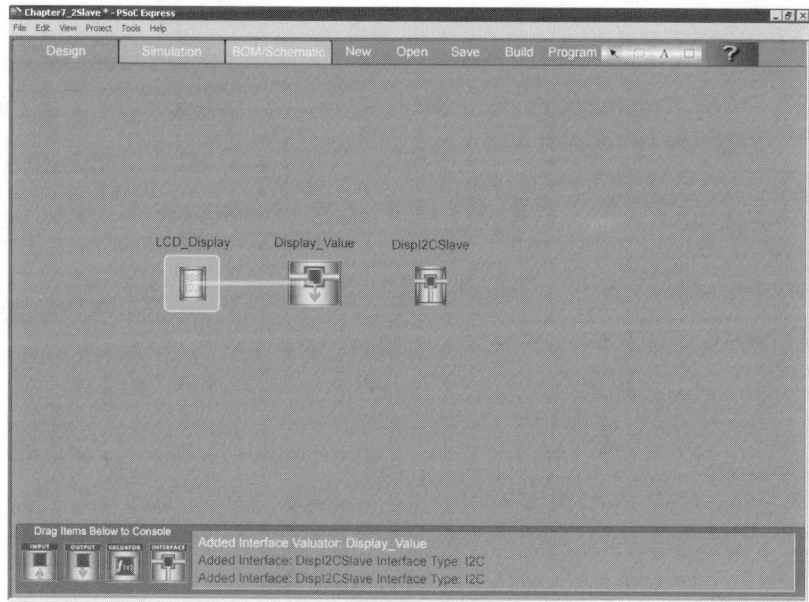

Figure 7-9

Implicit vs. Explicit Data Binding

Let's examine why there is no line connecting DispI2CSlave to other components. As discussed earlier, DispI2CSlave is the Interface that listens to I2C address 5 for commands and data from the Master to the Slave. Display_Value is the Interface Valuator where data arriving from the Master is stored. As already discussed, the Interface Valuator is just another name for a variable.

The association between DispI2CSlave and Display_Value is implied from the design desktop view. It's not difficult to understand when we look at how this association works using the graphic shown in figure 7-10.

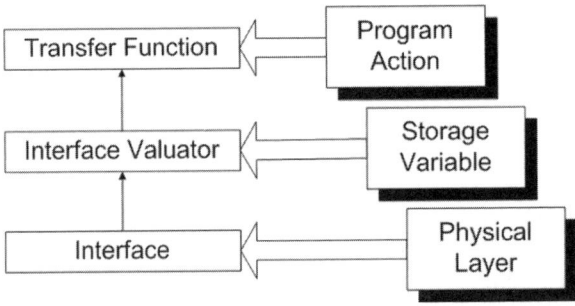

Figure 7-10

The Interface component is the physical link between the application and the hardware. The Interface component binds the hardware communications layer to the first available variable (Interface Valuator). Interface Valuators are Read/Write, and start at location zero (0) of the local Register Map.

The name of the Interface Valuator at Register Map Location 0 will accept the data, which in this case is the Display_Value Interface Valuator.

Referring once again to figure 7-10, the Interface Valuator provides local storage for the remote value. It is through this mechanism the remote value is not only copied to the local PSoC but is also made available to a local Transfer Function.

> **Note:** *The arrows are going in one direction only in figure 7-10. This is because the I2C master is currently a source of data only, and the value of the Interface Valuator is used only as input to the Transfer Function.*

Building the Project and Programming the PSoC

It's time to build and test this project. Click the Build tab, and choose the CY8C27643, 48 Pin MLF part, then press Next. Arrange the pins so that **pse_LCD_SHARED_0 LCDPin11** is connected to **P4 [0]** and **Slave5 I2CSDAPin** is connected to **P1 [0]** as shown in table 7-1, and figure 7-11.

PSoC Signal	Pin
pse_LCD_SHARED_0 LCDPin4	P4[5]
pse_LCD_SHARED_0 LCDPin5	P4[6]
pse_LCD_SHARED_0 LCDPin6	P4[4]
pse_LCD_SHARED_0 LCDPin11	P4[0]
pse_LCD_SHARED_0 LCDPin12	P4[1]
pse_LCD_SHARED_0 LCDPin13	P4[2]
pse_LCD_SHARED_0 LCDPin14	P4[3]
I2CSCLPin	P1[1]
I2CSDAPin	P1[0]

▲ Table 7-1

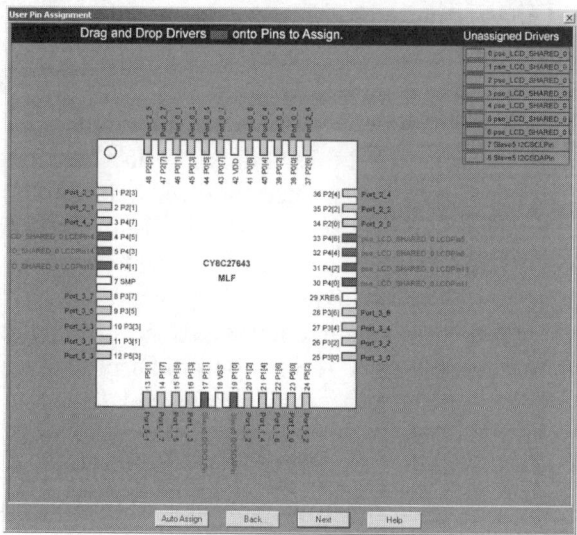

Figure 7-11

129

After the pin assignments are completed, press the Next>> button to finish the build. Once the build has completed successfully, press the Program tab. Remember the lower left quadrant of the board is being programmed, so remove the jumpers from that header to attach the MiniProg. Next, press the Program button. When the part has programmed successfully, remove the MiniProg and re-attach the jumpers. Apply power to the board through the mini-USB cable or a 9-volt battery. Note how the LCD updates concurrently with the seven-segment display. The first I2C Master/Slave project is now completed. Next, a return path to the I2C Master will be implemented by creating an Interface Valuator on the I2C Slave and an I2C Slave Monitor on the I2C Master.

I2C Slave Monitoring

By now, the use of PSoC Express and I2C communications should be demystified. If not then re-read this chapter again and it should start to become clear. If there is a comfort with I2C then let's move on to the next topic; reading slave values.

Earlier, when selecting the I2C Master there is a choice between an 8-bit I2C Master (0 to 127) and a Master that could have up to three additional address pins (11 bit). I2C can either 8 or 11 bits. Actually, I2C is either 7 or 10 bits when considering that only 7 bits of the 8 bits are addressable. For each I2C address used for sending data from the Master, there is a separate address used for return data from the Slave. If you multiply 64×2 the result is 128 or 7 bits that may be set from an 8-bit byte (0111 1111). Therefore, when transmitting to DispI2CSlave, address 5 is used. When receiving from the Slave, the lowest order bit is set. Adding a value of one to the transmit address. So the data request is address $(5 + 1)$ or 6. The lowest ordered bit (bit 0) in the I2C protocol is the direction bit, so transmitting to DispI2CSlave uses address 5 and receiving from DispI2CSlave uses address 6 (address $5 + 1$ (the 1 identifying receive mode)). Figure 7-12 illustrates how I2C addressing works. The top value in figure 7-12 shows the output address for DispI2CSlave, which is five. The lower portion of figure 7-12 shows the read address for DispI2CSlave, which is six.

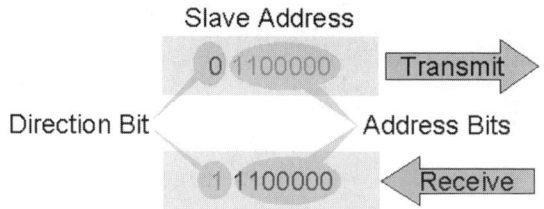

Figure 7-12

In the PSoC Express I2C Master project, an additional component is required to receive data back from the slave.

I2C Slave Monitoring in PSoC Express Means Location is Everything!

That's right! As discussed earlier, Interface Valuators are placed in the order in which they were created in the Register Map, starting at location zero. As also discussed, the position or order of Interface Valuators can be changed using the Project → Assign Register Map main menu.

When it comes to I2C slave monitoring, the same physical interface that receives data on the slave side, also transmits data from the slave side. However, the address of the data to transmit from the slave to the master is configured from the master. In addition, while the slave does transmit the data, the master controls when the slave sends the data via a data request. While this may seem confusing let's walk through an actual example as the current project is expanded.

Step 1 – Modify the I2C Slave Project

Start by doing a File → Save As, and naming the new project Chapter7_3Slave. Next, add a new component by choosing Input → Tactile → Potentiometer, naming it Remote_Display as shown in figure 7-13.

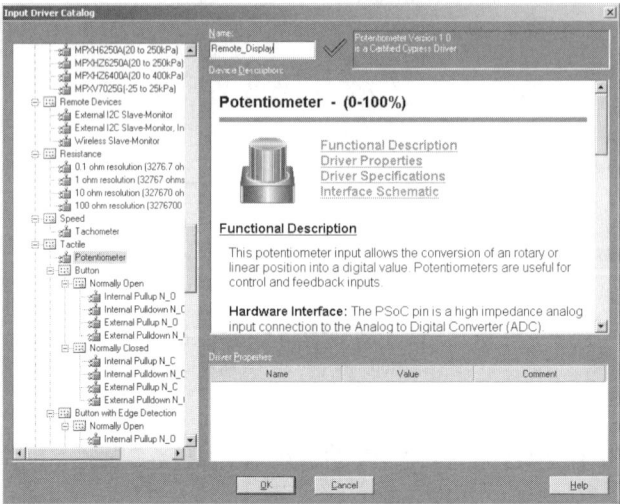

Figure 7-13

Press the OK button, and the design desktop will look like figure
7-14.

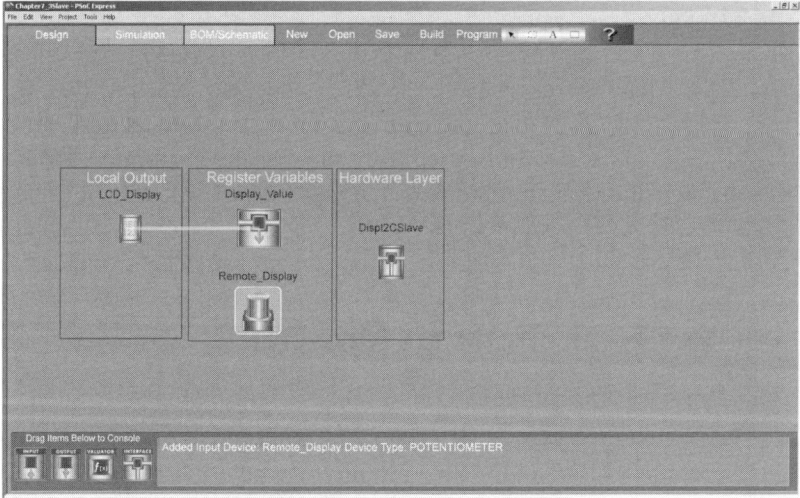

Figure 7-14

The potentiometer will be used to determine which field(s) are
output on the LCD Display. Since the value of Remote_Display has
nothing to do with any of the components on the desktop, there is no
need to add or change anything else in the slave portion of this

project. So, save and build this project by pressing the Save tab, followed by the Build tab. Press the Next button and assign the Remote_Display potentiometer to pin P0[1]. This will assure the slave actually reads the potentiometer. Then press Next to build the project.

After a successful build, view the datasheet to note the location of the Remote_Display register variable. To do this open the datasheet from the link on the completed Build screen, then scroll down to the Register Variables section, and locate Remote_Display object as shown in figure 7-15.

Table 2: Chapter7_3Slave Interface Register Map		
OFFSET	NAME	READ/WRITE ACCESS
0	Display_Value	RW
2	LCD_Display	RO
4	Remote_Display	RO

I2C Register Protocol Description (Requires an I2C Interface Object):

When writing one or more bytes, the first data byte is always the data pointer. The byte after the data pointer will be written into the location pointed to by the data pointer byte. The third byte (second data byte) will be written to the data pointer plus 1 and so on. The data pointer will increment for each byte read or written, but will be reset at the beginning of each new read operation.

A new read operation will begin to read data at the location pointed to by the last write operation's data pointer. For example, if the data pointer is set to 4, a read operation will begin to read data at location 4 and continue sequentially until the end of the data or the host completes the read operation.

Following each read operation the data pointer will reset to 4 and the next read continues sequentially from that location. This is true whether a single or multiple read operations are performed. The data pointer will not be changed until a new write operation is initiated.

If the I2C master attempts to write data to a read-only location or an undefined location, the data will be discarded and will have no affect. Data cannot be read outside the defined range. Any read requests by the master, outside the allotted range will result in invalid data being returned.

Figure 7-15

Looking at figure 7-15, Remote_Display is at location 4 and is one byte long. The several paragraphs below the Interface Register Map explain the I2C Protocol as implemented by PSoC Express. Go back and look at figure 7-2, then note the up and down arrows on the right side of the Register Map display. Remember these arrows allow the Register Map values to be re-arranged. Selecting one of the variables in either the Read/Write or Read Only window, then clicking the up or down arrows, notice that the highlighted variable moves up or down accordingly. These arrows will not allow Read-Only variables to be moved into the Read-Write section and vice-versa. Note the location of the Remote_Display register variable and size so Master I2C device may be modified.

Step 2 – Add the I2C Slave Monitor to the Master Project

One more component needs to be added to the I2C Master, it is a Slave-Monitor component. This component is located under Input, Remote Devices, I2C Slave-Monitor. Configure the driver as shown in figure 7-16.

Figure 7-16

Name this component Remote_Display to match the corresponding component on the slave device. There are three configurable parameters; they are:

▷ I2C_Address – The address of the I2C Slave to monitor

▷ I2C_SubAddress – Register Map location of the value to be Monitored (Read)

▷ Variable Type – Byte or Unsigned Integer

Our I2C_Address was originally set by the master at five, so let's set that number to five. The I2C_SubAddress is the Register Offset on the Slave of the variable we want to read. Looking back at figure 7-14, this value is set to four, so set the I2C_Subaddress to a four. While the length of the remote variable cannot be determined by looking at figure 7-14, it is known this value is between 0 and 100, a developer can be confident that it is defined as a byte. Knowing that, let's set the Variable_Type to a byte.

The purpose of the remote potentiometer is to allow the information displayed on the LCD to be determined by the potentiometer setting. To make this also work on the I2C Master, a change is needed to the Transfer Function of DispI2CMaster. Select DispI2CMaster, right-click and select Transfer Function. Then alter the existing function so there are three lines of expressions as follows:

```
if (Remote_Display >= 66) then (Elapsed_Minutes * 100) +
Elapsed_Seconds
```

```
if (Remote_Display < 66) && (Remote_Display >= 33) then
Elapsed_Seconds
```

```
if (Remote_Display < 33) then Elapsed_Hours
```

Depending on the potentiometer setting, Minutes and Hours, Hours, or Minutes will be displayed.

The Chapter7_3Master design desktop will now look like figure 7-17.

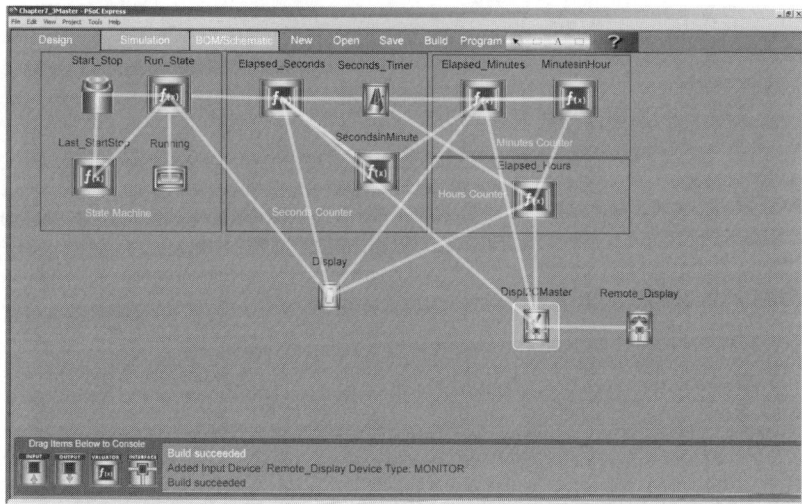

Figure 7-17

It's time to Save, Build, and Program the CY8C29666 part. Once programmed remove the MiniProg and replace the headers on the I2C pins to make certain the I2C interface will work. Then either connect a

USB cable from a PC to the board or attach a 9-volt battery. Experiment by pressing the button on the lower right quadrant to change the display states to the seven-segment display.

Notice that the LCD has the word Hours displayed on the top line. Turning the potentiometer on the lower left side of the board changes the LCD display from Minutes & Seconds to Minutes, then to Seconds depending on the potentiometer value.

Chapter Review

Now, there should be a basic understanding of how I2C communications work in PSoC Express environment. Transmitting data from a Master device is done using an Output component, while receiving data from a Slave device is done using an Input component. All data transfers are under the control of the I2C Master Output component on the Master device. This chapter has also taught the reader how to distribute control using the I2C bus among multiple PSoC parts. If you would like more information about the I2C protocol, visit the NXP website for I2C specifications at www.nxp.com.

Looking Ahead

In the next chapter, a serious look at WirelessUSB will be taken. Implementing the Master, Slave, and debugging topics will all be covered.

Implementing WirelessUSB

Chapter Overview

In the last chapter I2C Master and Slave interfaces were implemented using PSoC Express, adding new functionality to the hour meter design.

This chapter will go beyond I2C in teaching how to cut-the-cord for 1-to-1 wireless communications using WirelessUSB, another Master / Slave based communications technique for the PSoC.

> **Note:** This chapter is not for use with the World Tour board. Instead, this chapter uses the CY3630-DK WirelessUSB evaluation kit. Two PSoC Express drivers behave differently using the CY3630-DK. Normally-Open Push Buttons use Pull-up Resistors instead of the Pull-Down Resistors used by the World Tour Board. Also, the LED Drivers are designed where the PSoC pins sink the current. This means the LED Logic is inverted so the driver state of Off would actually turn on the LED.

WirelessUSB History

Cypress offers many wireless products. Since the first WirelessUSB product was introduced, range and data rates in the Cypress wireless products have been greatly improved. While these products are sold under the WirelessUSB name, they are actually 1-to-1 and many-to-1 wireless devices that operate in the 2.4 GHz range. Yes, they are commonly used for wireless USB HID devices such as Keyboards, Mice, and Game Pads. But, these devices are not dedicated to USB only type devices, and can be used anywhere other embedded wireless transceivers are used.

PSoC Express and WirelessUSB

Why use WirelessUSB? There are many answers to that question! WirelessUSB is inexpensive to implement as prices have dropped dramatically in the past few years, making WirelessUSB very price competitive with other wireless technologies, such as infrared (IrDA).

Next, there is a tremendous amount of flexibility gained in cutting-the-cord, even after adding up the costs associated with wireless development. And finally, the demand for the use of wireless devices is increasing as customers demand cutting-the-cord. The benefits gained from using wireless communications, combined with the ease of implementing a 1-to-1 wireless communications network with PSoC Express help you bring ideas to life in a fraction of the time previously required.

A wireless strategy for a new project or product can quickly be developed, without a large investment of time or money. This brings affordable wireless development to projects that were outside the reach of wireless in the past, and brings wireless within the realm of small companies that have a small engineering staff, or limited wireless expertise. But, these are just a few reasons to look at the WirelessUSB, PSoC Express combination. Imagine, full wireless development and implementation without ever writing a line of code!

Wireless communications may seem magical because data moves though the air without wires, mysteriously connecting devices together. There are many challenges that can be encountered during the wireless development cycle. These challenges can be difficult to resolve without proper training and diagnostic equipment. If you are designing your own transceiver boards you will need a good spectrum analyzer, wireless sniffer, or both; for viewing and debugging wireless data protocols. If you're building small quantities of products, and using off-the-shelf boards, you will find that using the WirelessUSB/PSoC Express combination will reduce development time, allowing you're product(s) to be price and feature competitive with systems costing much more.

A Brief WirelessUSB Primer

Any time two or more devices (or people) communicate, some type of protocol is needed. Imagine a room full of people, all trying to talk to the same person at once, no one would be heard. A protocol is implemented to referee which device talks, which device listens, and how data can be exchanged without constant collisions.

The PSoC Express WirelessUSB interface is a Master/Slave interface, which means the Master has control. Similar to the I2C interface, the PSoC Express WirelessUSB drivers gives developers control where the data buffer begins within the Device Register Map. But, WirelessUSB is unlike I2C in the regard there is no hardwired slave. Since there is no hardwired connection, multiple slaves can be within range at any given times. Since there are no wires connecting the Master and Slave devices, the Slave is "bound" to the Master the first time a connection has been established between the devices. After the first session has been established, the Slave will store information about the Master it has been mated with. These devices will remain "paired" until the firmware has been changed in the slave and a new program downloaded to the devices.

The WirelessUSB transceivers handle connection details. Multiple channels are scanned to select the channel with the least noise. The data packets are wrapped with Start-of-Packet (SOP) marker at the beginning, End-of-Packet (EOP) marker at the end, and Error Correction (CRC) bytes to provide the highest degree of reliability in establishing and maintaining the Master and Slave connections.

PSoC Express has two different types of WirelessUSB interfaces. This chapter only covers the Simple Packet Interface which has a fixed speed of 250Kbps. This interface only supports a single slave matched to a single master. The maximum number of bytes transferred per transaction is 15 and bytes sent are kept separate from bytes received. Fifteen bytes is plenty for a PSoC Express project.

A PSoC Express I2C Master is allowed access to the entire Slave device Register Map. A WirelessUSB Master is allowed separate access to the WirelessUSB slave send and receive data areas. Because access by the Master to the Slave send and receive areas are separate, developers will note more frequent use of the Offset parameter in the WirelessUSB component suite.

WirelessUSB has one more distinctive difference from I2C and that is the scheduling of data to and from the slave. In I2C the master sends and requests data. In WirelessUSB the slave controls when the data transfer occurs, although the Master still makes the data transfer request. And finally, all Reads and Writes are based on the Slave as both the source and target of data.

The Bind Process, the Master – Slave Link

One of the most important events in establishing WirelessUSB Master/Slave relationship, is the Bind process. Let's examine how the bind process works. There are two reasons for the bind process. First, the bind process dedicates the connection between the Master and Slave devices so the connection remains even if other WirelessUSB devices are nearby. The second reason for binding a Master and Slave devices, is to avoid outside interference to the link. Once a Master and Slave are "bound" information about the Master is stored in the memory of the slave device. Here is how the bind process works. During the binding process the Master determines if the slave is the same Type ID as the Master. If the Type ID's match, the Master will provide the slave with the manufacturing number of the Master which the Slave will store in permanent memory. In addition to identifying the Master, this manufacturing ID is used to also calculate network parameters, reducing the time needed to make a connection once two devices are "paired." This describes the Bind process and once two devices are "bound," they will remain so until the slave is reprogrammed.

After a Master and Slave are bound, on power-up the Master will scan available channels until a channel unused by other WirelessUSB Master devices is found with the least noise. Once a channel is located, the Master listens for a slave, periodically checking other channels for noise. If a channel with less noise is found, the Master will switch channels and continue listening for a slave.

When a WirelessUSB Slave powers-up that is already bound to a Master, the Slave selects a transmit channel. The Slave then transmits a connection request and awaits a response from the Master. If no response is received, the Slave will switch channels, starting the process over again. If no response is received the Slave will continue searching other channels until the Slave times-out. The Master and Slave change channels at different rates, so the highest degree of success in making a connection is attained. The Master listens for and only responds to requests from Slave devices. Even after the connection is established, the Master listens for the Slave to request and send data.

If the slave is not bound to a master, it will enter Bind mode on power-up. This is a blocking call, meaning that no other part of the program on the slave will execute until A) the Slave has been bound to a Master, or B) the Slave has timed out waiting for a response from a Master to bind with. This means that if a variable is initialized to a non-zero value, it should be set though the use of an Interface Valuator to be certain the value is set correctly if the Master and Slave do not successfully bind.

Unlike the Slave, the Master requires a "trigger" to start the Bind process. Typically this would be a button that would be pressed to initiate the Bind function after powered up. The Bind process on the Master is a also "blocked" call, until the Master has either A) completed the Binding process to a Slave device or B) has timed out awaiting a matching Slave device. No other part of the program will execute on the Master until one of these conditions has been met. It may take almost a minute for the bind process to complete after a power-up. If your applications don't respond immediately, wait a minute for the bind process to complete.

Designing with WirelessUSB

The best feature of WirelessUSB is the lack of a physical connection. The worst feature is debugging a WirelessUSB application. But, if the rest of this chapter is followed, debugging problems will be minimized and a comfort level of WirelessUSB will be attained. Before continuing make sure the above Bind process is understood.

WirelessUSB Performance

Let's begin with WirelessUSB link initialization. Other types of wireless networks seem to connect instantly. Don't expect this type of response from WirelessUSB, because it won't happen. First, a PC wireless LAN operates at between 10 Mbps and 100 Mbps (that's megabits per second). A WirelessUSB LAN operates at 250 Kbps (that kilobits per second). Kilo vs. Mega is no contest, Mega wins every time. So, linking a WirelessUSB master and slave together can vary in time from instantly to almost a minute. WirelessUSB shares the same 2.4 GHz band that other wireless devices use, so it may take time to find a clear channel depending on traffic.

WirelessUSB Power Requirements

Before starting the first project, let's touch on WirelessUSB power requirements and how they compare to PSoC power requirements. WirelessUSB requires 1.8 to 3.3 volts DC. Applying 5 volts to a WirelessUSB transceiver will likely destroy the unit. If a single voltage supply is desired, the PSoC can be set to low voltage mode, which is 3.3 volts. If running the PSoC at 5.0 volts is desired, then it is up to the developer to make certain the PSoC power is isolated from WirelessUSB power.

And a final warning about MiniProg power. When programming a PSoC in circuit with a WirelessUSB device, make certain the power setting is set to Reset. This will use the existing power source external to the MiniProg which will eliminate the potential of accidentally supplying 5.0 volts when programming.

A Developer's First WirelessUSB Project

Note: The Master device in this project is being developed first. The reason is because the project was designed and developed in advance of the text. In real-world practice there is no substitute for a good design. And with WirelessUSB that means a detailed layout of the Slave Register Map should be finished before starting a project.

Now that the fine points have been covered, let's begin the first project. Let's begin by developing the WirelessUSB master. Start PSoC Express or Select File → New → Save As, and name the project SimpleMaster1. The first component added will be a WirelessUSB Master CY3630 from the Output catalog as shown in figure 8-1.

Figure 8-1

Name this component WUSB_Master making certain that DO_NOT_BIND is selected in the pull down box above the parameter section. Next, chose 0 for Slave Device Type ID, and 0 again for Receive Base Offset. Choose 1 for both Bytes to Receive, and Bytes to Transmit parameters. When completed, press the OK button.

Next, select Tactile, Button, Normally_Open, Internal PullDown N_O push button, and name this component BIND_Button as shown in figure 8-2.

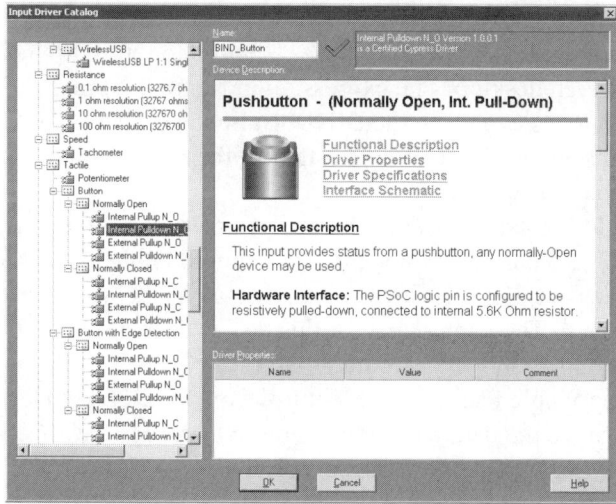

Figure 8-2

143

To complete this portion of the WirelessUSB master, right-click WUSB_Master, select Transfer Function, Priority Encoder and the following expression:

> *If* **(BIND_Button == BIND_Button__On)** *then* **WUSB_Master__BIND**

Figure 8-3 shows the completed expression window.

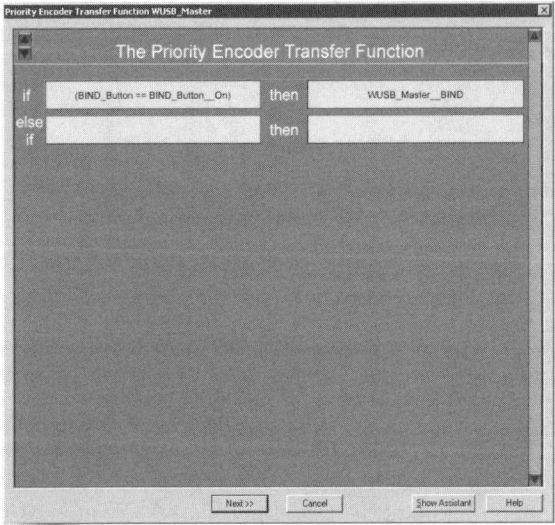

Figure 8-3

When completed, press the Next>> button to return to the PSoC Express design desktop. The expression in figure 8-3 binds the master transmitter to a slave when the BIND_Button is pressed. These two components and associated logic establish the initial connection between the Master and Slave devices.

Next, let's establish a data channel to transmit and receive data. Just like I2C, separate components are required on the master to send and receive data. For this first project, a data channel to the slave will be established. The component for this task is once again from the output catalog as shown in figure 8-4.

It is the Single Packet Slave Control from the Remote Devices category. Since the data will light a remote LED, choose a BYTE Variable Type, leaving the Offset at 0 as shown in figure 8-4.

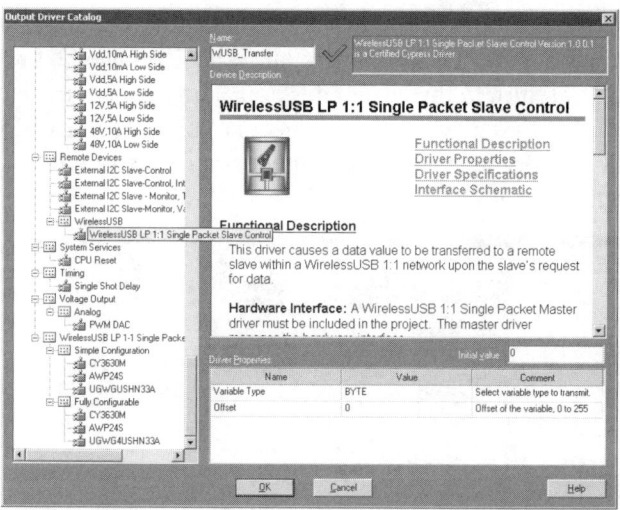

Figure 8-4

Note: The Offset used in this example was obtained from the datasheet of the Slave project. That project contains the component which will be controlled. In this design the component in the slave project is the LED that the Master device will gain control of.

To complete the Master part of this project select a Normally_ Open, Internal Pull-Down button from the Input catalog as shown in figure 8-5.

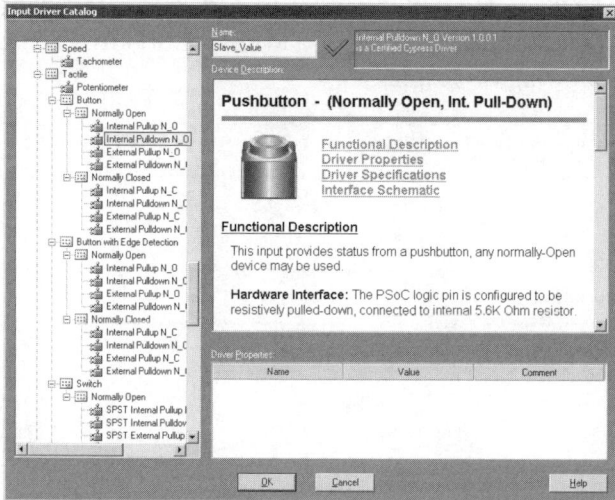

Figure 8-5

Name the component Slave_Value, since it will be sending a byte value to the slave device for processing. When completed, press the OK button to return to the design desktop. The final component needed for the master part of this project is a single color LED from the output catalog. Select the component and name it Status_LED as shown in figure 8-6.

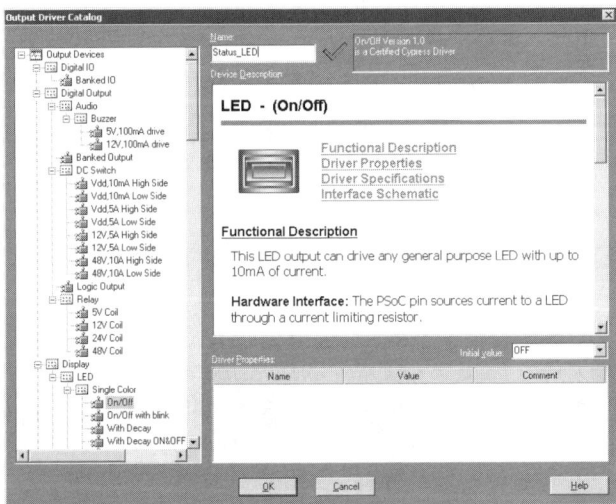

Figure 8-6

When finished press the OK button to return to the design desktop. It's now time to add the logic that will set the value and transmit that value to the remote slave. Right-click on the Status_LED, select Transfer Function, and choose Priority Encoder. Add the following two expressions:

```
If (Slave_Value == Slave_Value__On) then Status_LED__On
```

And

```
If (Slave_Value == Slave_Value__Off) then Status_LED__Off
```

Press the Next>> button to return to the design desktop which will look like figure 8-7.

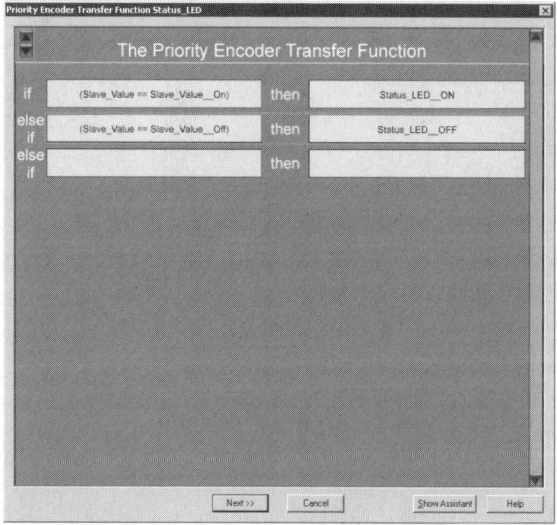

Figure 8-7

The first expression will turn on the LED when the Slave_Value button is pressed on the Master device and off when the button is released. Next, two states need to be converted to BYTE values then transmitted to the remote slave. Right-click on the WUSB_Transfer component, select Transfer Function, the add a Priority Encoder. Then add the expressions shown below and in figure 8-8.

If **(Slave_Value == Slave_Value__On)** *then* **1**

And

If **(Slave_Value == Slave_Value__Off)** *then* **0**

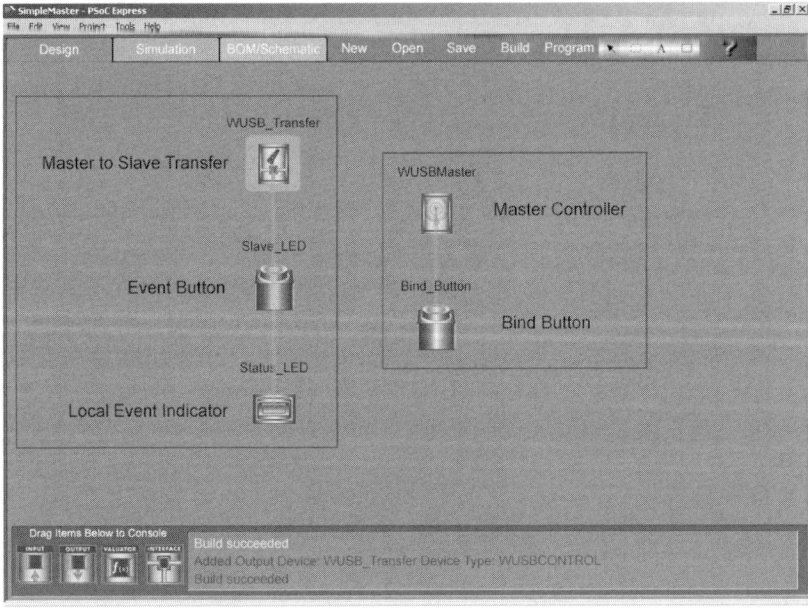

Figure 8-8

Looking closely it is apparent this Priority Encoder is similar to
Status_LED with one exception. In this exception, a byte value is
being set to 0 or 1, based on the state of the Slave_Value button. Figure 8-9 shows the completed design desktop with labels for each
object.

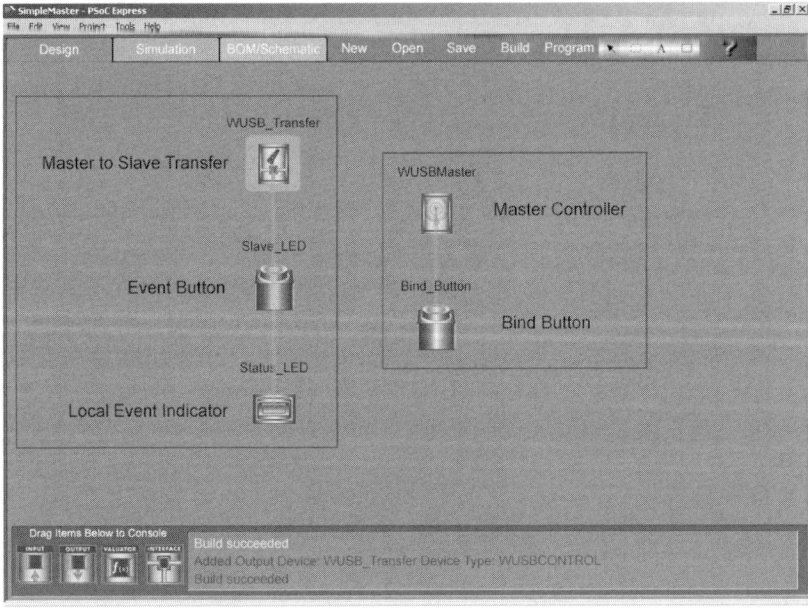

Figure 8-9

WUSBMaster establishes the link to the remote slave device. When developing with WirelessUSB it's important to remember that the link will be established to any slave that A) is the same TYPE ID as the Master or B) has already established a bound session. This link is required before any data exchange can take place. Without the link, there is no slave device.

After the link has been established, the slave control object (WUSB_Transfer) provides a channel which allows data to be sent to the remote slave. The event button and local event indicator on the master could just as easily be a potentiometer, temperature sensor, accelerometer, CapSense keypad or other Input device type. The Transfer Function associated with WUSB_Transfer is responsible for monitoring the state of the button input, converting it to a byte value, and placing it in the Register Map, and transmitting the value to the remote slave when requested.

Developing the WirelessUSB Master Project

> **Note:** The World Tour board has headers for WirelessUSB adapters but, due to potential power problems this project is built for the PSoC CY8C27443. This part was chosen because it is in a DIP package, works on the PSoC Eval1 board, and also works on the CY3630 board.

It's important to note that the Cypress WirelessUSB transceiver boards used here can communicate with any microcontroller that supports the SPI interface. As always, the schematics are created as part of the build process when using PSoC Express. The CY8C27443 is available on the PSoC Eval1 board or the CY3630 WirelessUSB Development kit. If a CD accompanied this book there is information on the CD on how to build this circuit using a breadboard and parts sources.

It's time to build the master project in PSoC Express. Click the Save tab followed by the Build tab. Select the CY8C27000 series as shown in figure 8-10.

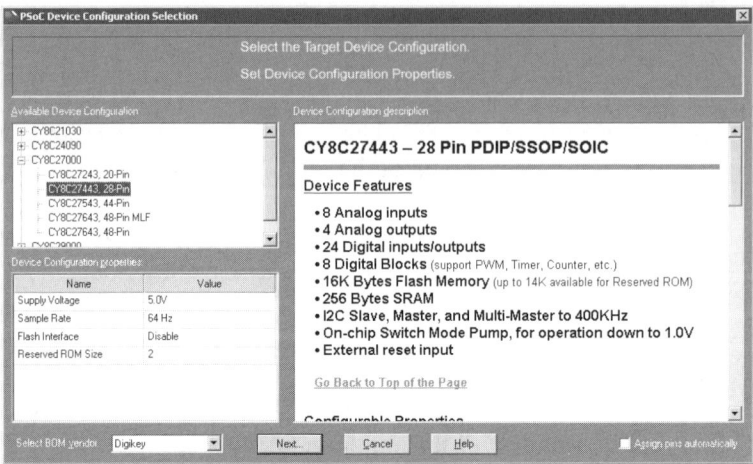

Figure 8-10

It's important to pay attention to the voltage setting here. By default the PSoC is driven by 5.0 volts with 3.3 as an option. Keep in mind that WirelessUSB is a 3.3 volt ONLY device. Next, assign the pins as shown in the following table and figure 8-11.

Signal Name	Pin
Bind_Button	P2[2]
Slave_Value	P2[1]
Status_LED	P1[2]
WUSB_Master IRQPin	P2[6]
WUSB_Master SSPin	P2[7]
pse_WUSB_SHARED_0 MISOPin	P2[0]
pse_WUSB_SHARED_0 SClkPin	P2[3]
pse_WUSB_SHARED_0 MOSIPin	P2[5]

▲ Table 8-1

This pin layout works well with the CY3630 and will work with other circuits as well. With the exceptions of Slave_Value, Status_LED and Bind_Button, all other connections are related to WirelessUSB. Table 8-2 has the definitions for this pin configuration.

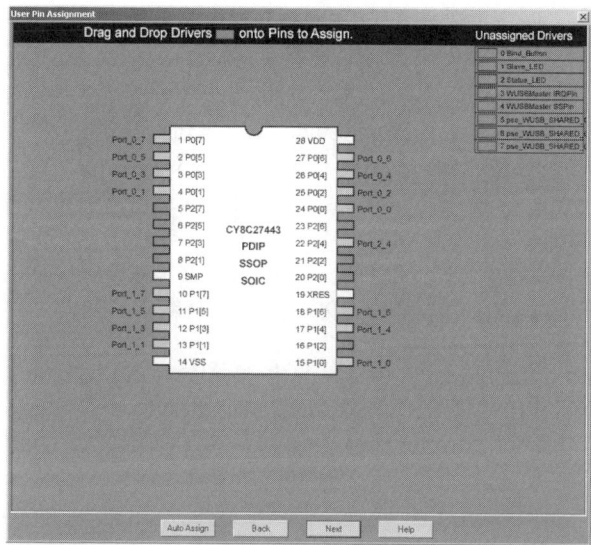

Figure 8-11

Signal Description	WirelessUSB Function
IRQ	Interrupt Output
SS	SPI Enable
SCK	SPI Clock
MISO	SPI Data Out Pin (Master In Slave Out)
MOSI	SPI Data In Pin (Master Out Slave In)

▲ Table 8-2

For those accustomed to using wired communication techniques, the absence of a ground signal should be noted. As shown in table 8-2, five lines are required to interface the CY6936 to the PSoC. It should be noted that the CY6936 is a 40 pin part. Among some of the other signals are Antenna, Clock In, Clock Out, Device Reset, PMU connections (2), Battery or VCC (3 each), I/O Interface Voltage, and GND connections (18). The numerous grounds are unused pins that are attached to ground to avoid their being in a floating state.

Chapter 8

Developing the WirelessUSB Slave

The Master can be programmed when the slave project is finished. Now it's time to build the slave device. When developing a WirelessUSB project, two instances of PSoC Express may be running at the same time. This will save time, and allows for faster changes. The alternative is to use two machines running PSoC Express, or switching between projects during the development cycle. Whichever method is chosen, remember this project is already debugged and should work without change.

Start with a fresh design desktop, then select an interface component from the bottom left of the display. Next, choose WirelessUSB, Single Packet Slave, Simple Configuration, CY3630M as shown in figure 8-12.

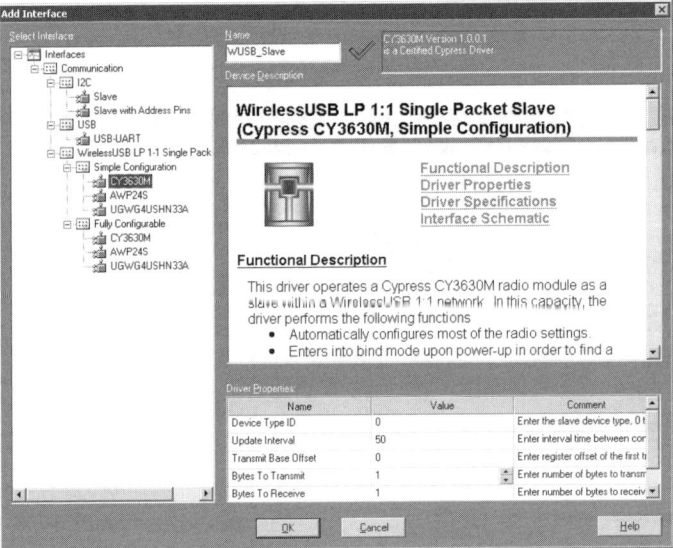

Figure 8-12

The slave uses the Interface component to establish the link with the Master. The Device Type ID must match the master Type ID for the link to be established. Note the second parameter is the Update Interval. This is the frequency at which the Slave updates the master.

This differs from I2C communications where the I2C master is used to send and request data. Remember, WirelessUSB uses the slave to send and request data from the master. The Transmit Base Offset in this project is set to 0, the number of Bytes to Transmit is set to 1, and the number of Bytes to Receive is also set to 1. After all of the settings match those in figure 8-12, press the OK button to return to the design desktop. Next, a variable needs to be created to hold data received from the WirelessUSB master device. This is done by adding an Interface Valuator and naming it Master_LEDValue as shown in figure 8-13.

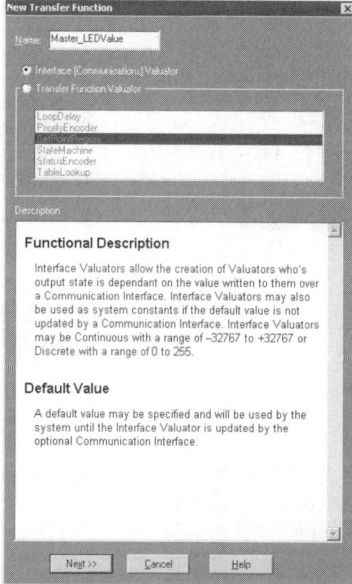

Be certain to check the Interface (Communications) Valuator, then press the Next>> button. The Discrete check-box should be selected, and a default value of 0 should be entered as shown in figure 8-14.

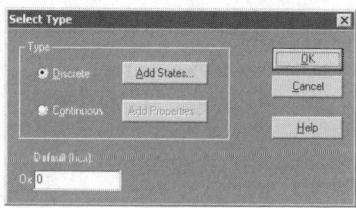

Figure 8-14

One more component is needed for the slave device so choose an Output component from the Display category, selecting a LED, On-Off Single Color as shown in figure 8-15.

Figure 8-13

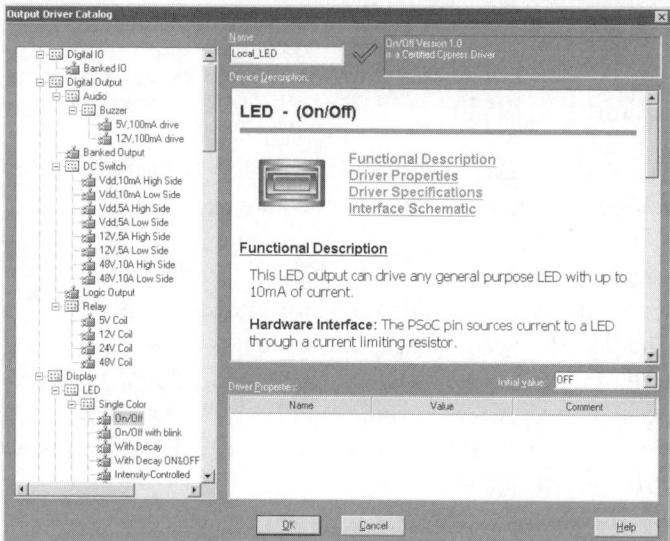

Figure 8-15

Chapter 8

Name the component Local_LED to reflect the status of the button on the Master WirelessUSB device. Press the OK button, then right-click the object and select Transfer Function. Choose a Priority Encoder and add two statements as shown below and in figure 8-16.

If (`Master_LEDValue == 1`) *then* `Local_LED__On`

And

If (`Master_LEDValue == 0`) *then* `Local_LED__Off`

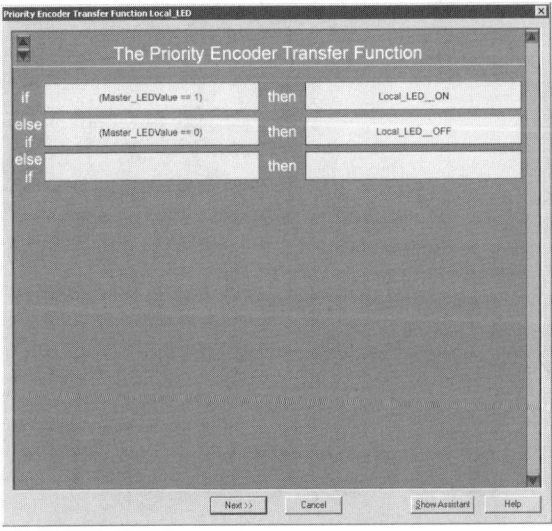

Figure 8-16

The first expression will set Local_LED__On if Master_LEDValue is equal to 1 (ON). The second expression will set Local_LED__Off if Master_LEDValue equals 0. When these expressions have been entered, press the Next>> button to return to the design desktop which should now look similar to figure 8-17.

The WUSB_Slave component is the link to the master device. The creation of the Interface Valuator, Master_LEDValue provides a variable to hold the byte-sized value read from the master. The transfer function of Local_LED acts upon the value requested by the slave and read from the master.

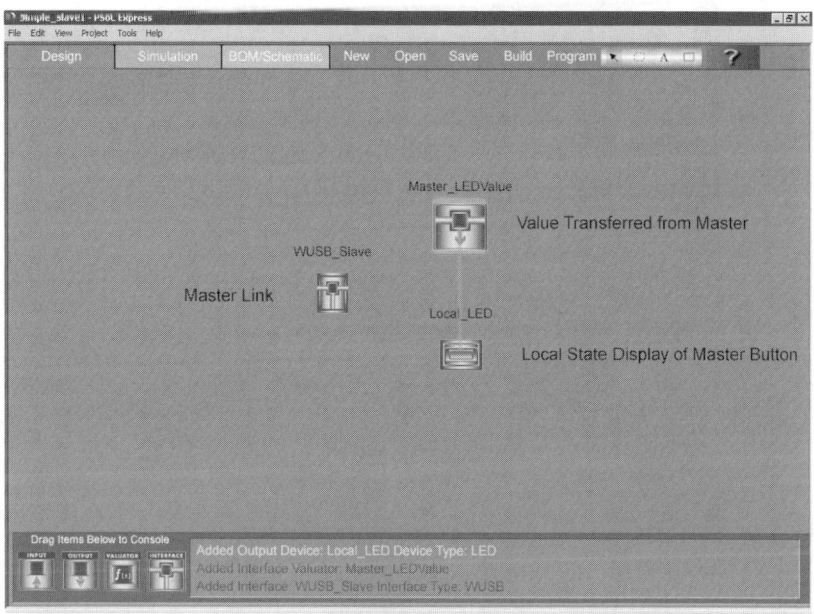

Figure 8-17

It's time to build the slave project. Set the pin assignments as shown in table 8-3 and figure 8-18.

Signal Name	Pin
Local_LED	P1[2]
WUSB_Master IRQPin	P2[6]
WUSB_Master SSPin	P2[7]
pse_WUSB_SHARED_0 MISOPin	P2[0]
pse_WUSB_SHARED_0 SClkPin	P2[3]
pse_WUSB_SHARED_0 MOSIPin	P2[5]

▲ Table 8-3

Now, program the Master and Slave boards. Once both boards have been programmed, turn Master on and press the first button. Nothing happens! As noted earlier, when the master is turned on it checks for noise, locating a channel most likely to provide error-free transmission. Depending on the environment (noise, RF interference, etc.) this can take up to a minute. While the WirelessUSB master is busy with this task, no other events on the master will be processed.

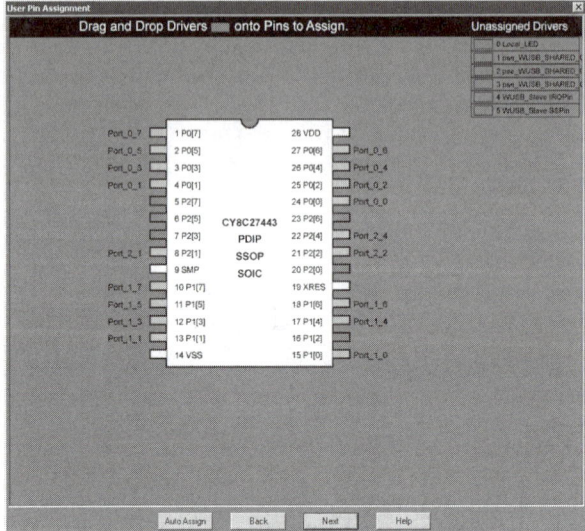

Figure 8-18

Once completed the local LED will light when the button is pressed, even if a connection to a slave has not been established.

First, Configure the CY6360 Boards

Start by marking the master and slave devices with a piece of tape marked appropriately "master" or "slave." This will eliminate any confusion on how each device should be programmed. If powering the CY3630-DK board using a 9-volt battery, please follow the instructions on setting the proper jumpers BEFORE turning the power on if using the CY6360 Kit. Otherwise the radios may be damaged.

Next, The Bind Process

The first step in powering up two WirelessUSB devices for the first time is to bind them together as a pair. The first step in this process is to make certain the master and slave devices are both turned on. Once both devices are on, press the Bind_Button on the master device. It may take up to a minute for the master to hear the slave and the slave to attach to the master. There are no indicators this process has completed successfully.

Now, Test the Project

After the bind process has completed, pressing the top button will light the top LED on both the master and the slave. Go ahead and experiment by:

▷ Communicating from different distances

▷ Placing different types of objects between the master and slave

▷ Try the devices outdoors

Project 2, Sending Data from the WirelessUSB Slave

With a little extra effort data can be returned to a WirelessUSB master the WirelessUSB slave device. Two new components are required and some existing parameters will need to be changed in existing components. Since the slave is the point of origination for the data, this project will begin by developing the slave side first. To begin, save the current project as SimpleSlave2. Since the changes required to the slave project are minimal, begin by adding a button from the input catalog as shown in figure 8-19.

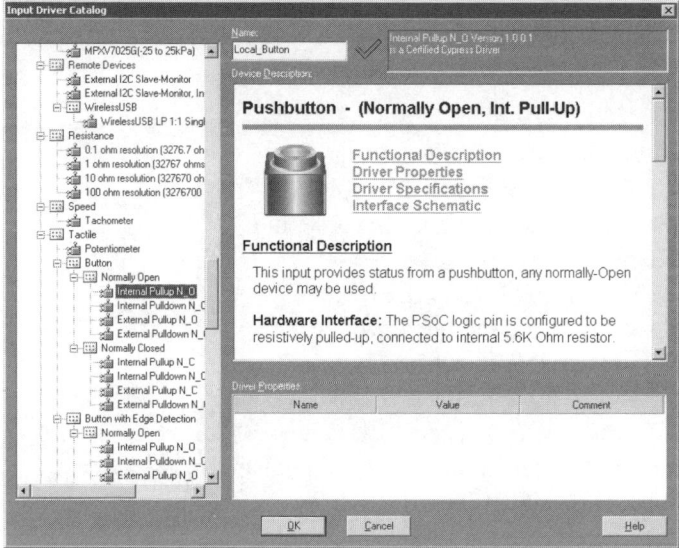

Figure 8-19

> **Note:** The pushbutton object selected is a normally open internal-pull-up type. This type of button is used on the CY3630 boards. If you are using a different board or design, be certain to use the proper button for that design.

The next and final step to finish the slave device is to change the WUSB_Slave component Transmit Base Offset parameter. Do that now by right-clicking the WUSB_Slave component, select properties, and change the Transmit Base Offset to 2 as shown in figure 8-20.

Figure 8-20

How did you arrive at a Transmit Base Offset of 2. Figure 8-21 shows the Register Map and variable offsets within the Register Map.

It is clear that Master_LEDValue resides at location 0 in the slave register map. That variable is defined as a discrete value, which means it is a byte variable. Located after Master_LEDValue is Local_LED which contains the value of the local LED state (On or Off). Local_LED is also a byte sized variable

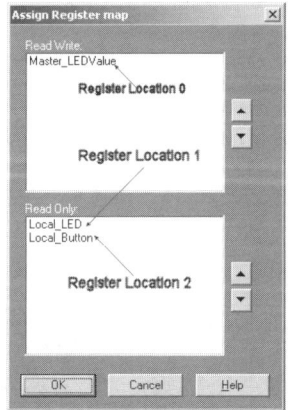

Figure 8-21

because the largest value an LED component can hold is 255. Local_Button resides at position 2 in the slave register map and because this button is either On or Off once again it's known this is declared as a byte variable. With all of these values known, it is easy for the developer to set the proper offset value to the location of the first variable to transmit back to the master device. In this case that location will be Local_Button, found at location 2, and one byte in size.

Planning Ahead for Base Offsets

One of the most confusing part of configuring WirelessUSB is setting the proper Base Offset for transmitted and received packets. Here are a couple of tips to help properly setup the Base Offsets. First, remember that all Base Offset values are on the slave device when calculating. The transmit buffer pointer on the Master will always point to the beginning of the Read/Write Register Map on the Slave. Drawing 8-1 illustrates the Register Map layout of the slave.

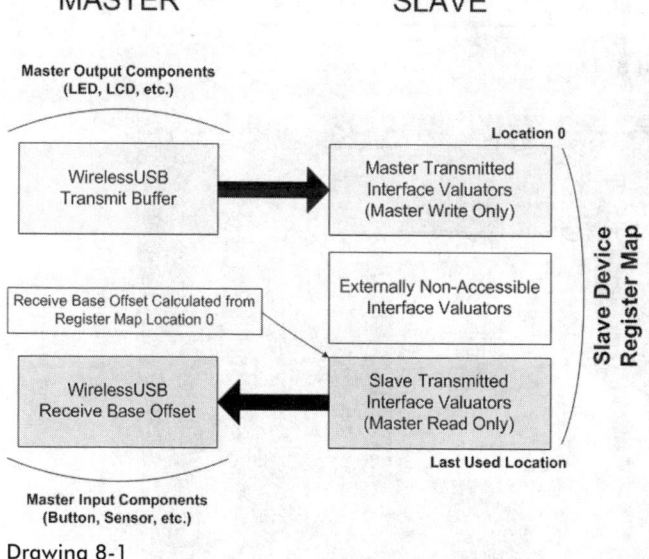

Drawing 8-1

Second, Output components on the Master whose values are transmitted to the Slave, are Write-Only via Transfer Functions on the

Master, but may be Read-Write on the Slave device. Variables transmitted to the slave may be Read-Write accessible to slave Valuators.

Third, Read-Write values that should not be accessible to a remote device should be stored in the Register Map after values available to remote devices. Following this Register Map area will be the Slave Transmitted Interface Valuators which are Read-Only to the Master.

Finally, remember the Master Receive-Base Offset points to the absolute location in the Slave Register Map where the first byte of slave transmitted data will reside. This may all seem confusing, but walking through the projects in this chapter will demonstrate how the remote variables are aligned.

Build the Project

It's time to save and build the project. The Local_Button pin needs to be added to the build pin assignment map as shown in table 8-4 and figure 8-22.

Signal Name	Pin
Local_Button	P2[1]

▲ Table 8-4

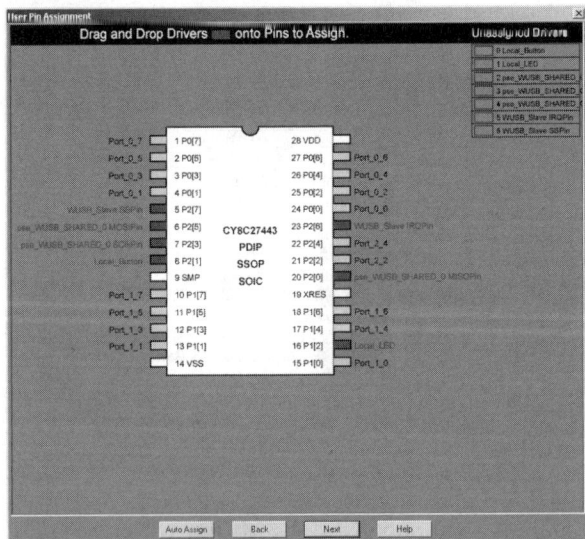

Figure 8-22

After attaching the pin for the Local_Button component, finish the build, then program the slave device. Remember to choose the "Reset" option when programming so the WirelessUSB transceivers don't get destroyed.

Modify the WirelessUSB Master to Receive Slave Data

Next, switch back to the master project. Two new components are needed and changes to a third component. Start by adding a WirelessUSB Slave Monitor component from the Input catalog by selecting Remote Devices, WirelessUSB, WirelessUSB LP 1:1 Single Packet Slave Monitor as shown in figure 8-23, and name the component Return_Data.

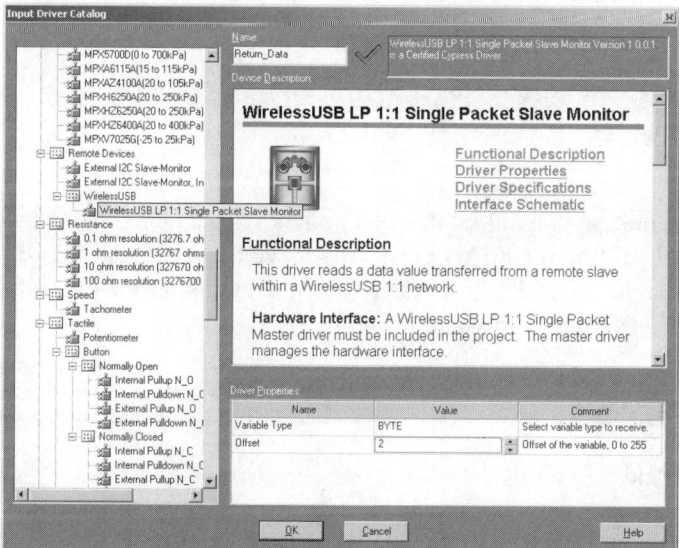

Figure 8-23

Note: The Offset changed to a value of two (2), to match the offset value entered on the slave device.

Name this component Return_Data and press the OK button. Next, add a Display → LED → On/Off LED component from the

Output catalog, naming the component Slave_LED_Status as shown in figure 8-24.

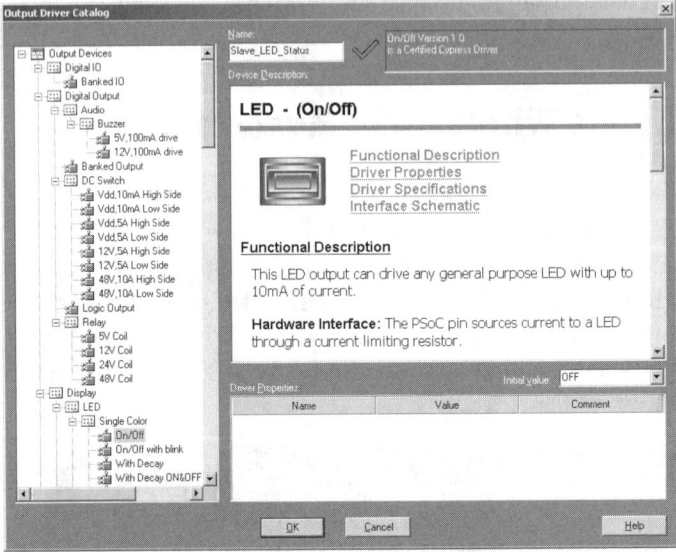

Figure 8-24

The Slave_LED_Status component will contain the status of the Local Button on the WirelessUSB Slave device. Press the OK button, then right-click, select transfer function, and enter the two lines of logic as shown below and in figure 8-25.

If (**Return_Data** == 1) *then* **Slave_LED_Status__On**

And

If (**Return_Data** == 0) *then* **Slave_LED_Status__Off**

The first expression will turn on Slave_LED_Status when Return_Data equals 1. Expression two will turn Slave_LED_Status off when Return_Data equals 0. The Transmit Base Offset in the WUSB_Master Component also needs to be changed to two (2) as shown in figure 8-26.

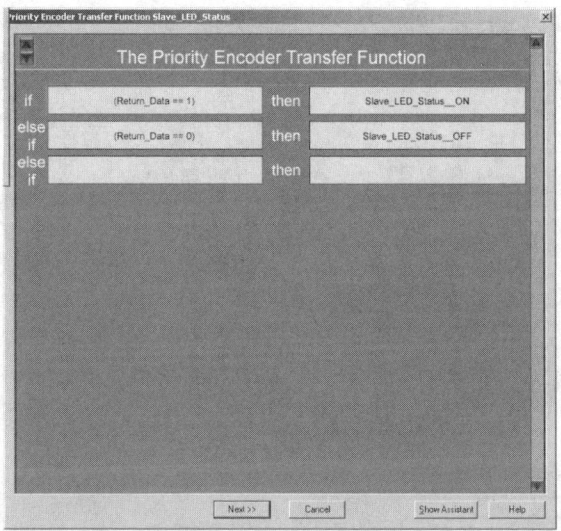

Figure 8-25

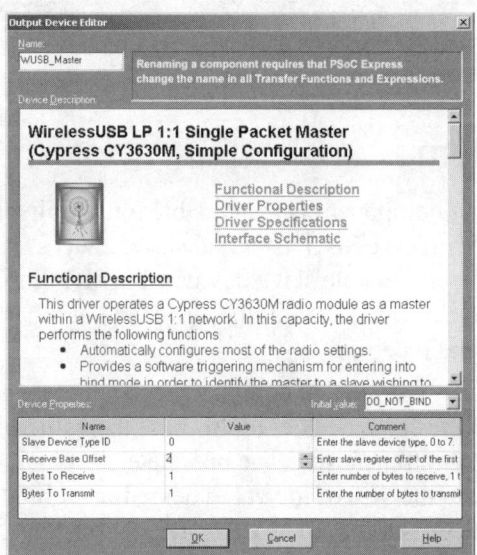

Figure 8-26

Now Base Offsets match for the data received from the slave. It's time to build and program the master project. The design desktop should look similar to figure 8-27.

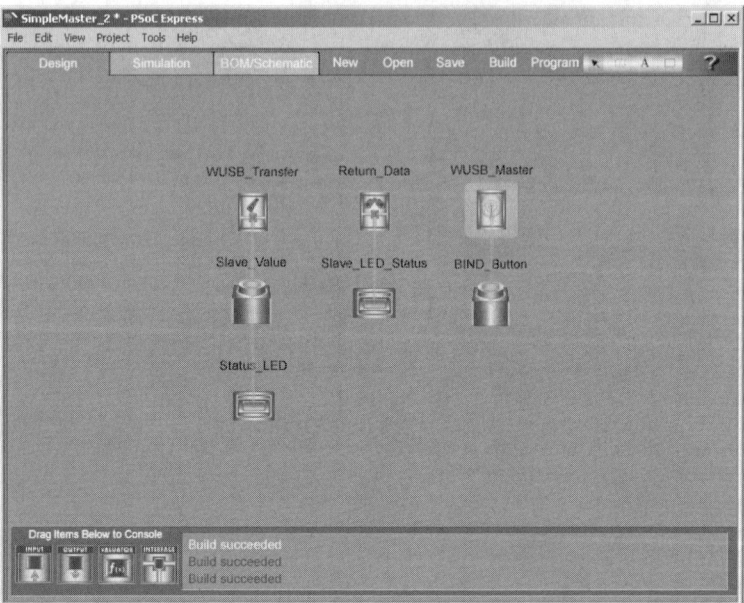

Figure 8-27

A Quick Project Recap

▶ The WUSB_Master component is responsible for establishing the link between the WirelessUSB master and slave devices. It also sets the Type ID for acceptable slave devices. Finally, this component sets the receive buffer offset on the slave, and number of bytes to transmit and receive.

▶ The WUSB_Transfer component contains the parameters needed to transmit data to the slave device. In this case the value of the Slave_Value button is transferred. The parameters set in WUSB_Transfer are the size of the value being transmitted (byte or integer), and the Offset for the Master Transfer buffer.

▶ A Packet Slave Control component is required for each value sent to the slave.

▶ The Return_Data component receives data back from a slave device to be processed on the master. In this project a single byte is returned with the status of a button on the WirelessUSB slave. The parameters are the same as the WUSB_Transfer object.

Save, Build and Program the Master. Then turn the Master and Slave devices on. The top button on the Master will light the top LED on the slave. The top button on the Slave will light the middle LED on the master.

Chapter Summary

This chapter has served as an introduction to WirelessUSB using PSoC Express. Some of the mystery of WirelessUSB has now been removed, and the basics of using simple packet transfers should be understood.

This chapter has just scratched the surface WirelessUSB development and in explaining how embedded wireless devices work. Explore and experiment on your own and above all, don't be afraid to make mistakes. Making changes using PSoC Express takes very little time and the experience can be very rewarding.

Looking Ahead

In the next chapter, we will explore the PSoC Express implementation of CapSense and how to develop and build a simple CapSense project on the World Tour board.

What is CapSense and How it Works

Chapter Overview

This chapter covers the PSoC CapSense technology. It begins with a brief history of capacitive sensing and then moves on to PSoC CapSense technology. The three CapSense technologies offered by Cypress are then explored. Two CapSense projects are then built with PSoC Express that demonstrate how easy it is to use CapSense technology. This chapter concludes with a brief review of CapSense a look ahead to the USB-UART technology in the next chapter.

What is Capacitive Sensing

Here is some history of capacitive sensing. In 1927 Leon Theremin developed a musical instrument named appropriately, the Theremin. This musical machine had two electrodes, one on the side for adjusting volume, the other on the top to adjust pitch. If you've ever heard the song *Good Vibrations* from the Beach Boys, the Theremin is used to make the unusual sound that is the main instrument of the song. Using hand motions, the pitch and volume of the Theremin are adjusted very rapidly to provide a very unique and quick changing sound.

Now, fast forward 80 years to 2007. Today proximity detection is used in a variety of applications, most are transparent to the user. The most common use of capacitive sensing is in the automotive industry, where these sensors are used for activation of the air-bags. Capacitive sensors are also used to determine the size of the occupant for air-bag deployment.

Cypress has taken a unique approach by combining capacitive sensing inside the PSoC to make the CapSense product line. This approach provides a very powerful solution, where the possibilities for this technology are virtually limitless. Here's how capacitive sensing works. Every object has density and most objects are conductive. For humans the electrolytes in our bodies determine the conductivity our body has. Conductivity is not static as it changes based on several factors. CapSense determines proximity by detecting sensor capacitance changes as a conductive object nears the sensor. Let's examine this a little closer. Photo 9-1 shows a close-up view of a CapSense button on the World Tour board. Notice the two traces. The amount of capacitance between these two copper traces will remain fairly static, so long as there are no other conductive objects that comes into contact with these fields. Notice the statement "fairly static." In truth there are numerous factors that contribute to the baseline value of a capacitive field. Humidity is one of those factors because air density of plays a big role in capacitance value. Putting a finger near the traces of a CapSense component will cause the capacitance of the field to change. Since the capacitance value is measured at a fixed frequency, it's fairly easy to track changes in the field. But CapSense is more than just a changing value. CapSense provides a second timer that compares the changes in the capacitive field, altering the baseline or base capacitive value that is being measured against.

In practice the capacitance is measured at a pre-set rate (determined by the conductivity of the object disrupting the field, object distance, and speed at which the object is approaching) and the change in the field capacitance indicates the presence of a conductive object within the field. In this example it would be a finger approaching the CapSense button on the board.

In this project, CapSense readings are being taken from a button that has been formed in traces of a circuit board. There are several advantages to this design. They are:

▶ CapSense Enables Creativity through a Unique Look & Feel

▶ There are no Mechanical Parts to Wear Out

▶ CapSense Buttons and Sliders are Almost Indestructible

▶ CapSense Buttons and Sliders Cost Pennies to Implement

These are three excellent reasons to use CapSense. CapSense can also be used in watertight applications, since the capacitance field can be easily detected through thin plastic coatings. How thin you ask? Well, that depends on which CapSense algorithm is used. Today there are three algorithms accessible from PSoC Express. They are:

▶ CSA – Successive Approximation

▶ CSD – Sigma-Delta Modulation

▶ CSR – Relaxation Oscillator

CSR was the first CapSense algorithm implemented in PSoC Express. It has been implemented for slightly over a year, is being superseded by the CSA and CSD algorithms. This shows how quickly the PSoC CapSense technology is advancing.

How is CapSense Useful

CapSense has many uses! Which CapSense algorithm isused depends on exactly what type of application is being developed. Here are some CapSense facts when used in PSoC Express:

▶ Supports up to 21 CSA Buttons, 16 Buttons using CSD and CSR technologies

▶ Supports Sliders with up to 20 Elements using CSA, 15 Elements using CSD or CSR

▶ Slider Scan Resolution can be Doubled using Diplexing

▶ Adjustable Sensitivity, Threshold, and Sampling Rates

▶ Baseline Update Algorithm for Temperature and Humidity Changes are Integrated into the Algorithm.

The CSA and CSD methods are equally preferred for buttons, sliders, or touch pads. Both methods support the use of overlays. One of the biggest determining factors in the choice of CSA or CSD is cost. The CSA component is only available in the CY8C20x34 devices, which are specifically designed as low cost CapSense devices. The lower cost devices have limited functionality outside of the CapSense function. The CSD component is available on a wider range of PSoC devices, making it more attractive when other mixed signal functionality is required in addition to CapSense justifying the higher part price.

The ground plane is very important in all CapSense solutions. Looking at the underside of the World Tour board, note there are no ground plane traces under the CapSense buttons. This is because the ground plane is used as a reference in CapSense applications. This means the ground plane design can have disastrous results if not implemented properly.

And finally, when designing with CapSense, board design is just as critical as the CapSense technology chosen. A very well operating CapSense product, or a very poor operating CapSense product are equally easy to design, so take time in advance of the project to read the application notes. Visit the Cypress web site and look for application notes pertaining to CapSense design before starting a new design.

Developing a CapSense Application

Developing a CapSense application in PSoC Express is easy. Choose a CapSense technology, adjust the parameters, test, re-tune the parameters, and when satisfied, build, program, and release the product. Since the World Tour board is being used, there are several developer kits that support CapSense development. Two of my favorites are the CY3213 and the CY3214. The CY3213 board is designed specifically for CapSense development. It contains an LCD, CapSense Buttons and Sliders plus connections for the MiniProg and the Cypress ICE unit. The CY3214 board has a USB host interface in addition to CapSense Buttons, Slider, MiniProg, and ICE connections, plus a generous breadboard area for testing new circuit designs. Photo 9-1 shows the CY3213.

Photo 9-1

This first CapSense project will demonstrate how easy it is to develop a minimal CapSense application using PSoC Express. Begin by starting PSoC Express, or creating a new PSoC Express project. This can be done by selecting File → New from the main menu bar. With a clean desktop choose File → Save As, and name this first project Chapter9_1 clicking the Save button when finished. Next, double-click on the Input catalog and select CapSense → CSR Button as shown in figure 9-1.

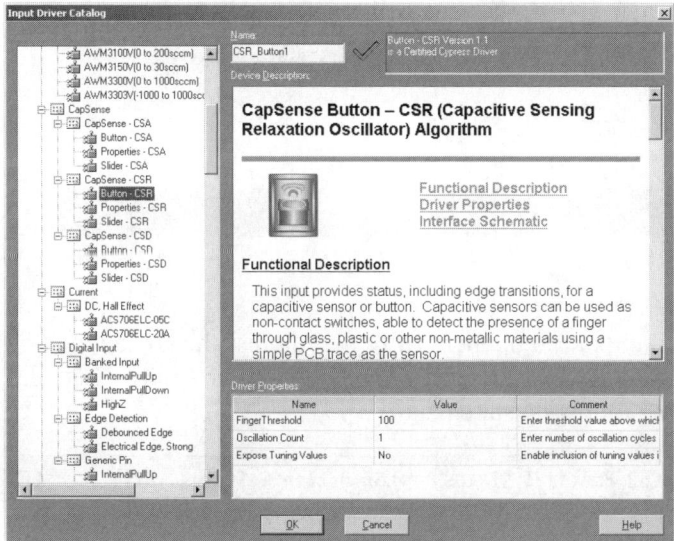

Figure 9-1

Name the component CSR_Button1 and leave the parameters at their default values. Next, add a single color, On/Off LED from the Output catalog as shown in figure 9-2.

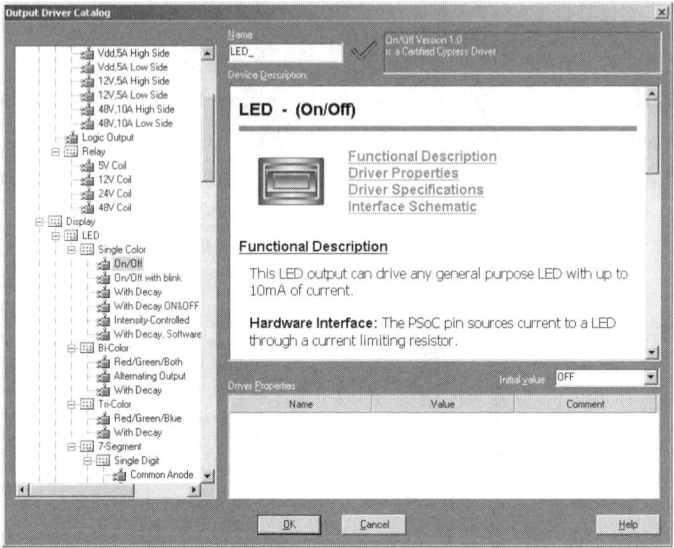

Figure 9-2

Name the component LED_1 and press the OK button.
Right-click LED_1, select Transfer Function, Priority Encoder, and
add the following statements.

> *If* (CSR_Button_1_Status == CSR_Button_1_Status__Off) *then* LED_1__OFF

and

> *If* (CSR_Button_1_Status == CSR_Button_1_Status__On) *then* LED_1__ON

Figure 9-3 shows the completed Transfer Function screen.

When a finger is detected on the CapSense button, the LED will
turn on, and when the finger is removed the LED will turn off. From
first appearance this looks very similar to a push button input, but
there are a couple of differences. First, there is no mechanical actuator
or contact, so the button is triggered by the change in the capacitive
field from the traces on the circuit board. Second, a push button has
no parameters because the type of button is selected from the component catalog and since a push button is mechanical it requires some
type of force to make it work. Not so with CapSense as the detection
of the finger (or change in the capacitive field) causes the trigger.

Proximity detection has much more potential than a mechanical actuator.

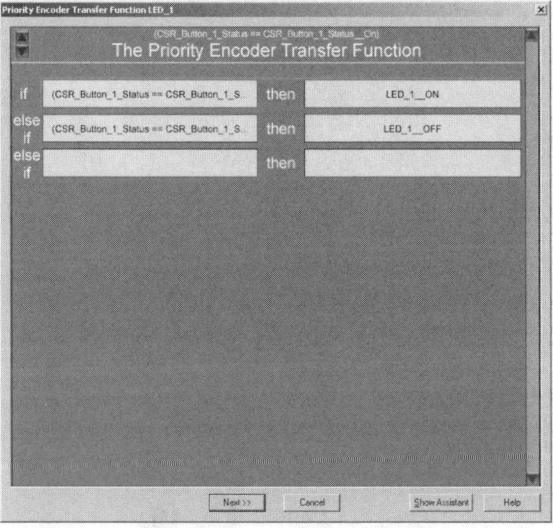

Figure 9-3

CapSense Parameters

The CapSense CSR button has only three parameters. They are:

▶ Finger Threshold – A capacitive value that when exceeded indicates the button is on

▶ Oscillation Count – The number of oscillation cycles over which a capacitance measurement is taken. By changing this value the resolution of the raw measurement can be adjusted. Increasing this value increases the resolution but also takes twice as long to obtain the value. If baseline and finger touch readings are very low, increasing this value will increase the difference between a finger touch and the baseline.

▶ Expose Tuning Values – Enable the visibility of the tuning values in the register map.

The default Finger Threshold is 100, Oscillation Count is 1, and the tuning values (in this project) are not visible. Build this project using the default values. First, Save the project, select the Build tab. For this

project select CY8C21434, then press the Next button. Assign the
LED to pin P2[0] and the CapSense button to pin P3[2] as shown in
figure 9-4.

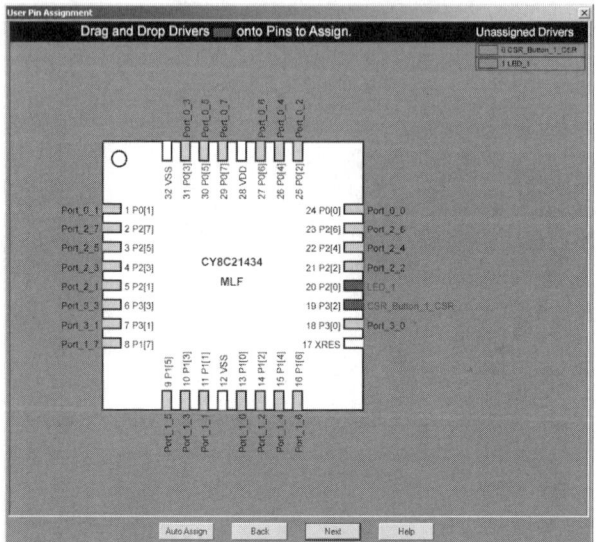

Figure 9-4

Remember this application will run on the upper left quadrant of
the World Tour board where the four CapSense buttons have
silk-screened numbers 1, 2, 3, and 4 marked in their centers. After a
successful build, attach the MiniProg, then Program and apply power
to the board. Put a finger over CapSense Button 1, and one of the
LEDs will light up.

Put a piece of paper between the button and your finger. The button still lights up. As more layers of paper are added note that more of
your finger has to be covering the CapSense button to turn the LED
on. As the paper thickness grows, eventually the LED will no longer
light.

Next, try covering the CapSense button with different types of
materials. Notice that only materials with conductive properties turn
the LED on. Plastic bottle caps, plastic film containers, and/or business cards or other paper products do not turn the LED on because
they are non-conductive or just too thick.

Controlling Additional CapSense Parameters

Go back to the Input catalog under CapSense → CSR and add a Properties component. This adds two more settings for CapSense CSR control as shown in figure 9-5.

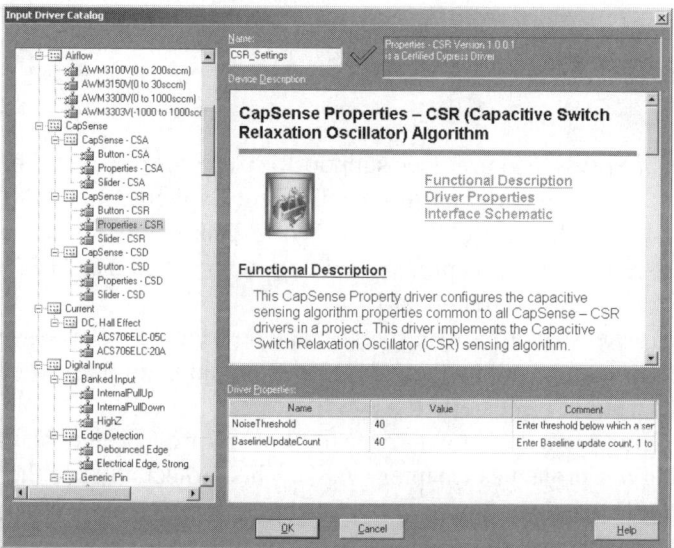

Figure 9-5

Now there are five parameters that can control CapSense behavior. In addition to the three mentioned earlier, we now have control over Noise Threshold and Baseline Update Count.

▷ Noise Threshold – Determines where the noise level filter is placed using a value from 0 to 255.

▷ Baseline Update Count – Determines the frequency of how often the parasitic capacitance values changes. This value can be from 1 to 255.

So what do these values really mean. Finger Threshold combined with Noise Threshold determine what level of noise should be filtered and what value of capacitance indicates the presence of a conductive object. Adjusting these values can easily cause a CapSense button to always be on or off. Raising the noise level to a large value can filter out a valid button press and lowering the Finger Threshold can make CapSense believe there is always a conductive object present when

175

there really isn't. Make small adjustments to these values when you develop. Altering the Baseline Update Count should only be altered on an experimental basis. If this count is too high, the response to environmental changes will be too slow, resulting in missed readings. If the value is too low this can result in false readings. In short be very careful when altering this value.

A CapSense Slider Project

PSoC Express also provides support for CapSense Sliders. This next project is going to demonstrate a different CapSense method (CSD) used on a slider control. Since the World Tour board doesn't have a slider component, this project will be developed on the CY3213 CapSense development board.

How easy can PSoC Express make developing a CapSense Slider with Diplexing? Almost any developer should be impressed with this project, so let's get started.

Once again, begin with a clean PSoC Express design desktop, saving our project as Chapter9_CSD. This project will use the Sigma-Delta algorithm or CSD. Select the Input catalog, choosing CapSense → CSD → Slider → CSD, enabling Diplexing as shown in figure 9-6.

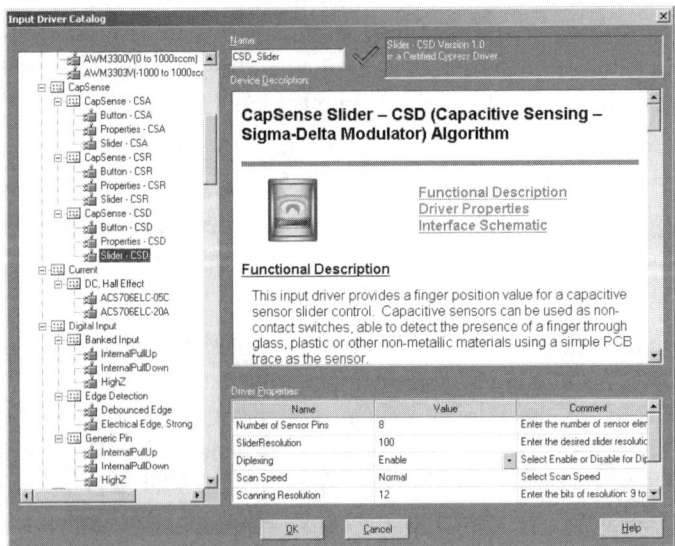

Figure 9-6

Except for Enabling Diplexing, leave all other properties set to their default values. Name this component CSD_Slider and press the OK button when finished.

Next, add an LCD Horizontal Bar Graph from the Output catalog, naming the component Bargraph_1, and setting Max Value to 100, Units to "Position," and Initial Value to 0 as shown in figure 9-7.

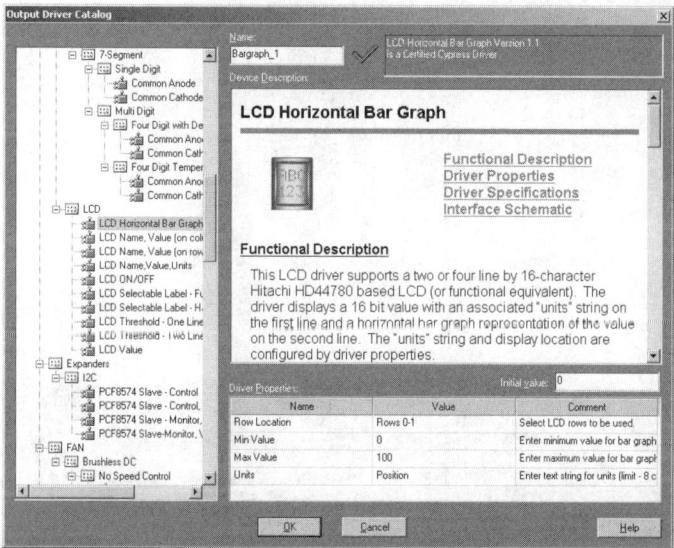

Figure 9-7

Press the OK button when finished, then right-click and select Transfer Function. Choose Priority Encoder and press the OK button. There is a single statement for this Priority Encoder, it is:

```
If 1 then CSD_Slider_Position
```

The completed Transfer Function window is shown in figure 9-8.

That is all it takes to make a working slider in PSoC Express. The design desktop should look like figure 9-9.

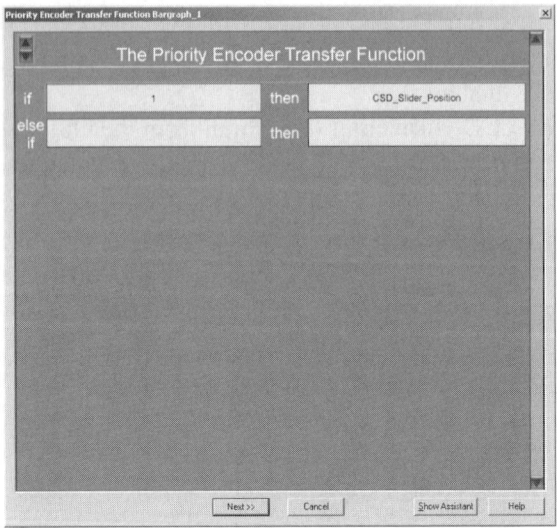

Figure 9-8

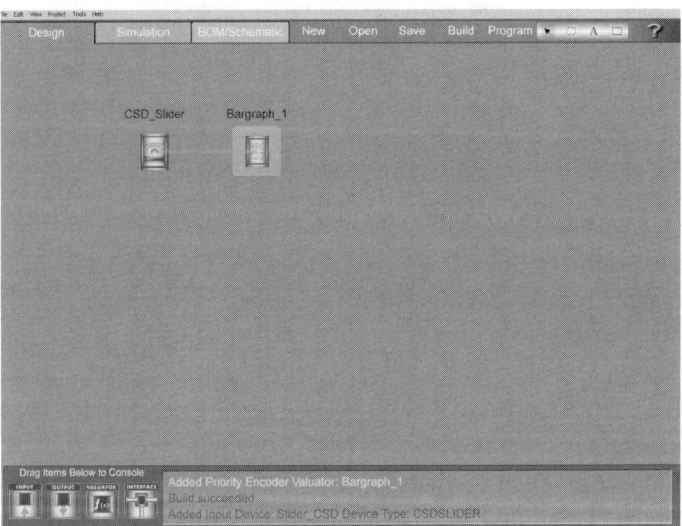

Figure 9-9

Now it's time to build the project. Remember this project is for the CY3213 board which contains a CY8C21434 part. Choose Save, Build, and select the CY8C21434 part as shown in figure 9-10.

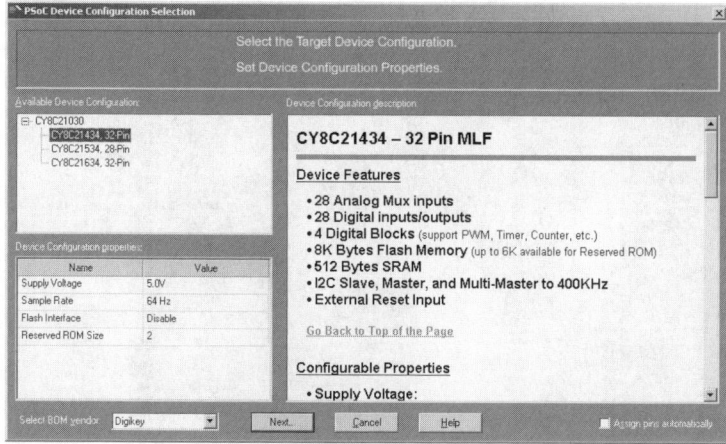

Figure 9-10

The pins need to be placed before the build can be completed. Place the pins as outlined in the following table:

Description	Pin Assignment
pse_LCD_SHARED_0LCDPin11	P2[0]
pse_LCD_SHARED_0LCDPin12	P2[1]
pse_LCD_SHARED_0LCDPin13	P2[2]
pse_LCD_SHARED_0LCDPin14	P2[3]
pse_LCD_SHARED_0LCDPin6	P2[4]
pse_LCD_SHARED_0LCDPin5	P2[6]
pse_LCD_SHARED_0LCDPin4	P2[5]
pse_CSD0 CSD_FdbkResistorPin	P3[1]
pse_CSD0 CSD_ModulatorCapPin	P0[3]
CSD_Slider_CSD_Slider00	P0[0]
CSD_Slider_CSD_Slider01	P0[1]
CSD_Slider_CSD_Slider02	P0[2]
CSD_Slider_CSD_Slider03	P2[7]
CSD_Slider_CSD_Slider04	P0[4]
CSD_Slider_CSD_Slider05	P0[5]
CSD_Slider_CSD_Slider06	P0[6]
CSD_Slider_CSD_Slider07	P0[7]

▲ Table 9-1

Chapter 9

Figure 9-11 shows the completed pin assignments.

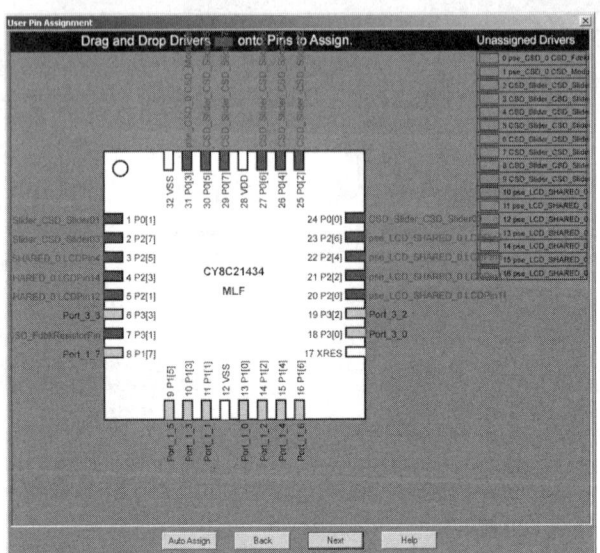

Figure 9-11

Press the Next button to complete the Build. While waiting for the build to complete, connect the MiniProg to the CY3213 board. The MiniProg connection is located between the ICE connector and the 9-volt battery connection in the upper right of the CY3213. Once the build is completed, Program the part. When the programming is finished apply power to the board either using the MiniProg or by attaching a 9-volt battery.

The LCD should display a 0 at the top left of the display with the word "Position" on the right. Both should be on line 0 of the display. Starting at the left, slide your finger towards the right of the slider and notice how a bar graph on line 1 of the LCD follows. Experiment by placing your finger at different positions and note how the slider will always appear to the point where your finger is touching.

Next, run your finger on the back side of the slider and note how the results are the same. This illustrates how CapSense can work through a circuit board or other non-conductive surface with no ill effects.

Chapter Review

This chapter has touched on a very small portion of what CapSense can do and how CapSense works. Hopefully, this chapter has been helpful in getting developers started with using CapSense in PSoC Express and in showing how easy CapSense is to implement using PSoC Express. Experiment using CapSense and PSoC Express. You will find that CapSense is a valuable asset to your embedded toolkit and once mastered, is an excellent replacement for mechanical buttons and potentiometers in many projects.

What's Ahead

The next chapter will conclude the use of the World Tour board using components from the Input and Output catalog. The topic is developing a USB Virtual COM port application. Combining PSoC Express with USB-UART technology allows for quick and easy USB implementation.

Chapter 9

Using the USB-UART in PSoC Express

Chapter Overview

Almost any embedded developer has used, or wanted to use USB in an embedded system at one time or another. This chapter examines how easy a USB-UART interface is implemented in PSoC Express and compares this to other USB-UART bridge products. A USB-UART bridge project will be created to show just how easy it is to implement a USB-UART application with PSoC Express.

Cypress in the USB Market

If you've had the pleasure of working with native USB implementations before, then you probably already know that Cypress has a 40% share of all USB chips sold worldwide. I've worked with Cypress in prior writings and their USB developer kits are easy to understand and allow developers the ability to get up and running quickly for any type of USB device (custom, HID, etc.). The product mentioned is sold as the EZ-USB product line.

The Purpose of the PSoC Express USB-UART

Typically, when thinking of a USB-UART bridge interface, a virtual com port that bridges a USB interface to a legacy serial port on a PC comes to mind. While there are plenty of these devices on the market, the PSoC Express implementation is not the same. The PSoC Express approach to USB-UART is similar to the I2C and WirelessUSB interfaces. Like those interfaces PSoC Express exposes the PSoC Slave device Register Map to a remote USB Host via a Virtual COM Port (VCP).

What differs from I2C and WirelessUSB interfaces is that the Register Map is accessible by a Host PC and not another PSoC device. This connection literally brings the ability to have a PSoC communicate with the World. Even so, communications for the projects in this chapter will be limited to a host computer. This allows customization of a PSoC based device by a host computer in both an organized and customized fashion.

Designing a PSoC Express USB-UART Bridge

The question always arises as to what the usefulness of a USB-UART bridge is other than legacy RS232 serial applications. The answer is: there are many other uses. Depending on the host PC application, the fact a legacy RS232 port is used can be completely transparent to the end user. Here are a few examples of USB-UART applications:

▶ Motor Speed Controls
▶ Remote Temperature Sensors
▶ Fan Control
▶ GPS Receiver
▶ External Status Indicators for the Handicapped (Light, Touch, or Sound based)
▶ Numeric Input Keypads
▶ CapSense Keypads
▶ Cash Register Inputs
▶ Cash Register Outputs

With a list like the one above another reasonable question is: How easy is it to implement a USB-UART application that can monitor and/or control an embedded PSoC based project. The answer to that question depends on how comfortable the developer is programming for the host system (Windows, MAC, Linux). If the developer is experienced in host software development, then developing a custom host monitor/control program is an easy task. But if the developer has never programmed on the chosen host, this could be a very big task. While this chapter doesn't cover PC programming, experience will be gained in how to send and receive data from the World Tour board. The good news is that the process is the same for all of the PSoC USB parts supported by PSoC Express.

To begin, projects will use the HyperTerminal program that comes with all recent versions of Windows, and there will be screenshots of a simple application that was written to communicate with the World Tour board. That application is available on the CD.

The PSoC USB-UART Application

Before a developer begins developing custom USB-UART applications, some time should be taken to design the embedded application, host data interface, and host side application. The possibilities of how a PC and PSoC can be used together are virtually infinite. The example being shown here is simple, but much more sophisticated programs can be developed with a little experience. The PSoC USB possibilities are so great, that an upcoming tutorial DVD will be dedicated to this topic.

Start PSoC Express, or start a new design, and save the design as Chapter10_1. From the Input catalog, choose Tactile → Potentiometer, and name the component Potentiometer_1 as shown in figure 10-1.

Chapter 10

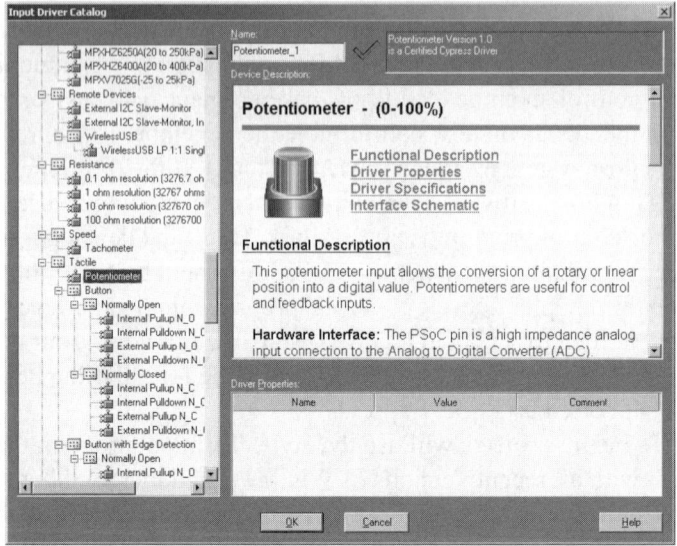

Figure 10-1

Next, select the Output catalog, choosing Display → LED → Intensity Controlled, and name this component LED_1 as shown in figure 10-2.

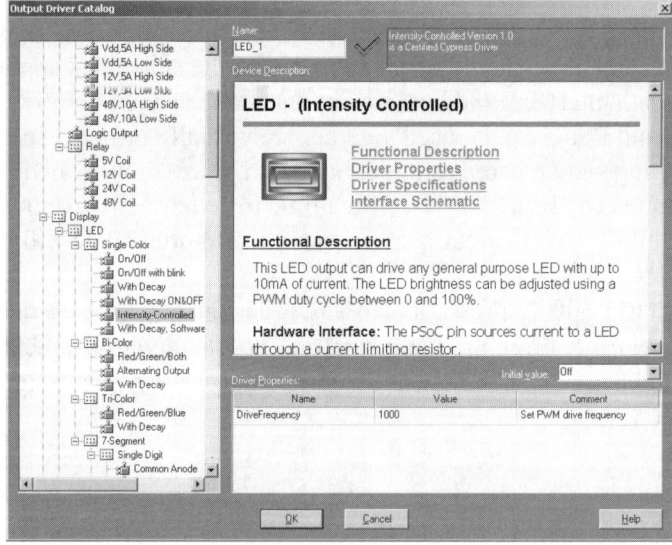

Figure 10-2

Leave the Initial Value and Drive Frequency parameters set to their default values. Now, choose the USB-UART component from the

Interface catalog, naming this component USB_Intfc as shown in figure 10-3.

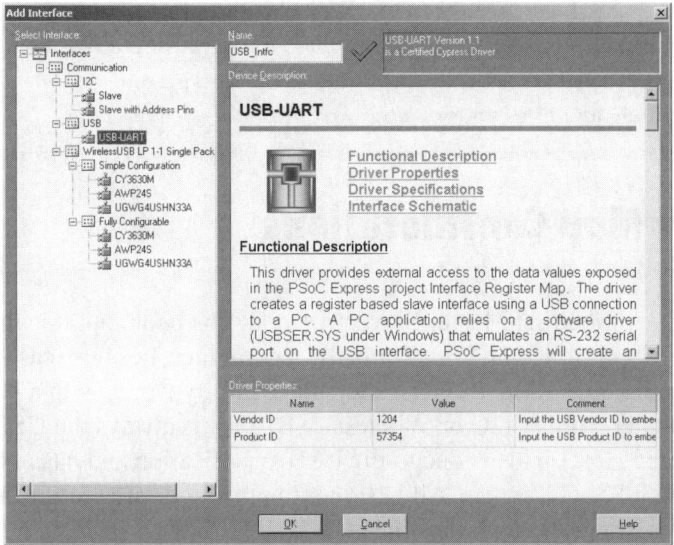

Figure 10-3

Leave Vendor ID and Product ID set to their default values of 1204 and 57354 respectively. When finished, press the OK button.

What Are the VID and PID and Why Are They Important?

The Vendor ID (also known as VID) is a unique number assigned by USB.org. Each USB vendor has a unique ID which is used in combination with the Product ID (also known as PID) to determine which device driver should be loaded.

Since the World Tour board is being used, Cypress has supplied their VID and assigned the PID internally to 57534. When the PSoC is programmed and a USB cable is plugged into the board, these IDs will be transmitted to the host so the host can determine if the driver is A) already available, B) needs to be loaded, or C) non-existent on the current PC, requiring a search for the driver.

Chapter 10

Note: Do not use the VID and PID from this project in your own projects. If the wrong PID or VID is used, it could cause the wrong driver to be loaded causing the Windows Blue Screen of Death. PIDs can be obtained at www.usb.org. While there is a fee for a PID, this is a one-time expense and uniquely identifies your company as the hardware provider.

Register Map Considerations

This isn't the first Master/Slave project in this book, but it is the first project controlled and monitored by a computer. For this reason let's examine how PSoC Register Map accessibility works with a USB host computer. Unlike I2C or WirelessUSB, a PC is always the USB Master (aka Host). This is due to the USB specification and has nothing to do with PSoC Express. All USB communications are seen from the Master point of view. This means a Write is always data from the Master to the PSoC, and a Read is always from the PSoC. In USB terms these are actually called OUT and IN data transfers.

All Reads and Writes are always initiated by the PC. When the PC Writes data, the PSoC updates it actions and when the PC Reads data, the PSoC serves the request.

From the Master view of the system, Potentiometer_1 is a read-only device, and since it is an Input component, it appears in the Read-Only section of the Register Map in PSoC Express. The Register Map can be viewed by selecting Project, Assign Register Map from the main menu in PSoC Express. Note that LED_1 is listed in the Read-Only area as well. For this project Read-Write access to LED_1 is required. If we were to write to a read-only Register Map value, the write will simply be ignored on the PSoC.

So, to control the intensity of LED_1 from the PC, it must be done through the Transfer Function of LED_1. Looking back at how all Master-Slave relationships work in PSoC Express, there are some basic rules that always apply. The first rule is:

A remote device NEVER alters the actual status of an Input or Output Component.

Every time the value of an Input or Output component is changed, it is done through the Interface Valuator component. To gain access to the intensity value of LED_1, an Interface Valuator is required as shown in figure 10-4.

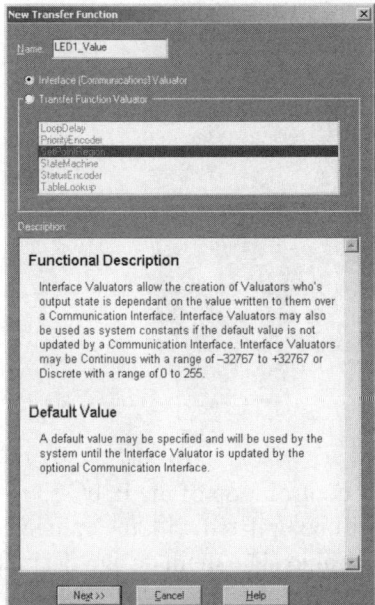

Remember to click the Interface Valuator checkbox, name the component LED1_Value, then click the Next>> button, which will display the window in figure 10-5.

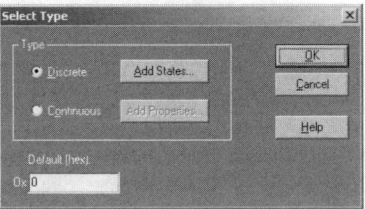

Figure 10-5

Figure 10-4

Choose a Discrete type, a default value of 0, then press the OK button when finished. Now, a Transfer Function needs to be added to LED_1. This will allow the Intensity to be updated when changed on the PC. Select LED_1, right-click and select Transfer Function. Choose a Priority Encoder, then press the Next>> button. Enter the single statement as shown below and in figure 10-6.

> *If* 1 *then* **LED1_Value**

Chapter 10

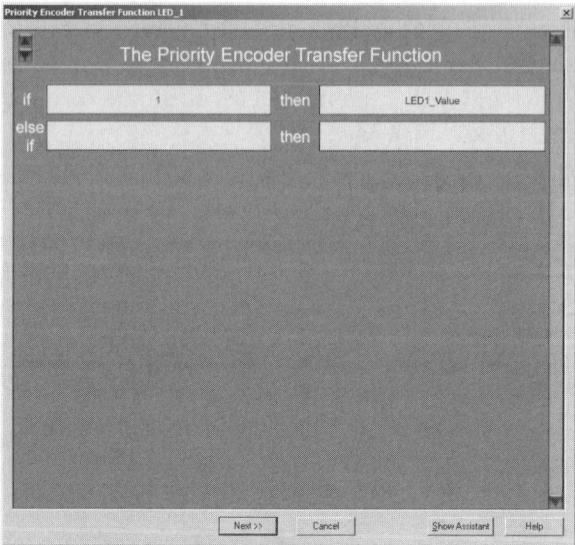

Figure 10-6

Each time through the main control loop of the PSoC Express program, the intensity of LED_1 will be updated with the value contained in the Interface Valuator LED1_Value. The main design desktop should now look similar to figure 10-7.

Figure 10-7

Remember the logic for Potentiometer_1 has not been implemented yet, so while Potentiometer_1 is on the design desktop, LED_1 is currently the focus of this project.

Before building this project, let's look at the Register Map to see how LED_1 and LED1_Value are arranged. Click Project → Assign Register Map and arrange the order of the Interface Valuators and components like figure 10-8.

LED1_Value will hold the value written from the PC. By rearranging LED_1 after Potentiometer_1, the Read/Write and Read-Only values are now next to one another. If the last variable in the list does not display the length in the datasheet don't worry since the length is

Figure 10-8

known to be one, since it was declared a Discrete (byte) value. Potentiometer_1 is also a byte value so it to, is a single byte in length. The length of LED_1 is also known to be a single byte in length, since it contains values from 0 to 100 (just as Potentiometer_1). When the register map is in the same order as figure 10-8, press the OK button to continue.

Chapter 10

Building the USB-UART Project

Press the Save tab followed by the Build tab. Choose the CY8C24894 part as shown in figure 10-9.

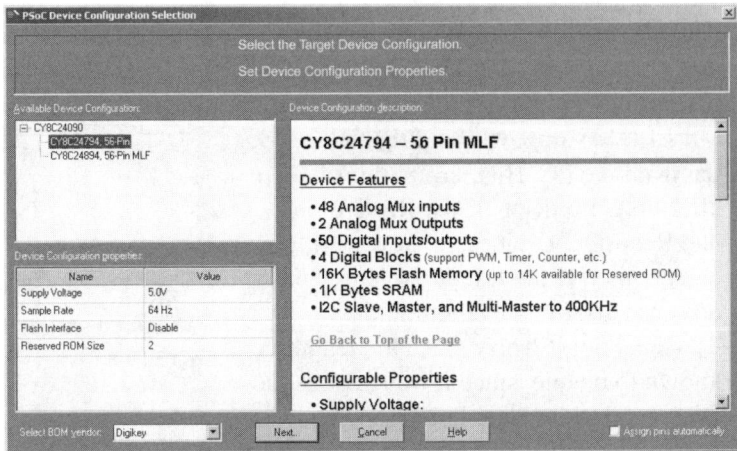

Figure 10-9

Press the Next button. LED_1 should be attached to pin P2[5] and Potentiometer_1 should be attached to pin P0[1] as shown in figure 10-10.

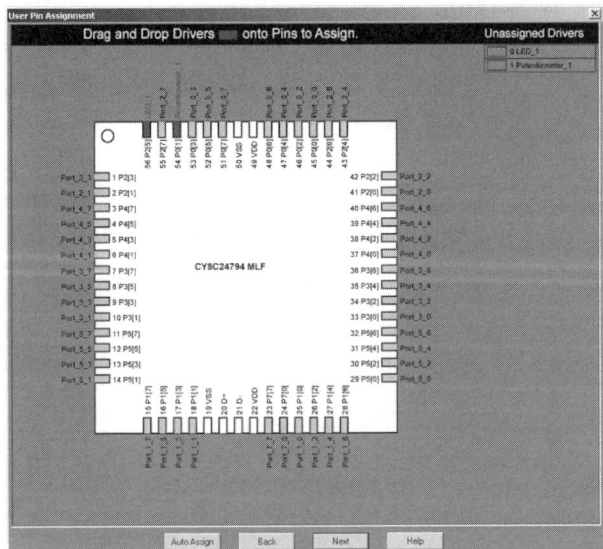

Figure 10-10

Looking at figure 10-10, note the USB VSS, D+, D–, and VDD pins are automatically assigned. This differs from I2C and WirelessUSB where there are options on where to place the I/O pins. Using PSoC USB parts, the USB core is permanently assigned to the USB pins, so no placement is necessary. To continue, press the Next button to finish the build.

Testing the Design

Once the build is completed, the commands to control and monitor the USB-UART can be found in the data sheet. The Register Map layout is contained there as well, as shown in figure 10-11.

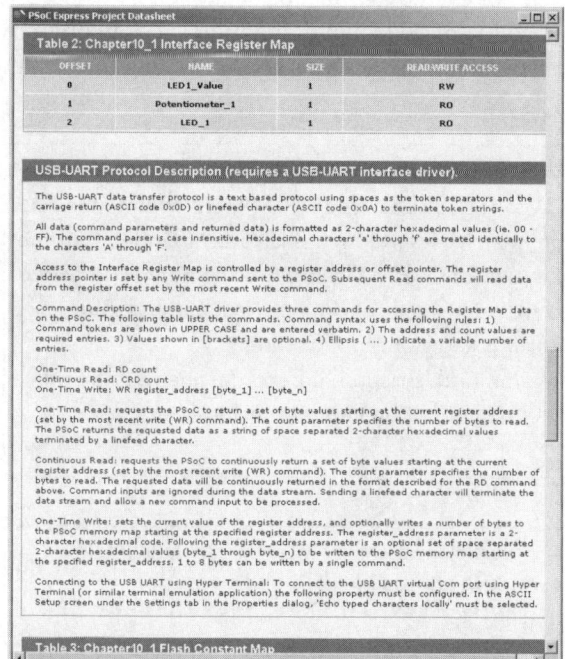

Figure 10-11

Note the Interface Register Map is identical to the manual assignments we made earlier. Also note that the length of the last value in the register map is also printed so we can view the total length of our Register Map area, which in this case the length is three.

Following the register map layout in the datasheet, is the description of the USB-UART protocol. This is the roadmap for accessing the USB-UART interface. There are only three commands. They are:

Write (WR) Command

Syntax: WR address Hexbyte1 Hexbyte2 etc.... [ENTER or LF]

The WR indicates the command type, which in this case is a Write command. The address value, is the beginning address (or offset) in the register map of the first location on the Slave that will be written to by the Master (Host). Following the address are the values to be written with each byte separated by a space (decimal 32). The command is terminated by a line feed (decimal 13). Any type of variable can be exchanged but each byte must be separated by a space. So if an integer Interface Valuator is declared, the high and low order bytes will need to be separated with a space before writing them to the Slave device.

> **Note:** The WR command establishes the starting position in the Slave Register Map for all subsequent RD (Read) commands. A WR command must be issued first. It is recommended that the first command issued after establishing a USB connection with a PSoC Express developed application, be a WR command to establish the starting Register Map location.
>
> Once a WR command is issued, it becomes the permanent starting location and cannot be changed using future WR commands.

> ALL commands issued from the host MUST BE IN UPPERCASE ONLY. Using lowercase characters will return an error.
> ALL BYTES SENT TO THE SLAVE MUST BE SEPARATED BY A SPACE (Character 32).
> ALL BYTES RECEIVED FROM THE SLAVE WILL BE SEPARATED BY A SPACE.
> ALL VALUES SENT AND RECEIVED ARE IN HEXADECIMAL (Base 16) FORMAT.

Read (RD) Command

Syntax: RD Count [ENTER or LF]

The RD (Read) command is followed by the number of bytes to read from the slave. In the above example, 2 bytes will be read starting at the address defined in a prior WR command or location 0 if no prior WR command was issued.

Continuous Read (CRD) Command

Syntax: CRD Count [ENTER or LF]

The CRD (Continuous Read) command is identical to the RD command except that data will be read from the slave device continuously on each pass through the main program loop on the PSoC.

Let's continue with this project. Make certain the MiniProg is connected to the upper-right programming header, then select the Program tab. Upon completion, exit the Programming software, and disconnect the MiniProg from the USB cable. Once the MiniProg has been removed, plug the USB cable into the World Tour board, and a message will appear on the host PC that a new device has been found. If the USB-UART has not been used before, follow the instructions in the next paragraph. If the USB-UART has already been used in a prior application, the driver should already be installed.

Chapter 10

If this is the first time using the USB-UART interface, Windows will guide the user through the installation process. The USB-UART driver is located in the main Project folder, inside a sub-folder also named the same as the main project folder, in a second sub-folder named lib. The Windows Installer should manually be pointed to this folder, if it is not already in Windows path. Once located, a message will appear stating the driver is not certified, click the Continue Anyway button to finish installing the driver.

Connecting to HyperTerminal

Start the HyperTerminal program, which is located at Startup → All Programs → Accessories → Communication → HyperTerminal. Default values of 9600 baud, 8 data, 1 stop, and no parity bits will work perfectly. You will need to manually choose the COM port the USB-UART is attached to, then open that port. If everything is working correctly, enter the following command string:

WR 00 20 [ENTER]

The above command writes a HEX 20 (decimal 32) to location 0 of the register map (LED1_Value). If executed correctly the HyperTerminal Display will look like figure 10-12.

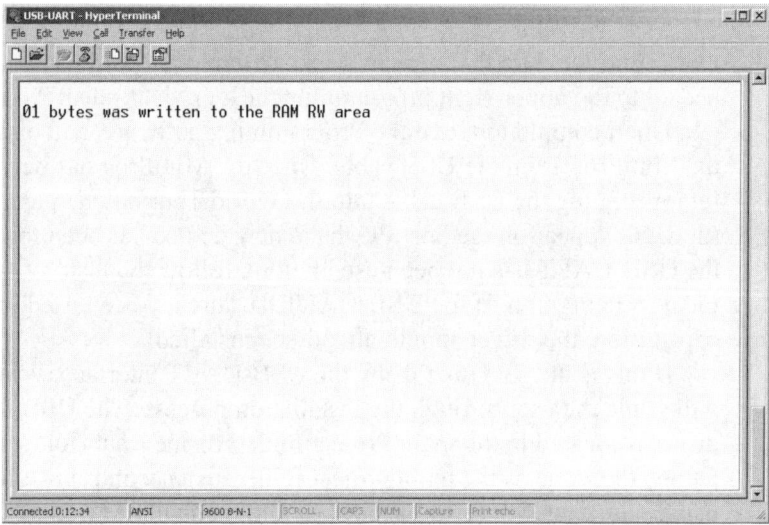

Figure 10-12

The message indicates that 1 byte was written successfully to the Slave Read/Write Register Map area. If you received a different message, remember that 2 HEX characters must be entered for each value, separated by a space and the command must be in CAPS. After typing the above command the LED closest to the USB connector in the row of LEDs will be dimly lit.

Next, read a value from Potentiometer_1. To read, write the following in HyperTerminal:

RD 02 [ENTER]

The read location was established by the first WR command issued. Since LED1_Value resides at location 00, location 00 will be the first value read. To obtain the value of Potentiometer_1, two bytes will need to be read, location 00 and location 01. Location 01 contains the value of Potentiometer_1 as shown in figure 10-13.

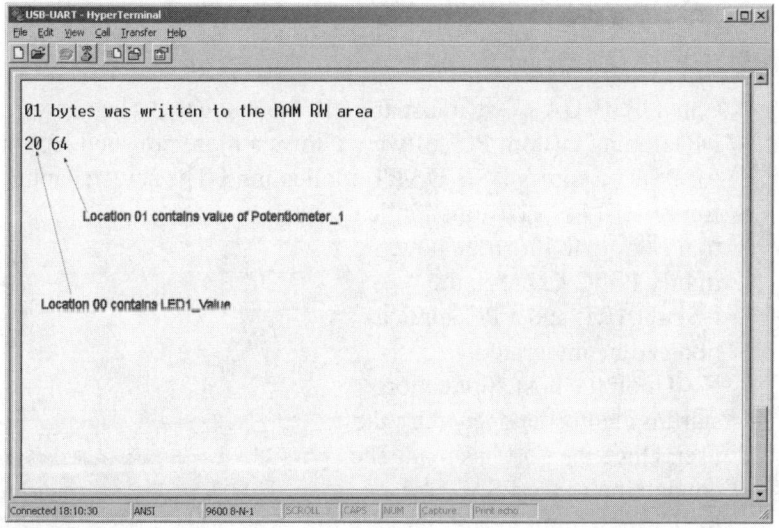

Figure 10-13

The first value returned contains the LED1_Value we wrote earlier (WR 00 20) and can be ignored. The second value returned contains the current setting of Potentiometer_1, which is currently set to 64 hex (100 Decimal) the upper limit.

Changes Required for Production

In a production environment it's doubtful end users want to use HyperTerminal to communicate with a PSoC Embedded System. There are many tools available to help developers automate these tasks. When developing the host software, it's important to remember that two independent systems need to communicate. If communications will be bi-directional, use a Windows Timer object to do Reads. The same timer can do periodic writes or a write can occur when a

Windows control has changed or a Windows event has triggered. Visit this author's web site at www.psoc.time-lines.com for additional USB-UART software and hardware tools in coming months.

Custom PC Software using the USB-UART Bridge Device

Can a USB-UART be transparent to the end user? The answer is yes. Developing custom PC software allows a more polished look-and-feel for PSoC Express USB-UART applications. The screen capture in figure 10-14 is a custom application I wrote to illustrate how tightly PSoC Express, the USB-UART, and a PC application can be integrated.

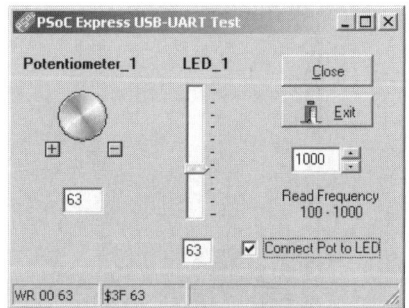

Figure 10-14

Upon the host application startup the Port is opened by the user. Once the port has made the connection to the PSoC Slave, the Close string replaces the Open string on the Open/Close button. A Windows timer establishes the frequency of the reads. The round dial on the far left reflects the data value read from Potentiometer_1. The slider in the middle allows the PC application to control the intensity setting of LED_1 by writing the LED1_Value. If the connect check box is set, the slider becomes a read-only component attached to Potentiometer_1 on the World Tour board that changes in sequence with the value written to LED1_Value. This logic allows a logical connection to be established by writing the data read from Potentiometer_1 to be written to LED1_Value.

While this is a simple demonstration, it shows only a fraction of what can be accomplished when PSoC Express, the USB-UART, and a PC application are combined.

Chapter Review

Once again, a lot of material has been covered on an advanced subject. I hope that reading this chapter has given you creative inspiration to try your own designs using the USB-UART and a PC application. These combined technologies allow you to develop a USB-UART application in a few hours. Speaking of hours, how much time did this project take me to develop? That is an excellent question. The PSoC Express USB-UART project took me 15 minutes from beginning to end. Remember that I've been using PSoC Express full-time for over 7 months. But, even a beginner should be able to develop this application in a couple of hours, once you've mastered the other aspects of PSoC Express. The custom PC application took me about four hours of development to complete. Of the four hours, roughly half that time was spent selecting and tweaking the screen based controls. So the PC application was actually working in two hours time.

A Look Ahead

In the next (and final) chapter on using PSoC Express, we cover how to implement custom "C" code in the custom.c file. Yes, PSoC Express does give developers to write code outside the design desktop.

Custom Programming with PSoC Express

Chapter Overview

Well, you've hung in there to reach this, the final chapter of PSoC Express projects. This chapter deals with writing custom code when an application requires additional functionality that is beyond PSoC Express normal logic. PSoC Express allows a developer to add additional functionality through the use of custom C code. In addition to this being an advanced topic, knowledge of the C language is also a requirement to understand how a PSoC Express application can be modified. While the example in this chapter is simple, it will clearly outline the steps needed to properly add custom code to a PSoC Express project.

PSoC Express Source Files

Unlike past chapters, this chapter digs right into the actual source files created by PSoC Express. Actually, that's one source file, "custom.c." Care should be taken in this chapter because modifying PSoC Express source files can lead to frustration and ill-functioning or non-working PSoC Express applications. So there are two pieces of advice offered next.

First, make source code modifications in small steps, adding a few lines of code, saving the source code, doing a Build in PSoC Express, Programming, Testing, and starting the cycle over again. This minimizes changes between testing, thus reducing the amount of code that will need to be sifted through. While this appears to take more time because development is tested more frequently, this approach pays off when a bug is discovered. Instead of hundreds of lines of code that may need to be sifted through, only a few lines added between testing, make finding and fixing bugs much quicker.

> **Note:** Making too many changes between builds can be costly as well. In a worse case situation, it may be necessary to purchase a PSoC ICE Cube for source level debugging. While the ICE Cube is a $600 investment, it also includes a C compiler license, and is an excellent value. In fact purchasing the PSoC ICE is strongly recommended.

The second recommendation offered here is to recommend that the objective of the modified code is clear, concise, and understood thoroughly by the developer. If possible make certain the modifications have been documented before making the code modifications. This will keep the risk of errors and bugs to a minimum.

There are many source files that make up a PSoC Express project but only one source file (custom.c) and one header file ("custom.h") where code changes are made. Keeping custom code limited to these files makes it easy to remember where custom code should be placed and greatly reduces the change for serious problems resulting from code changes.

Source File Layout of a PSoC Express Project

Before starting the actual project, let's take a sneak peek at the finished project and the modified source files. While this may seem somewhat backward, it will give some background that should make understanding the process easier. Figure 11-1 is the completed design of the project for chapter 11 named Chapter 11-1.

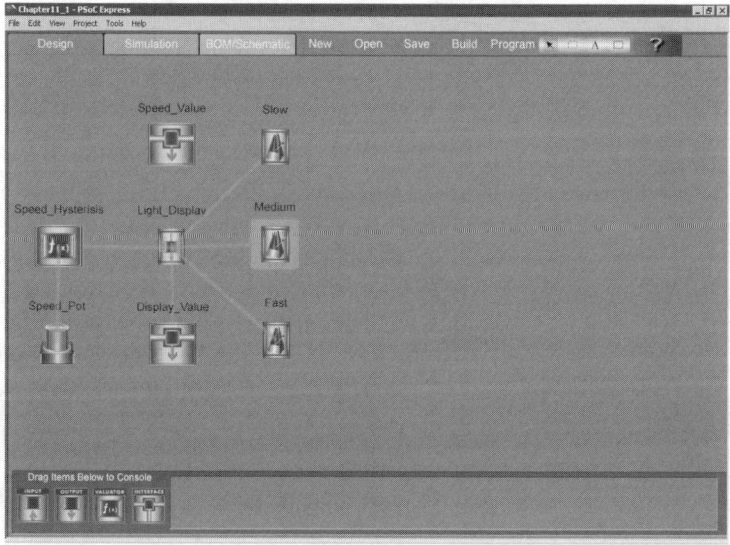

Figure 11-1

The step-by-step process to build this project will be covered later in this chapter. At the center of this design is a Banked Output component named Light_Display. Light_Display can be shown at one of three speeds. They are: Fast, Medium, and Slow. Light_Display can also be set to Off and On. The Speed_Pot Input component is used to provide the setting for the display state and speed through the Valuator Speed_Hysterisis. Speed_Hysterisis has set points at 20, 40, 60, and 80 percentiles. 00-20 is Off, 20-40 is Slow, 40-60 is Medium, 60-80 is Fast and 80-100 is On.

Display_Value holds the next value for Light_Display, and this variable is exposed to custom code. Figure 11-2 shows the directory contents of the source files for this project (Project 11-1) after the first Build has been completed.

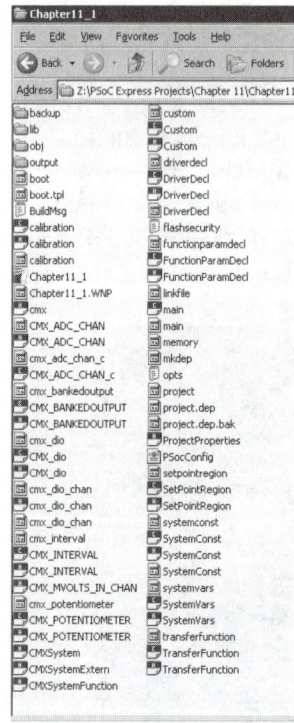

Figure 11-2

There are a large number of files, but they have logical names that are organized by categories, component types and Valuator types. Each component chosen from the Input and Output catalogs have a corresponding source file that begins with the letters CMX. In the listing to the left, the following component source files are shown:

CMX_ADC_CHAN
CMX_BANKEDOUTPUT
CMX_INTERVAL
CMX_MVOLTS_IN_CHAN
CMX_POTENTIOMETER

These files represent the component types used in the design. There may be more than one component of a given type, but the source file appears only once. Valuators also appear as source files. Here the SetPointRegion and TransferFunction source and header files are also shown. The DriverDecl, SystemConst, and SystemFunction header and C files are where other constants and variables are defined.

Custom.c and Custom.h is where all of the custom code will be placed in this project.

PSoC Express C Interface Code

In this project, the PSoC Express design desktop is used to add Input and Output components, Valuators, Interface Valuators, and Transfer Functions. The values assigned to the Banked Output component are added, and each value in the array is cycled through. This demonstrates the best of using PSoC Express and manual code by allowing a developer to setup the Interval Generator, Input, and Output components in PSoC Express, then adding the values to be output in "C".

This approach allows a developer to use a single Interface Valuator to cycle through an array created outside the PSoC Express design desktop. If this project were done completely in PSoC Express, a new Interface Valuator would be required for each array element and making changes would require adding, changing, or deleting additional Interface Valuator components.

Before starting to customize PSoC Express code, it's a good idea to have the PSoC Express portion of the project simulated, working, built, and tested if possible. Remember, the project has to be built for the custom.c and custom.h files to be created.

Interface Valuators make excellent conduits to custom "C" code in PSoC Express. In addition, using Interface Valuators as conduits, makes debugging easier because Interface Valuator values can be sent to a LCD with little trouble. This project will begin with the PSoC Express portion first.

The PSoC Express Project

Start PSoC Express or if PSoC Express is already running, choose File → New from the main menu bar. Next, choose the Input catalog → Tactile → Potentiometer, and name this component Speed_Pot as shown in figure 11-3.

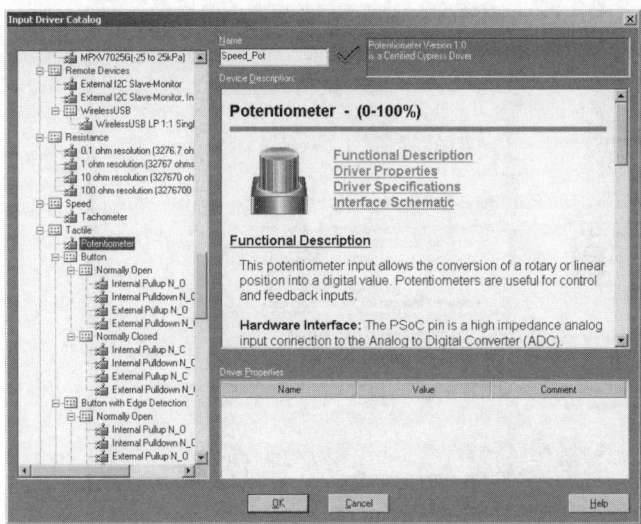

Figure 11-3

This component will be used to control the On, Off, and Speed functions of the Banked Digital Output component. Next, select a

Valuator, choosing Set Point Region type, then name this component Speed_Hysterisis. Press the Next>> button and add the settings as shown in figure 11-4.

There are five different thresholds in figure 11-4. They will be (from lowest to highest) Off, Low Speed, Medium Speed, High Speed, and Off.

Once again select the Input catalog. Now add three Interval Generators, naming them Slow, Medium, and Fast setting their parameters as shown in figures 11-5, 11-6, and 11-7 respectively.

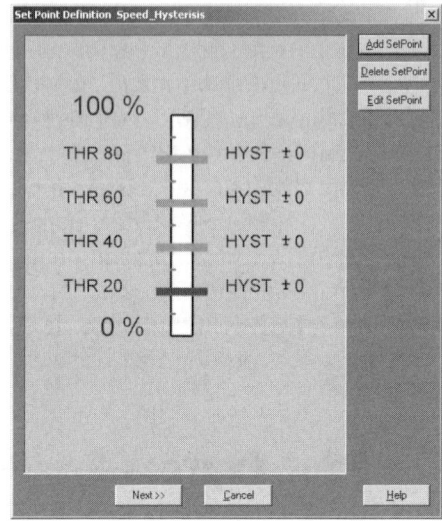

Figure 11-4

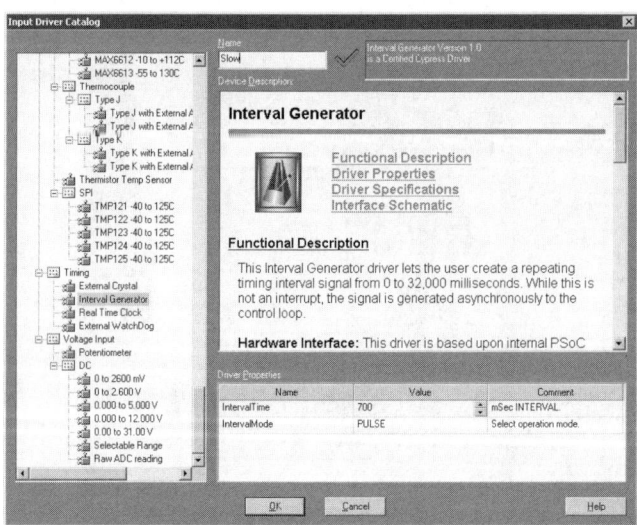

Figure 11-5

Figure 11-5 shows the Slow Interval Generator. Note the Interval Time of 700.

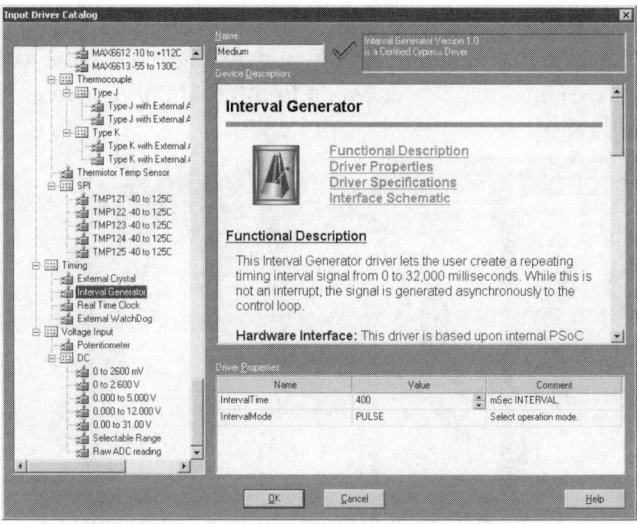

Figure 11-6

Figure 11-6 shows the Medium Interval Generator. Note the Interval Time of 400.

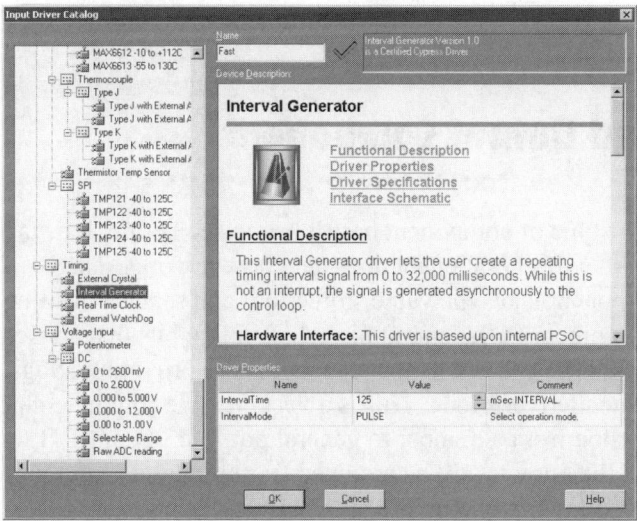

Figure 11-7

Figure 11-7 shows the Fast Interval Generator. Note the Interval Time of 125. These three Interval Generators will provide us with a delay based on the position of the Potentiometer Speed_Pot.

Now, select the Output catalog and select Digital Output, Banked Output component, naming this component Light_Display, setting the pin count to 6, and the Driver Mode to Internal Pull Down as shown in figure 11-8

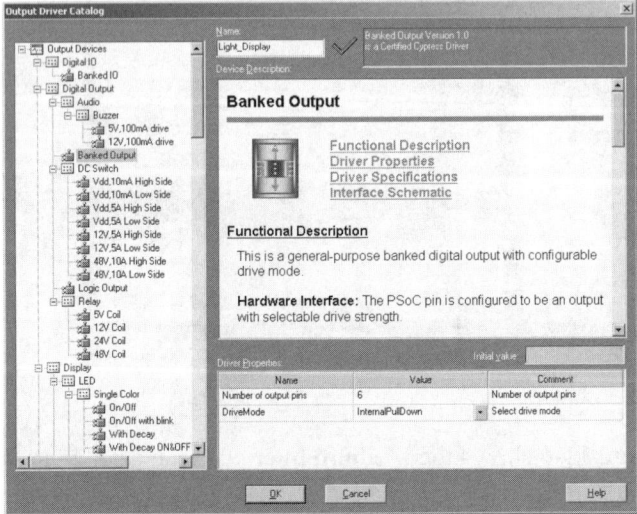

Figure 11-8

The Banked Output Component

Since this type of component hasn't been used before, let's take a brief look at what this component does, and how it works. The Banked Output component takes the value stored to it and sends that value out as a binary number to the output pins. The binary bits that are set to one provide a logic 1. The bits that are set to zero providing a logic 0 in the selected Driver Mode. This is a very flexible component providing a conversion from a number to general purpose I/O pin TTL logic. In this case the outputs will be assigned from bottom to top for the row of LEDs, allowing output as a simple light display.

Just above this component in the Output catalog is the Banked IO component. The difference between this component and the Banked IO component is simple. Banked IO is useful when the next value output is based on the existing Input value of the pins, or a DIP switch needs to be read. Banked Output on the other hand, does not possess the capability to read back a value.

Completing the PSoC Express Project

To complete the PSoC Express portion of our project, add an Interface Valuator to the desktop, naming it Display_Value as shown in figure 11-9. Accept the default values for type Discrete, and 0 for the default value.

Next, select the Light_Display component, right-click, and choose Transfer Function, and select the Priority Encoder. Enter the expressions as shown below.

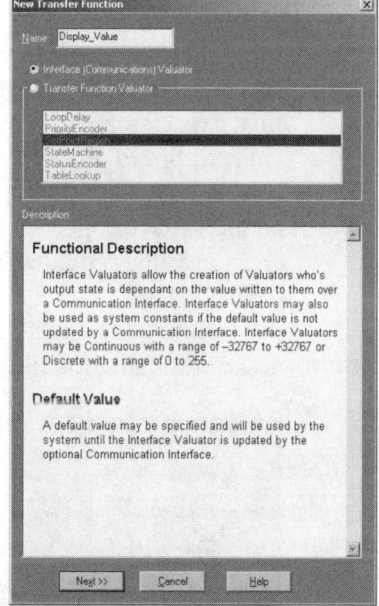

Figure 11-9

If (Speed_Hysterisis == Speed_Hysterisis__0_00_to_20_00__) *then* 0

If ((Speed_Hysterisis == Speed_Hysterisis__0_20_to_40_00__) && (Slow == Slow__Triggered)) *then* Display_Value

If ((Speed_Hysterisis == Speed_Hysterisis__0_40_to_60_00__) && (Medium == Medium__Triggered)) *then* Display_Value

If ((Speed_Hysterisis == Speed_Hysterisis__0_60_to_80_00__) && (Fast == Fast__Triggered)) *then* Display_Value

If ((Speed_Hysterisis == Speed_Hysterisis__0_80_to_100_00__)) *then* 63

The first expression will set Light_Display to 0 (Off) if the Speed_Pot value is in the 0 to 20% range. The next expression will set

Light_Display to the value of Display_Value if the Speed_Pot is in the 20-40% range, and the Slow Interval Generator has been triggered. The third expression will set Light_Display to equal Display_Value if the Speed_Pot value is between 40-60%, and the Medium Interval Generator has been triggered. The fourth expression will set Light_Display equal to the value of Display_Value if the Speed_Pot is set to 60-80%, the Fast Interval Generator has triggered. The fifth and final expression will assign the value of 63 to Light_Display if the value of Speed_Pot is between 80-100%.

This PSoC Express project will adjust Light_Display speed based on the value of Speed_Pot. Display_Value will contain the next array element value provided by the "C" code we will add to custom.c in the next step.

Before adding the custom code, click the Save tab. The design desktop should look like figure 11-10.

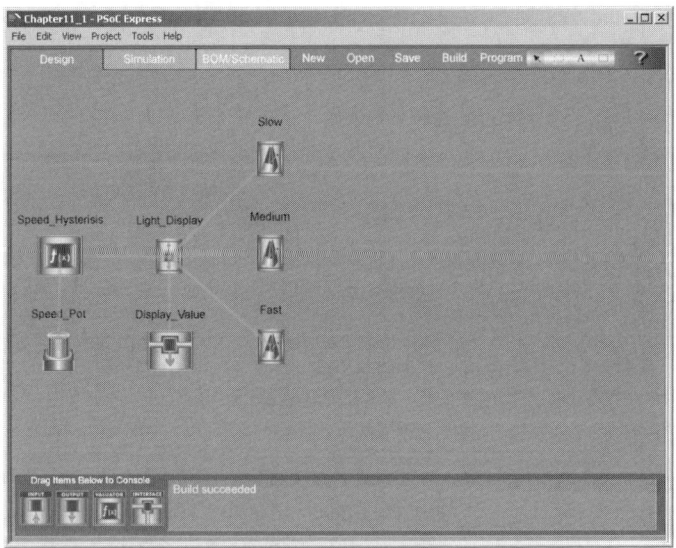

Figure 11-10

Let's Build the current project. This needs to be done at this time so that A) the custom.c and custom.h source files that are needed will be created and B) It is known the project compiles without errors. After pressing the Build tab, choose the CY8C24894 part as shown in figure 11-11.

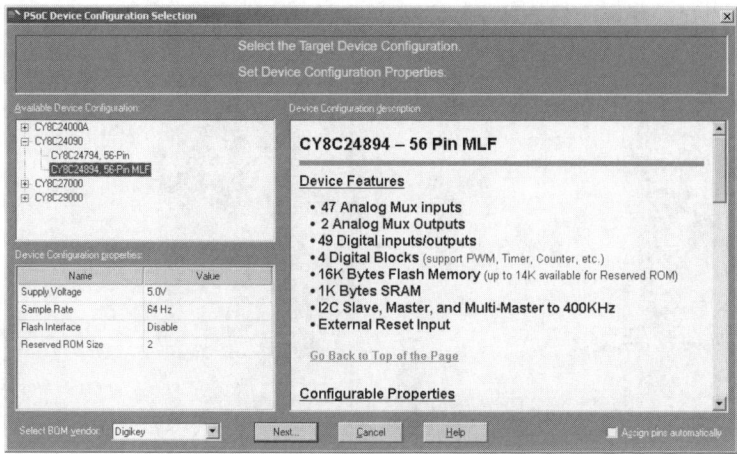

Figure 11-11

Now it's time to position the pins. Assign the outputs as shown in table 11-1.

Pin Definition	Assignment
Light_Display_bit0	P2[5]
Light_Display_bit1	P2[3]
Light_Display_bit2	P2[2]
Light_Display_bit3	P2[1]
Light_Display_bit4	P2[0]
Light_Display_bit5	P2[4]
Speed_Pot	P0[1]

▲ Table 11-1

The pin assignment window should look like the one in figure 11-12.

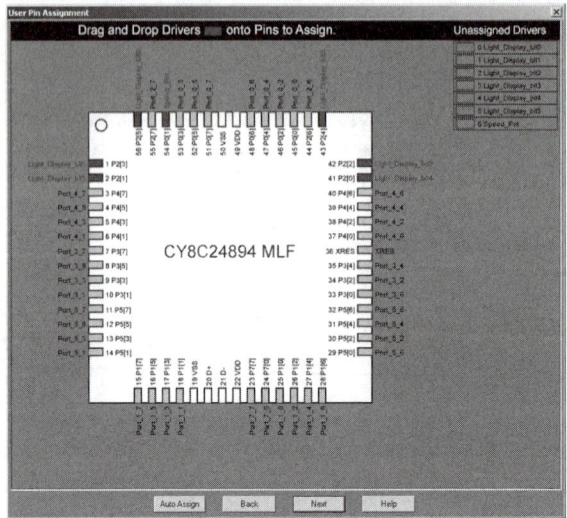

Figure 11-12

The project should now build without errors.

Modifying Custom.c and Custom.h

The C language rules that apply to PSoC Express have already been discussed. For the most part, the same "C" language syntax and rules apply to PSoC Express that apply to PSoC Designer. The "C" manual can be found either on the CD that accompanied this book or on the Cypress web site.

Now it's time to modify the custom.c and custom.h files. Using Notepad, open the custom.h file located in the X:\Chapter11_1\ Chapter11_1 folder. Once opened make certain the files have the three lines of code as shown in figure 11-13.

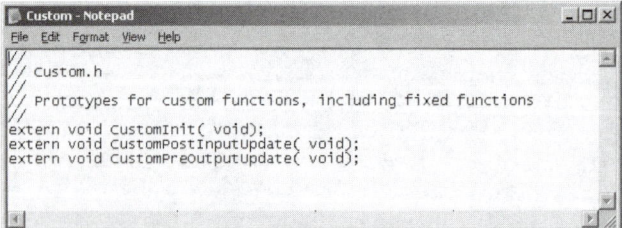

Figure 11-13

Now, start a second copy of Notepad and open the custom.c file located in the same folder as custom.h. There should be three functions to match the declared functions in custom.h as shown in figure 11-14.

Custom - Notepad

File Edit Format View Help

```
//
// Custom.c
//
//   Custom functions for insertion into PSoC Express projects, including fixed functions
//

#include "custom.h"

void CustomInit()
{
}

void CustomPostInputUpdate()
{
}

void CustomPreOutputUpdate()
{
}
```

Figure 11-14

When declaring new functions, add the function declarations in custom.h, and add the code for the functions in custom.c. For this project, let's keep things simple, so all of the modifications and additions will be made to custom.c.

Ten lines of code need to be added to custom.c. The file shown in figure 11-15 contains the modified code along with comments describing what the code in each line performs.

Custom - Notepad

File Edit Format View Help

```
//
// Custom.c
//
//   Custom functions for insertion into PSoC Express projects, including fixed functions
//

#include "custom.h"
#include "CMXSystemExtern.h"
#include "functionparamdecl.h"

const BYTE sequence[]={12,18,33,18,12,0};                  // <- Array of values to be displayed on LED's
int loop;                                                  // <- counter that holds current array element value

void CustomInit()
{
 loop=0;                                                   // Initialize loop value to zero at startup
}

void CustomPostInputUpdate()
{
        // No altering or massaging of Input Data so this function remains empty
}

void CustomPreOutputUpdate()
{
 if (sequence[loop] != 0) {                                // <- If array element value is not zero
  SystemVars.ReadWriteVars.pse_Display_Value = sequence[loop]; // <- Assign array element value to Display_Value
  loop++;                                                  // <- Addvance to next array element
 } else {                                                  // <- Array Element value is zero
  SystemVars.ReadWriteVars.pse_Display_Value = 0;         // <- Assign Display_Value the value of zero
  loop = 0;                                                // <- Reset loop counter to first array element
 }
}
```

Figure 11-15

Chapter 11

Let's examine the finished custom.c file. Begin by including the CMXSystemExtern.h and functionparamdecl.h files in custom.c. These files define the PSoC Express variable (SystemVars.Read-WriteVars.pse_Display_Value) that will be altered.

Next, a BYTE array named sequence is declared. Note the "const" keyword that prefixes the array definition. This keyword tells the compiler to store the array in the E2Prom area of the PSoC instead of using RAM. This is done to save RAM area for program code. Next, a loop of type "int" is declared to hold the value of the array element currently pointed to. Since the custom code only affects output components, no changes are needed in the CustomPostInputUpdate() function as noted in the listing.

In the CustomInit() function initialize the loop counter to 0. Most C compilers assign a zero value automatically when the value is declared outside the braces of a function, as done here. But assigning the value assures the LEDs will be off when the program initializes. Next, look at the CustomPreOutputUpdate() to check the value of the current sequence array element to make certain it is zero. If it isn't 0, then assign the value of the sequence array element to the pse_Display_Value. This cycles through the sequence array until the zero value at the end is detected. When that zero value is detected, a zero is assigned to pse_Display_Value to turn off the LEDs and the loop counter is reset to zero, setting the sequence array element pointer back to the beginning of the array preparing to start the cycle over the next time through the main program loop.

After making the above modifications to custom.c, save the file back to disk from Notepad before doing a Build. This is an important step; otherwise, none of the added code will be included during the build process or executed when the program runs. After saving custom.c back to disk, switch back to PSoC Express and press the Build tab.

Once the project Build has finished, Program the part, then power up the project. When Speed_Pot is set at 0-20% no LEDs will be lit. When Speed_Pot is set at 20-40% the LEDs will move from the center to the edge very slowly and then turn off for one cycle. Setting Speed_Pot at 40-60% increases the flash rate slightly, setting Speed_Pot at 60-80% will flash the LEDs very fast. When Speed_Pot reaches 80% or higher, the LEDs will all be lit constantly.

Build Errors when using Custom Code

If Build Errors are encountered, the error message is usually descriptive enough to help quickly locate and fix the problem. One of most common source of errors is misspelled variables or function names, additional braces, or illegal syntax. Earlier in this chapter it was suggested making custom code changes in small steps, thus avoiding a long list of error messages and allowing for frequent testing.

Chapter Summary

In this chapter modifying PSoC Express code has been explored using the Windows Notepad program. Hopefully, you have become more comfortable with using PSoC Express and how quickly and easily you can develop with this tool. I encourage you to test the boundaries and see what interesting products and programs you can develop on your own.

Book Summary

This is the last chapter of projects. The resources chapter follows, with the subject index after that. If you acquired this book from Cypress, all of the projects will work with PSoC Express 2.2 and the World Tour board. If would like a CD of the projects developed for this book, along with additional projects and tools, you can order the accompanying CD using the order form at the front of the book.

If you purchased this book theCD should be included. The CD includes additional information, tools, and the actual projects developed for this book. PSoC Express, USB-UART software, additional projects, and notes that didn't make the book can also be found on the CD.

All of the projects can be developed from scratch using the step-by-step procedures outlined in each chapter. All of these projects were developed using PSoC Express 2.1 and have been tested to work. These working projects have been the basis of each tutorial.

Chapter 11

After seven months of working daily with the product, I can tell you first hand that I can now develop the most complex projects in less than a few hours. In the process of writing the advanced topics section, I became very comfortable with WirelessUSB, CapSense, USB-UART, and modifying the Custom.c file.

I did have to download and use the C compiler manual as a reference, but once I did that, there were no more build errors. All of my build errors using custom code were either syntax errors or misspellings.

PSoC Express is a very powerful and useful tool. Whether you use it for prototyping, project development, or jump-starting a PSoC Designer project, PSoC Express is a very capable and powerful tool. During the course of writing this book I have used this tool extensively and to be very honest, have found very few bugs in the generated code. In the current version (2.2) I have not found any logic errors at all.

I have also found that using PSoC Express has made me more productive in PSoC Designer, which somewhat surprises me. Moving between the two products is easy, quick, and simple. I hope this book gives you confidence and positive experience with PSoC Express and the PSoC line of parts.

There will be several training DVDs available during 2007 that cover PSoC Express topics in more detail. Check my web site at www.time-lines.com or www.psoc.time-lines.com for more details, pricing, and availability dates.

Chapter 12

Resources

Overview

Throughout the course of writing this book, I found many useful products and tools. All of these tools were used in developing this book.
As always, I like to pass on useful products and tools, so my readers
can benefit from these products as well. This chapter is broken into
three sections. They are:

▶ Hardware

▶ Software

▶ Other Tools

Each item has the product name, company information, description, a
photo (if available), personal comments, price, and web site information. Every product in this section has been used by me for the
production of this book.

Hardware

WirelessUSB Adapters

ArtaFlex
215 Konrad Crescent Markham
ON L3R 8T9 Canada   Phone:
905.479.0148   Fax: 905.479.0149
www.artaflex.com

Artaflex manufacturers several WirelessUSB
adapters for both short and long range applications. The AWP24S is supported in PSoC
Express and is shown in figure 12-1.

I have used the Artaflex products and they
work very well with PSoC Express.

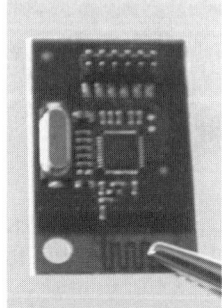

Figure 12-1

WirelessUSB Products

Unigen-USA
45388 Warm Springs Blvd.
Fremont, CA 94539-6102   Phone: 510-668-2088   Fax:
510-661-2770
www.unigen.com

Unigen also manufactures a line of
WirelessUSB boards. Figure 12-2
shows the UGWG4USHN33A board
which is also supported by PSoC
Express.

I have also used the Unigen
board with PSoC with excellent success as well.

Figure 12-2

SoCsicle Development Board, PSoC Express for Programmers - DVD, and PSoC Projects for Beginners - DVD, and "The Beginner's Guide to PSoC Express"

Timelines Industries Inc.
5107 Greenwood Pl
McHenry, IL 60050-2376   Phone: 815-759-1404
www.time-lines.com or www.psoctraining.com or
www.psoc.time-lines.com

Timelines builds and manufacturers the SoCsicle, a PSoC based project and development board that is in the form factor of a 48 Pin DIP. SoCsicle has 2 LEDs, an onboard CapSense button, and four five pin headers for piggyback boards. SOCsicle will also fit a solderless breadboard. The SoCsicle Start Kit includes 1) A SoCsicle board, 2) *The Beginner's Guide to PSoC Express: Microcontroller Development without Writing Code,* 3) CD with projects, PSoC Express, and other goodies, 4) DVD with over 10 tutorial projects in full color video to get started, 5) Wireless Breadboard, and 6) All the components for the projects on DVD.

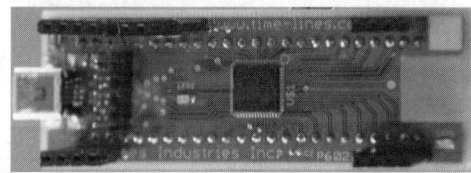

Figure 12-3

Software

Eagle Layout Editor

CadSoft Computer, Inc.
801 South Federal Hwy., Suite 201
Delray Beach, FL 33483-5185   Phone: 1-800-858-8355
Fax: (561)-274-8218
www.cadsoftusa.com

This company is U.S. Sales and support for the Eagle Layout Editor, a very well done electronics layout program. I've been using Eagle for the past four years and it is an excellent value. It is easy to use and rivals programs costing many times its cost.

EAGLE
www.cadsoft.de

Figure 12-4

Chapter 12

B2 Spice Version 5

Beige Bag Software Inc.
623 W. Huron, Suite 2
Ann Arbor, MI 48103   Phone: 734-332-0487   Fax: 734-332-0392
www.beigebag.com

This company makes a dynamite product called B2 Spice. This is one of the nicest simulation programs I've seen and it works in conjunction with the Eagle Layout Editor. Special Offer! The folks at Beige Bag Software have been kind enough to offer 20% off their regular prices. Just visit their website and follow the instructions in the coupon below.

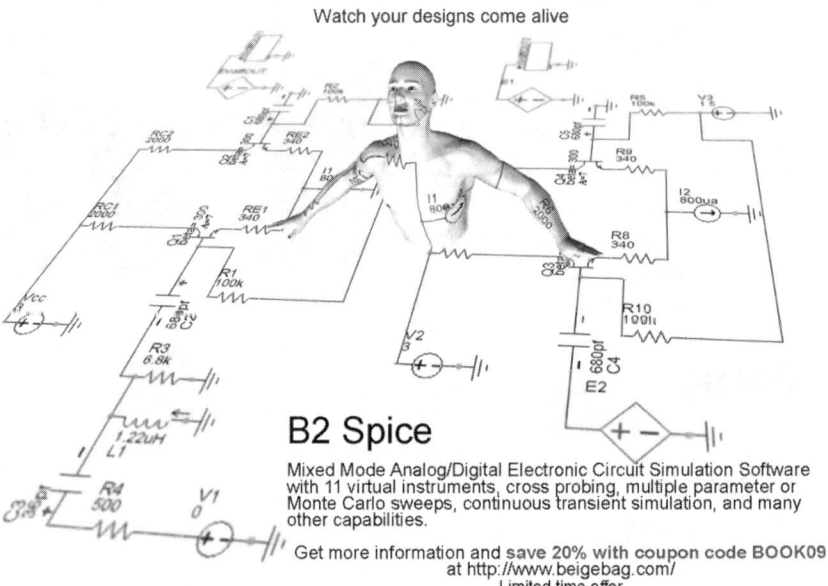

Watch your designs come alive

B2 Spice

Mixed Mode Analog/Digital Electronic Circuit Simulation Software with 11 virtual instruments, cross probing, multiple parameter or Monte Carlo sweeps, continuous transient simulation, and many other capabilities.

Get more information and save 20% with coupon code BOOK09 at http://www.beigebag.com/
Limited time offer

Other Tools

ELAB-80 Oscilloscope, Logic Analyzer and Frequency Generator

Dynon Instruments
19825 141st Place NE
Woodinville, WA 98072   Phone: 425-402-4034 (Sales)
Fax: 425-984-1751
www.dynoninstruments.com

The ELAB-80 is an excellent USB based digital Oscilloscope. This device is actually five instruments. They are:

1. 80 MHz Dual Channel Oscilloscope

2. 16 Channel Logic Analyzer

3. 100 MHz Waveform Generator

4. Dual Programmable Power Supplies

5. Dual Programmable Clocks

I've been using this product for about a year for all my writings. This device is an excellent value and built to take the abuse that happens in a lab.

Dynon Instruments also manufacturers avionics equipment and instruments so they know how to build a rugged precision device. This product costs $495 which is a real steal for the value.

RF-Field Strength & Spectrum Analyzers

Aaronia AG
Gewerbegebiet Aaronia
DE-54597, Strickscheid (Germany)   Phone: ++49 (0) 6556 93033
Fax: ++49 (0) 6556 93034
www.emf-meter.com

This company makes a unique line of Spectrum Analyzers and Field Strength Meters. What makes their products unique is that each product comes with a whip antenna that can be replaced with a directional antenna. The unit is designed to fit on one hand and can be operated

Chapter 12

with just one finger. For more detailed data analysis, the device can be connected to a PC for both off-line analysis of captured data and real-time collection, analysis, and storage. Figure 12-5 shows the handheld device and features.

Aaronia provided a unit that I used for testing the field strength of the WirelessUSB devices. This unit uses rechargeable batteries, and is very high quality. I briefly used the analysis software but in the short time I did use it, I found it very comprehensive and easy to understand.

When visiting the Aaronia site, make certain to choose the English version of the site if you are from North America.

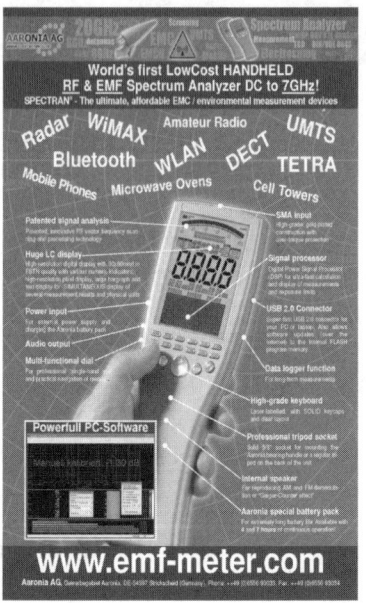

Figure 12-5

LCD Displays

Matrix Orbital
302-524 17th Ave SW
Calgary, AB T2SOB2   Phone: 403-229-2737   Fax: 403-229-1963
www.matrixorbital.com

Matrix Orbital manufactures a variety of LCD displays. Their displays are the Cadillac of LCDs. I've used their products for the past 4 years and their quality is unsurpassed. What makes them unique is they offer I2C versions of their graphics and text displays. Figure 12-4 is one of the I2C displays I frequently use with the PSoC.

Figure 12-6

USB Analyzer

Total Phase, Inc.
735 Palomar Avenue
Sunnyvale, CA 94085   Phone: 408-850-6501   Fax: 408-850-6501
www.totalphase.com

These folks manufacture both full-speed and high-speed USB analyzers. Their products are very reasonably priced (full-speed USB analyzer is $400) and support Windows, Linux, and MAC operating systems out-of-the box. I've used their products in articles and training sessions, and love how easy they are to use, and the well organized desktop they provide in their software. And their software development kit is part of the price. Figure 12-7 shows a photo of their Beagle full-speed USB analyzer.

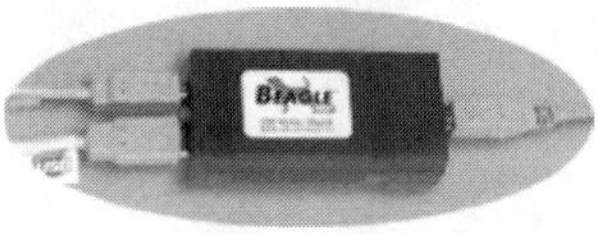

Figure 12-7

And last, don't forget to check the Cypress web site. The Cypress site is located at: www.cypress.com.

Index

Discount Offer:

As our way of saying thanks for purchasing this book, we would like to offer a 10% discount good towards any single Timelines Industries product. For a list of products please visit www.time-lines.com, www.psoc.time-lines.com, or www.psoctraining.com. When ordering use coupon code CYP239 to apply the discount on a single item.

This Offer Expires 12/31/2007

Notes

Notes

Notes